C000271421

The Mirror
of the
Mind

Seeing personally, seeing really and seeing sanely

Trevor Rollings

The Mirror of the Mind

Copyright ©Trevor Rollings 2020
All rights reserved

Printed by Kindle Direct Publishing 2020

tjrollings@gmail.com

Also available by the same author
in the series
Empires of the Mind

We are More than our Brains
Putting our minds to neuroscience
No Man is an Island
How pain, suffering and hope bind us to each other
The Mosaic of the Mind
Where does our mind go in sleep, dreams, hypnosis and meditation?
In Our Right Mind
Sex, drugs, kicks and control

For my grandchildren

The gift of words
and the joy of learning.

Contents

Mirror Mirror

Mirrors and copulation are abominable, because
they increase the number of men.
Jorge Luis Borges

When we look in the mirror, we assume that we see an accurate reflection of reality, but that depends on how clean the glass is. It may be dirty, cracked or shattered. As Francis Bacon wrote four hundred years ago, at the start of the modern scientific adventure, 'The human mind is like a false mirror, which, receiving rays regularly, distorts and discolours the nature of things by mingling its own nature with it'.

In other words, it is the mind that sees, not the brain, and what it sees is often what it projects, not what is actually there. Consider Edouard Manet's painting 'A Bar at the Folies Bergère' overleaf, which leaves us with more questions than answers. We, the viewer, stand looking at a barmaid in front of a large mirror, which reflects all the drinkers behind us, some of whom may be staring at our back, making us feel self-conscious.

The Mirror of the Mind

The girl at the bar
Manet's 1882 painting challenges our assumptions about looking, seeing and understanding what is reflected.

What is the girl thinking, and how can we possibly know? Her face gives little away. If we are the person looking at the girl, why is our reflection not behind her, out of our line of sight? Are our senses giving us a warped view of reality?

If we are male, are we the man on the right of the picture? If he's not us, who is he? He seems to be leaning in very close to her, a possible rival for her attention, challenging our male gaze. If we are female, we still feel challenged, because we can't be sure whether we have her full attention. Is she playing mind games with us, or barely noticing us? Is it her voice we are hearing, or our own? Should we be worried? How do we know we are not hallucinating the whole scene, and that we are not going mad? Do we need therapy?

In this book we look at three aspects of our experience which help us to understand what we see in the mirror of our mind: theory of mind, reality testing and staying mentally balanced. To sharpen the focus, we zoom in on autism, schizophrenia and psychosis, three different mind-worlds which challenge our assumptions about empathy and trust, reality and imagination, normality and sanity.

Seeing personally

Seeing into other minds

Social brain - theory of mind – mother/child dyad – point of view – mutuality – empathy – social grooming – mirror neurons - shared gaze – social learning

- We are natural minders, born with a social brain into a world of mind, and equipped with a theory of mind to access it.
- Our journey into mind begins in the womb, then in our mother's arms.
- By the age of four, we realise that other minds do not see the world as we do.
- We progress from literal pointing to metaphorical understanding of someone else's point of view.
- This tunes us in to the needs of others, makes us receptive to the ways of our tribe, and enables us to understand cultures different from our own.
- It also alerts us to the fact that we can manipulate others by telling fibs when it suits us.
- We need both of these insights of theory of mind, the prosocial and the antisocial, because as the story of Robinson Crusoe illustrates, we are lost without the stimulus, opposition and company of other minds.
- We revel in mutuality, but we soon learn that our delicate social relations collapse if we are unable to hide our thoughts from each other.

The Mirror of the Mind

- Not only has theory of mind driven the growth of our big brain, it is also the fount of reciprocity, empathy and conscience.
- The evolution of theory of mind is on full display in the antics of our closest primate relatives.
- Neuroscientists have identified mirror neurons in the brain which make us great mimics of those around us.
- In our early years, our mirror neurons incline us to be copycats, but as we grow, we begin to exercise greater choice over what and who we wish to emulate.
- The eyes and face play vital roles in our 'reading' of other minds.

A minded world

Our common sense folk psychology is based on a double conviction: not only do we possess a mind of our own, but we are able to see into other people's minds, even the minds of strangers. This core belief, which psychologists call theory of mind, is so integral to how our mind has evolved that we never question it. There is no other way of seeing ourselves. The only time we notice it is when it breaks down, or is absent, in conditions such as autism, schizophrenia and psychopathy.

Theory of mind starts very early, in the dynamic of the mother-child dyad. She greets us not as a bundle of needs or a packet of information, but as a person waiting to be known. As early as in the womb, she bathes us in her idea of the world as a minded place. Several months before we make our grand entry, we hear the give and take of her conversation through the walls of her uterus, and feel the complementary rhythms of her moving and resting.

Our brain is primed to reflect and reach out to her mind the moment we appear, a rude awakening assuaged by the comfort of her physical contact, skin on skin. We feel her warmth, hear her voice and smell her milk. The to-and-fro of breast feeding, alternately sucking and pausing for respite, is a foretaste of the turn-taking of conversation.

In her arms, we gain our first experiences of the miracle of love, in the gentle reciprocity of sleep and waking, pain and relief, helplessness and rescue, suffering and redemption. If we open our mouth, she opens hers too, an act of synchronised mimicry that forges a preverbal bond through social interaction. As natural mimics, we laugh at the sound of her laughter, and cry at the sound of other babies crying.

Mother/child dyad
Our journey into mind begins here, in our mother's arms and eyes, being nourished, touched, spoken to, smiled at, played with and loved.

We respond to her moods, constantly looking to her for security, edgily checking out any stranger who hoves into view. If we fall, we turn to her for consolation and reassurance. During these early months, our mind is one with her mind, and we are in effect one person. This closeness of attachment is a crucial step towards our gradual individuation. Our intimacy of exchange will directly affect our later intellectual growth, emotional development and self esteem.

She constantly encourages us through a special kind of sing-song language called motherese, addressing us *as if* we have a mind. For deaf mutes, denied the sound of the human voice, touch alone is enough to trigger the mind-reading module in their mind's ear.

At first our mother's face is an unfocused round blob, but we are primed to recognise her smile, and return it by about six or eight weeks, acknowledging the presence of another mind. This drive is so strong that even blind babies smile, proving that our sense of other minds is made in the mind's eye of the imagination.

When we gaze into our mother's eyes, we synchronise our brain patterns with hers. When she looks away, we follow her direction of gaze, so that her field of attention becomes ours. This is the birth of theory of mind: we realise that there is something in her mind that is not yet in ours.

The Mirror of the Mind

When she reads to us, or tells us a story, we achieve shared attention, which is the key to the passing on of learning and culture. Joint concern also has a moral foundation. When we rock our dolly or cuddle our pet, we are not just copying our mother but imagining another creature's need for comfort, learning to see through the eyes of another. We want to 'help'.

> *We realise that there is something in*
> *her mind that is not in ours.*

This instinct starts very early, primed as a sure-fire algorithm, so intuitive that it is wordless. When toddlers are shown a video in which the 'characters' are geometrical shapes, one acting as 'helper' coming to the rescue of a smaller 'victim' being pushed around by a larger 'bully', they always choose the 'helper' to play with afterwards. They anthropomorphise the shapes, even though there are no facial expressions on display. As we discover when we stumble over our sums at school, our brain is primarily social, not mathematical. We find a logic puzzle much easier to solve if it is couched as a *people* problem, not a number one.

Natural minders

We are natural minders, primed to seek out other minds, interact with them and model their behaviour. This instinct for reciprocity is not however automatic or straightforward, as reflected in our proverbs. We offer 'a penny for your thoughts', giving the lie to 'I can read you like a book'. On Monday we say 'absence makes the heart grow fonder', but by Friday 'out of sight, out of mind' better fits the bill.

We are natural animists, attributing a motive to everything around us, even inanimate objects. If our car refuses to start in the morning, we take it as a personal slight: 'she' wants to upset us. We are echoing the sentiments of our ancestors on the savannah, who believed that everything in nature has its own spirit, trying to express itself in human terms.

This inheritance is reflected in our language: the river *seeks* the sea, the sun *hides* behind a cloud, the wind *tries* to get in the door, willows *like* to have their feet in water. We attribute intention to animals too: the mother bird *fusses* over her chicks, the geese *decide* to fly south in autumn, the tiger *wants* to grow his stripes, our cat *hates* getting wet. Shown a picture of a wave towering over a small boat, we assign intention where none can exist: the wave is *threatening* the tiny vessel which *cowers* below.

We can't help this, because we are natural vitalists: there is an energy or life force in every cell or creature that *wants* to grow to maturity. Nature is not only alive, it also tries to talk to us. 'We find human faces in the moon, armies in the clouds', wrote the philosopher David Hume.

'We find human faces in the moon, armies
in the clouds', wrote the philosopher David Hume.

First we name our pet, then our doll, and eventually the gods who move our imaginations in mysterious ways. We echo an ancient urge to see mermaids in the waves, hear a voice in the thunder and sense a lady in our luck. When our dog pines when left alone, we assume a personal connection: *she* (not it) is missing *us*. We name the stars and mountains, even humanise our machines: may God bless all who sail in *her*.

John Ruskin called this the pathetic fallacy, informing all our moods. When we are happy, we say the sun has got his hat on, but when we are late for an appointment, we blame fate, the rain, the traffic, anything, as if everything has a mind to conspire against us.

Some say we are natural theists, assuming a power greater than ourselves and yearning for connectedness. We attribute a minded creator where there are only natural causes. Our brains evolved as part of nature, and it is only in modern times that we have abstracted ourselves from it as objective observers. But primal drives and instincts remain, our evolution as a social animal predisposing us to seek out mind, attribute meaning to actions, distinguish people from things, second-guess intentions and model our behaviour on those close to us. If we are surrounded by panicking people, our heart rate will rise in 'copy cat' response, and religious enthusiasm is not far behind.

Our emotions are primed to infer feelings and our brain to second-guess intentions. The mere act of seeing someone perform a good deed inspires a like-minded kindness in us, and watching someone weep makes us tearful. We recognise intuitively who is good, who to trust and how to love. We are happy to see others happy, and happiest when we make them happier.

> **The pathetic fallacy**
> John Ruskin (1814-1900) coined this phrase, based on our habit of attributing mind to nature, or projecting our own feelings (pathos) onto it. The rain pelts against our skin, and the blackbird greets the dawn.

We understand ourselves only in proportion to our ability to enter different mind-worlds.

Our early play confirms the reciprocal nature of human interaction: when I roll the ball to you, you roll it back, in a game of rewarded anticipation. As our games become more complex, they strengthen our models of how things work, and our beliefs about how people react. Unstructured play makes us stronger reality-testers, because it carries our interest beyond our own point of view.

Our instinct for mutual recognition in a minded world has been variously called an I/Thou nexus, 'we' thinking, inter-subjectivity, between-ness, biological bonding and neural fusion, depending on which theory we prefer. What matters is that we are learning to put ourselves inside the minds of others, and to share their perspective. We understand ourselves only in proportion to our ability to enter different mind-worlds.

The Mirror of the Mind

Theory of mind

In our early years, up to the age of four, we lay the foundations for theory of mind, faster and stronger if we face the competition of siblings. Our attempts to navigate the perilous shoals of other minds and negotiate a complex social identity confront us with a stark truth: other minds do not see the world exactly as we do.

But it takes a while to make this cognitive leap, as shown in the 'broccoli test'. A researcher offers a fourteen-month old girl broccoli or ice cream. Having tasted both, she invariably chooses the ice cream. The researcher then makes it plain that he doesn't like ice cream, pulling a 'yuk' face when he eats it, but responding to the broccoli as 'yum'.

The researcher then asks her to pass what she thinks is his favourite food. She invariably passes the ice cream, on the basis that 'you're bound to like what I like'. By around eighteen months, she shows a distinct advance in mind-reading. She is more likely to pass the broccoli, because she has arrived at a key insight: 'your taste is different from mine'.

This finding is replicated in many similar experiments. Imagine that we are two two-year-old children hiding a toy in a room with an adult present. We hide it together, but you then leave the room, while I stay. While you are out of the room, I see the adult move the toy to a different hiding place, so that I now know the new hiding place, while you don't.

When you come back in, I am asked where *you* think the toy now is. I point to the new hiding place, not the old one, because I don't yet understand that, while you were out of the room, I came into possession of knowledge that you cannot possibly have. I can't see that you are harbouring a false belief about the whereabouts of the toy, unless and until I pass on to you what I know.

Grasping that we perceive the world from different points of view can be a great asset, enabling us to be empathetic and considerate, automatically preferring helpers to bullies. But it can just as easily open the doors of deception. I now know that I can *plant* false beliefs in your mind to further my own interests, hiding my prized possessions from you. Just as important, you can do the same, playing a double-bluff on me.

In our first three years we are behaviourists, judging people by their actions, but by age four we become mentalists, capable of imagining mind-scenarios that are neither real nor true, reflected in our play: you be the goodie and I'll be the

13

baddie. We can play party games like blind man's buff, realising that the blindfolded person can't see what we see, needing us to be their eyes for them.

Broccoli or ice cream
I prefer ice cream to broccoli any time, but I accept that you'd much rather have broccoli. There's no accounting for taste. Broccoli-flavoured ice cream, anyone?

At this age, hide and seek is great fun, but we don't quite 'get' it, because we have yet to realise that 'my I' is not the same as 'your I'. At first we put our hands over our eyes: if I can't see you, you can't see me. We leave our leg sticking out from the curtain, not realising we have to hide our whole body, not just our eyes. When given a second chance to hide, we go back to the same hiding place, thinking that's the last place you'll look to find us.

Seeing things from other people's point of view
is the foundation stone of empathy.

We gradually begin to appreciate that each of us sees from a different line of sight. I have to see in my imagination what you see in reality: my leg sticking out gives me away. This 'seeing things from other people's point of view' is the foundation stone of empathy, when we start to see metaphorically: 'I can see things from your perspective'. But it is also the beginning of lies and deceit: if I can hide my body from you, perhaps I can hide my thoughts too.

14

The Mirror of the Mind

Back on the savannah

In the nursery, we spend as much time learning to get on with other children as we do stacking bricks, if only because our playmates keep trying to knock our bricks down, or steal them. It was the same for our ancestors on the savannah. There were always others to look out for, and a complex social world to navigate.

Daniel Defoe's 1719 novel 'Robinson Crusoe' remains a popular story, based on the adventures of a real castaway who spent four years on a remote island. Its intrigue lies in the fact that we did not evolve on a lonely atoll, locked in our own nervous system. From the moment we are born, our eyes and ears search the room for human presence, our social brain desperate to connect with the group mind. Robinson is in danger of losing his mind unless a Man Friday arrives to shape his thought-world, because to be ourselves at all, we need other people. The gifts of language and love are pointless without them.

Robinson Crusoe
The ship has gone down, and Robinson finds himself alone. But this is not our natural state. Desperate for company, he spends his long days scanning the horizon for the sight of a sail.

Mind, consciousness and culture are wasted on a desert island, with no-one to share them. Without the sounding board of other minds, there is no communion, meaning or personhood, only relentless sense data. Our gregarious nature as a species means that the solitary life is unnatural to us. We instinctively form bonds and alliances, but exile, ostracism and solitary confinement are feared punishments, because rejection causes real physical pain.

We are born into a biological bind, which is at heart a moral one: we have to look out for our own interest, but we have to negotiate other people's needs and demands too. It is not enough to master physical space: we also have to build bridges across the chasms between us. The physical world comes as given, but our social world has to be personally connected.

Nature gives us a head start by priming us with emotions to bind us together. Nearly all of our emotions are socially triggered, brought into play to help us steer our passage through group politics. Millennia later, we still find ourselves dominated by our emotions, as dangerous and contagious as ever. Like our ancestors, we are still driven as much by envy and status anxiety as by hunger and sex.

What use are happiness, sadness, fear, anger, surprise and disgust except to dissolve the boundaries between our isolated minds? Even shame binds us together. We can feel embarrassed on another's behalf, or stand condemned by the actions of someone close to us. Even though we ourselves are innocent, we feel the judgment of hundreds of pairs of eyes boring into our soul.

Emotions are triggered by hormones, especially oxytocin, without which we would be unable to play together without squabbling, stay together as a family, extend the hand of friendship or melt into the arms of our beloved. Our hormones can however as easily trigger suspicion of strangers and antipathy towards the 'out group' if we allow them to. Not for nothing are our dreams dominated by the other people in our lives, because our hot-blooded emotions need as much sorting and processing as our bloodless ideas.

When it comes to reading other minds,
intuition beats logic every time.

These deep impulses work at the level of instinct, giving us our 'folk psychology', much derided but nearly a hundred per cent reliable, because it works on the default assumption that our minds mirror each other. This is more a gut feeling than a rational calculation, because when it comes to reading other minds, intuition beats logic every time.

Theory of mind is therefore anything but theoretical: it is as practical as our arms and legs. Without it, we would have no way of passing on our complex culture, which means there would be no progress. Parents, elders and teachers rely on our 'teachability'. They are primed to envision what our learning mind needs to know, and we are programmed to model our mind on theirs, simulating their mental state. We achieve this not by uncritical imitation, but by discriminating emulation. In effect, we exchange minds with our mentors, not directly, but as a slow awakening.

Mutuality

Our sense of 'what it's like to be another human being' is what gives us our mutuality, or moral entanglement with each other. The African concept of *ubuntu* or human-kindness captures this perfectly: I am because you are. By extension, we are who we are because others are as they are, experiencing similar thoughts and feelings.

> **Ubuntu**
> This Zulu expression was popularised by Archbishop Desmond Tutu (b 1931). It means 'I am because you are', or 'A person is a person through other people'.

The psychologist Carl Rogers urged that, before we reply to a point during a discussion-verging-on-argument with someone, especially if things get a little heated, we say in our own words and to our opponent's satisfaction what we think has just been said, after which the favour must be returned. When we do this, we find ourselves engaged in a dialogue, not forcing two monologues past each other. Getting inside the skins of others, or walking in their shoes, is our chief defence against bigotry, selfishness and summary judgement.

Early in our evolution we learned that we do not stop at our own body boundary: we are inter-subjective and inter-dependent, especially when young. Mothers spend as much time communicating feelings as teaching words: 'you'll make mummy sad if you do that'. Our survival in small vulnerable family groups demanded that we anticipate the intentions of those around us, and appreciate the consequences of our actions: hostile or friendly, manipulative or caring, deceitful or trustworthy.

Morality and consciousness are integral
to the rise of Homo sapiens.

Our close-knit communal living with all its cliques and counter-plots drove the evolution of mind to its present levels: we are self-aware because we are social, and vice versa. Morality was the father of consciousness. Morality and consciousness are not mere evolutionary spin-offs or afterthoughts: they are integral to the rise of Homo sapiens. We could be neither Homo nor sapiens without them.

If I am to avoid punishment, I must project my mental space onto yours so I know how to avoid violating it. This calls for a lot of grey matter working at a high level, but it complicates as much as it simplifies. We know, but only to the extent that we are known. Our lives have meaning only in relation to each other's, because our interests do more than overlap in our neocortex: they overlay each other.

The eighteenth century economist Adam Smith gave the name sympathy to our ability to change places with each other in our imagination. We need to be both spectators and agents if we are meaningfully to exchange contracts or form associations. Without sympathy we cannot establish trading networks, political systems and social relations which are built on trust, mutuality and consensus. For this insight, he is regarded by many as the 'father of economics'.

But he went an important step further. Our interdependence engenders a moral sentiment that allows us to express benevolence to our fellows in times of need. If someone reaches out an open hand to us as we pass by, it offends the spirit of charity to leave it empty, just as we feel deeply offended when someone refuses to take our hand offered in friendship.

Sympathy helps us to breach the gap between our otherwise separate bodies, transforming our naked ego into a cultured self. We are born into a complex social pact, where one plus one equals three. Outside of the reciprocity of human communication, our mind/brain has no role or fulfilment.

The Mirror of the Mind

In Smith's vision, sympathy is always a positive inclination, but that is not necessarily the case with empathy. Neuroscientists have identified up to as many as ten 'empathy circuits' in the brain, but psychologists have made an important distinction between cognitive and emotional empathy.

Shakespearean villains such as Iago and Edmund have cognitive empathy: they know the minds of their victims so well that they are able to deceive, manipulate and torture them. What Iago and Edmund lack is emotional empathy, which would temper their villainy, because it would enable them to feel the pain of their wickedness as keenly as those they torment.

Psychopaths possess cognitive empathy in abundance, but not emotional empathy. Their sympathy stops at their own skin, never blossoming into compassion. They are social isolates, frozen in their hearts, unmoved by the look of pity, impervious to the suffering they cause. They break the primal social contract of *ubuntu*. Not all psychopaths wish harm to others, or behave criminally, though all criminals by definition display a blatant disregard for the feelings of their victims. Such contract-breakers are judged by the rest of us as in need of either psychiatric help or incarceration.

Iago and Edmund are only actors playing a part, but our ability to see through fictional eyes and feel vicarious suffering means that theatre, novels and films can throw open the windows of the mind as powerfully as any everyday experience. Research suggests that our emotional intelligence can be sharpened by entering imaginary worlds, but sympathy means little unless it makes a difference to how we treat each other in the real world. Many Nazi SS officers had fine libraries, but they were also sadistic killers.

Social grooming
To gain a glimpse of the evolution of empathy, and how it makes humans different, we need only look at the social shenanigans of our nearest relatives, the highly gregarious troops of gorillas, chimps and baboons, less so orangutans, which are fairly solitary.

Most monkeys and primates have a social brain like ours, spending hours getting to know each other through mutual grooming as the glue of their society. This serves the triple purpose of ridding their fur of parasites, reinforcing hierarchy and strengthening social bonds.

19

The Mirror of the Mind

> **Male gorilla**
> Yes, I've got theory of mind too. I need it to stay one step ahead of all the young pretenders who would dearly love to steal my harem from me.

This leisurely practice is not a waste of time, but the driver of having a bigger brain, characteristic of our branch on the evolutionary tree. Though dominant male gorillas spend most of the day lying around, when trouble breaks out, they need every brain cell to second-guess the alliances and machinations of rivals if they are to keep upstarts in their place. They live in small networks of around a dozen or so, and they need to keep tabs on who owes whom a favour, and who is trying to infiltrate the harem.

Social grooming is not however just about controlling sexual access and maintaining male hierarchy. Bonobos, slightly smaller versions of chimpanzees, do not guard their females so jealously. The females respond by offering sex more freely, as a result of which there is less group conflict.

We humans perform our own kind of social grooming, not by picking each other's fleas, or in order to wield power, but by sharing gossip and rumour. Half of our communicating is about each other, and if we want more scandal, we can turn to social media and celeb tittle tattle. We too are social primates, living in small closely bonded family groups.

We can reach out to the wider family of mankind,
not as rivals, but as partners.

This need not make us insular, racist or chauvinist towards the female of the species. We become prosocial by networking more widely with on average about a hundred and fifty 'contacts' whose lives and concerns we vaguely share, more if we go digital. As well as our tight-knit group of immediate friends that we confide in or swear loyalty to, we can reach out to the wider family of mankind, not as rivals, but as partners. As well as being self-interested mind-readers, gifted with clever theory of mind, we are also caring empathisers, inextricably connected to the needs of others.

Animal skulduggery
Monkeys and apes give interesting insights into the evolution of theory of mind. Female hamadryas baboons have sneaky sex with young male pretenders out of sight of alpha adult males. Like naughty children, they know how to avoid surveillance, and fear the penalty of being caught.

Chimpanzees, our nearest primate relative, are even cheekier. They give false alarm calls to fool the troop into scattering, so that they can bag the bananas for themselves. Such selfishness is balanced by the fact that they have been observed consoling each other after a fight, which means they are capable of emotional empathy as well as cognitive scheming. This is confirmed in the laboratory, where they have shown reluctance to pull a lever which they know will inflict pain on a fellow chimp.

In captivity, they manipulate attention and know how to act dumb, if only to frustrate a researcher they have taken a dislike to. They have been seen to point out to a second chimp that has just entered the enclosure where something is, showing that they know that the other chimp doesn't know. They too appreciate line of sight, taking a fruit that they know another chimp cannot see, so as not to arouse envy or anger.

Human children reach this stage of cunning around the age of two and a half, but for chimps, this marks a plateau of cognitive and emotional empathy. They don't grasp that line of sight is irrelevant if the other chimp is blindfolded. In a similar vein, they have been seen to beg for food from a blindfolded keeper, unaware that she cannot see their held out hand. They cannot put themselves in the position of another mind, and their lack of language means they cannot articulate what beliefs another mind may entertain.

We tend to credit our pets with theory of mind: our dog knows when we are coming home, or about to take it for a walk. It is more likely exhibiting superior sensory awareness, working on habit or picking up subliminal signals from us. A gun dog may seem to be 'pointing' at something, but it is merely thrusting its nose in the direction of a smell. It doesn't *know* it is helping the hunter.

Most animals are behaviourists, not mentalists, reacting to what they see on the outside. This persuades us that our pets cannot judge us, or shame us, which is why most of us have no qualms about swearing, stealing, urinating or performing sex in front of them.

Elephants, chimps and dogs don't tell deliberate lies.

There is some evidence that elephants understand when a human points, which should heighten our respect for them, because pointing is a higher cognitive activity, presuming the ability not just to symbolise an object, but to envision that symbol in another's mind. But as far as we know, elephants, chimps and dogs don't tell deliberate lies, or know what it is like to be the victim of a deception: we leave that higher level of cunning to humans.

A camouflaged lizard does not *intend* to deceive its predators: its cunning trick is merely an effective evolutionary ploy selected over thousands of generations. A lapwing runs along the ground trailing a wing to distract a fox near its nest, but this is instinct at work, not conscious cunning. The lapwing doesn't 'know' it is being deceptive, and the fox does not 'know' it is being duped. Such a simple trick pales into insignificance alongside the devious mind games that humans play with each other.

But we can give a wild gorilla some credit worthy of a member of the Mafia. If it has been threatened or harmed by a human, it may not react instantly, but nor will it forget. Instead it will serve its revenge cold, possibly months later, exhibiting a kind of calculated cunning we normally associate with our own species. Such machination requires great brain power. Scientists are brainy too, but few go into politics. Perhaps it is simply because they are not very good at telling lies.

The Mirror of the Mind

Mirror neurons

In recent years, mirror neurons, triggered as early as one hour old, have been identified in the brain, 'lighting up' on a 'monkey see, monkey do' basis. If I see you yawn, the 'mirror effect' will be triggered in my brain, and I will yawn too. If I see you join a queue, I might join you just in case there's something good on offer at the end of it. These 'copycat' brain cells are hailed by some as doing for psychology what DNA did for biology, explaining not only how our brain establishes theory of mind, but also providing the foundation for empathy.

Mirror neurons engage us in far more than mimicry: they go to the heart of what it means to be self aware humans. It might appear that as babies we merely imitate those around us, but something much more profound is going on. Biologists debate long and hard whether we are creatures of instinct or learning, only to conclude that we are both. It has to be this way. We are primed to imitate, but also to expand our understanding in the process.

Take smiling for instance. This is a programmed response at around six weeks old, which is greeted with 'Oh look, she's smiling'. Now we know what a smile is, how to do it again, when it is appropriate, and what response it gets. This feedback is even more important when we start moving our limbs. In copying others, we discover our own body, and how to control it.

Beyond our early weeks and months, very little of our behaviour is pure mimicry. We might stick out our tongue in response to an adult doing so, as a kind of instinctive response, but we might just as easily stick it out for the fun of it. Later on at school, when our cortex has started to wire up, and social learning comes into play, we think twice about the consequences of sticking our tongue out at the school bully. A knee-jerk response gets a warm reaction in the nursery, but in the playground we soon learn that it might get us in trouble.

Mirror neurons involve more than recognising ourselves in a mirror, vital though that is. By age of twenty months, we pass the 'red spot' test, reaching to touch a red spot painted on our forehead, not the one on the face reflected in the mirror. That's *me* I'm looking at. In this way mirror neurons play a key role in drawing the boundary between my body and yours, or 'self' and 'other'.

The Mirror of the Mind

The looking glass self
Our mirror neurons fire when we see someone we know, or detect meaning in a gesture, but as this painting by René Magritte shows, try as we may, we never see ourselves as others see us.

Very few animals are capable of this act of self-recognition. Dogs never manage it, though elephants and dolphins do. A male hedge sparrow in the breeding season attacks its own reflection in a garden mirror to the point of exhaustion, seeing itself as a potential rival.

When neuroscientists talk of mirror neurons, they mean something more than the looking-glass self, or falling in love with our own reflection, like Narcissus gazing into the pond. They believe they have discovered specialised neurons that operate as neural wifi, like a second pair of eyes. Our motor neurons fire in sympathy when we see someone kicking a ball, as an automatic imitation reflex, even though our leg stays still.

On the outside, we are behaviourists,
but inside, we are mentalists.

Dedicated cells in our prefrontal cortex are activated when we witness an *intentional* movement. Random motions around us are ignored, but when someone picks up something and hands it to us, a signal is registered in our consciousness: there is a *motive* to this action, which triggers a mirrored response. This happens in the part of our brain that processes language, so our mirror neurons are closely tied to our capacity for anticipating the future, reading people's minds, expressing our feelings and experiencing empathy.

Even before we learn to talk, we start to read the minds of adults. At one year old, if we see dad drop an item of clothing on the way to the washing basket, we pick it up and put it in for him, because we know his hands are full, he might not have noticed it, and we have read meaning into his journey. On the outside, we are behaviourists, observing his actions very closely, but inside we are mentalists, inferring his psychological goals. We even copy his actions that on the surface seem pointless. We might not grasp his intention, but we realise that what he is doing matters to *him*.

The foundation of empathy

This is not just social contagion, like breaking into a yawn because others around us are doing so. Mirror neurons engage us more fully. When we are in the presence of others, we 'catch' their mood: our pulse rate rises, our empathy is stirred, our face breaks into a smile. Reading their emotional state from their face and body language, our heart rhythm aligns with theirs. We cannot feel their pain or joy directly, but their emotions become our feelings. We can't help flinching when we see someone being hurt, or feeling pleased to see them happy.

We have to go through the looking glass, to the
interactive human world on the other side.

This is the basis of empathy, but if we are to go *through* the looking glass, to the interactive human world on the other side, we need to convert empathy into compassion: what are we actually going to *do* to help this person, right this wrong or develop this friendship? Compassion is not an instinct granted us by our sure-fire mirror neurons, but a moral habit we painstakingly learn through our culture, interactions and decisions to commit ourselves.

We experience this difference between self-indulgent empathy and targeted compassion when we visit the cinema. We forget the strong feelings aroused by the film as soon as the credits roll, because our mirror neurons switch off. Feeling empathy in the cinema is temporary, fictitious and at no cost to ourselves, something we leave behind in the auditorium.

The Mirror of the Mind

Compassion is our practical response when we see someone outside on the street in *real* distress. Suddenly our whole moral being is engaged. We are propelled from automatic response to considered reflection, from make-believe to real life, from isolation to connectedness. Otherwise we are little different from the Nazi concentration camp commandants who wallowed in escapist movies at night, only to resume their extermination of 'Untermensch' in the morning.

If we find this comparison offensive, that is good, because it means we are making a clear distinction between mindless mimicry and mindful emulation. We model our values on those we consider worthy of imitation, and this is a matter of judgment after deep reflection, not a facile game of 'Simon Says'. We are all natural mimics, but that is not the same as becoming an SS sadist just because everyone else around us is behaving like one.

The Good Samaritan
Traditionally the Jews and Samaritans hated each other, but it was a Samaritan who stopped to help this Jew who had been left bleeding by robbers, and whose needs had been ignored by his own people.

The Holocaust shows how empathy can be dangerous when the mirror is distorted to include the in-group, but to exclude the out-group. In the parable of the Good Samaritan, a Jew has been robbed and left bleeding beside the road. Many of his own kind ignore him, but a passing Samaritan helps the injured man. Traditionally Samaritans and Jews hated each other, but the Samaritan is able to express empathy as compassion, because the mirror of his mind has no blind spots. Instead of passing by looking the other way, he commits himself to an act of charity.

The Mirror of the Mind

Copycat behaviour

If we use mirror neurons to explain everything, from the picking up of a silly habit to our capacity for compassion, we risk trivialising the complexity of human choices. We don't learn to dance by watching others do so. We have to get up on the dance floor and stumble a few times, until we slowly begin to master the steps.

Similarly we don't ape the behaviour of others willy-nilly, or cross our legs just because everyone else in the room is doing so. When we learn to speak as a child, we don't spout fixed phrases, but generate a huge diversity of possible sentences from grammatical sub-structures coded in our brain. Our mimicry, if such it is, is infused with insights, goals, values and meanings.

Mirror neurons have been key drivers of our evolution and culture, but they are not simply agents of slavish imitation. There must also be conscious discrimination at work, otherwise we would end up picking our noses or killing Jews, just because we see others doing so. Motivation is more important than mimicry.

We are nevertheless dedicated followers of fashion, 'putting on the style'. In one chimpanzee troop, the dominant female was observed to stick a piece of grass in her ear. Within a week or so, other chimps were 'trending' with her. Being a copycat however comes with a health warning, especially with suicides, which tend to happen in local clusters. We do better to stick with copying someone's golf swing in order to beat them next time.

Bash the Bobo doll
If I see an adult bash the doll, I'll do likewise. But what if I see it being offered kindness?

The Mirror of the Mind

We copy bad things depending on our role models and impressionability. In the 1960's, Albert Bandura spent many hours observing children in the company of adults. In the room was a large inflatable Bobo doll. If the adults treated it violently, and then left the room, the children often followed suit, the reverse happening when the adults had been seen treating it affectionately.

He concluded that we learn a lot of our kindness or nastiness through social learning, or the observation, imitation and modelling of the behaviour of peer and adult role models. Neuroscience confirms this, the 'kick the ball' network in the brain of a footballer lighting up more readily than a non-player, suggesting that mirror neurons can be both the products of learning and the causes of our actions.

This does not mean that we are merely the reflection of our mirror neurons, nor do they 'explain' autism, empathy, fads, fashions or the acquisition of language. If we merely mimicked those around us, we would struggle to respond to the pain of others, tune in to their emotions, fathom their intentions or learn to love them.

If all we see is our own reflection,
we are in love with our own vanity.

Put to sensitive use, mirror neurons help us to see what others reflect back to us. We can pick up wordless signals in a conversation, judge whether we are listening closely enough, work out how to handle a delicate topic, tune in to what lies behind the tone of voice, decide when it is time to move on. If instead all we see is our own reflection, we are in love with our own vanity.

My mother knew all about mirror neurons long before they were discovered. As a young boy, I soon learned that the worst justification I could give for bad behaviour was 'but that's what all the other kids do'. She wasn't a moral philosopher or a neuroscientist, but she left me in no doubt about whose neurons I should be mirroring.

The eyes have it
Whoever our role models happen to be, our identity begins to take shape in our early years, not in a vacuum, but through the prism of our social interactions. Our

28

rate of progress is linked to our ability to enter the perspective of other minds, triggered through the eyes, and starting the moment we are born.

Mirror neurons work invisibly, out of sight, but eyes are the windows of the soul, giving us in-sight into other minds. It is as if we are born to gaze into each other's eyes. The poet John Donne writes of the eyebeams of lovers entwining, sparking spontaneously from one mind to another. If this sounds too romantic, we need only to recall how the bully uses his eyes to terrorise us with his baleful glare, or what happens if we stare too long at the Gorgon.

Blind children are not excluded from the transformative power of social intelligence. They 'see' with metaphorical eyes, fully aware of concepts such as hiding objects, noticing things, drawing attention to what they have, and pointing towards sounds. What their eyes fail to tell them is compensated for by their ability to read tone of voice, share attention and think symbolically. Their advantage as they grow is that they might be less vulnerable to being deceived visually, because they 'see' things for what they truly are.

If we are normally sighted, by the age of one we are expert in directing our gaze, and establishing mutual gaze. We can detect when someone is giving us the eye. By the age of three, we begin to realise that seeing leads to knowledge in *another's* mind: we don't want mother to *see* us doing what we know is naughty.

Catching the eye of another is to establish joint attention, and the length of look determines the nature of our relationship, from furtive glances to hard stares. Mutual gaze is a sign we are getting on with someone, and we tend to spend longer with those who return our gaze. We get on best with those who meet our eyes with engaged interest, not a blank look, suggesting they like us, possibly even think like us.

We hate being stared at.

We are the only primate with white eye sclera, allowing us to be great gaze-spotters. This is important, because the eyes can betray the heart. When we are trying to convey something important to someone, we check their eyes to see how much is going into their ears. When we're being teased, we check the eyes for a hint of a smile. When we want to make a serious point, we look away like a stargazer, but when we've made our point, we look back in expectation of a reply.

The Mirror of the Mind

We suspect anyone who keeps glancing sideways while we are talking to them. They must be plotting against us, just as a lover who keeps gazing at someone else in the room no longer has eyes only for us. When we want to be really sure about somebody's good faith, we look them straight in the eye. If they can't look straight back at us, or if the smile looks false, we are put on alert. If we're angry with them, we give them the evil eye. We avert our gaze if we are embarrassed, or lower our eyes if we want to show submission.

If we know each other well, we can catch each other's mood in a single glance, but when looking becomes staring, we are unnerved. We hate being stared at, and possess an uncanny awareness of when someone has their eye on us, like a nesting bird sensing the beady eye of the hawk overhead.

The all-seeing eye
Smile, you're under surveillance. The electronic eye lays bare your secrets, and from it no thoughts are hid.

Surveillance cameras on every street corner give us a kind of security, but also make us feel uneasy. In crime black-spots, posters of large penetrating eyes deter thieves and muggers. Conscience is our sublimated hatred of being watched, the outer eye fashioning our inner guilt. If we conform to the law, it is because we have internalised the gaze of others. One of the appeals of cinema is that we can peer into the private thoughts of strangers, but not be gazed on in return. Film makes voyeurs of us all, allowing us to avoid eye contact, and to see without being seen.

The Mirror of the Mind

Making the point

In films and fiction, our mind-reading capacity enables us to follow the narrator's point of view. This begins with intuiting the potent significance of the raised index finger. At first we use it to signal 'I want that thing', but gradually we realise we can use it to share what is in our mind.

John Everett Millais' 1870 painting 'The Boyhood of Raleigh' depicts the great Elizabethan seafarer as a young boy. He and a friend gaze intently at an old sailor who is pointing over the horizon. We sense that soon they will all three turn their eyes out to sea, sharing the same vision of the New World of Virginia that Raleigh will go on to claim for his Virgin Queen.

The Boyhood of Raleigh
Over yonder lads, far beyond the horizon, in a country of the mind.... Look, you can almost see it.

Without theory of mind, such dreams cannot be shared. Eyes establish joint attention, beginning with young children learning to follow their mother's eye direction. Pointing is unique to humans. It is present in rudimentary form in chimps, usually towards a threat or food source, but never to share interest, or to project an imagined world beyond the horizon. We may think our pet dog can follow our pointed finger, but it is more likely relying on other signals we unwittingly give off.

We must follow the pointed finger of our imagination.

If we are to broaden our minds, we must think like a historian, archaeologist or anthropologist, endeavouring to understand the countries of the mind that

31

The Mirror of the Mind

flourished long ago, or that exist in the present in cultures different from ours. We must follow the pointed finger of our imagination, using a technique called *verstehen*, trying to get inside other people's skin. If not, we are trapped in the present, sequestered in our ignorance, like a teenager unable to grasp that our parents have been through what we are going through, and have something to teach us.

We point so that others can see our point of view, and to do so, parents and teenagers have to put themselves in each other's shoes, to see from where they stand. I know the shortcuts, and I know that you don't, and I want to share them with you. I have to see life from your perspective. As we shall see later, autistic children struggle with this concept, which is why they rarely point.

Playing mind games

Intentionality – game theory – mind games - reading faces - lies and deceit – dirty politics – social media – privacy

- We are natural animists, instinctively attributing intentions to the actions of others, even inanimate objects.
- As a scientific theory, theory of mind explains a great deal about how our social mind works, but because the mind is fickle, it cannot account for the unpredictability of our mind games with each other.
- This is because we can never see right into the human heart, least of all our own.
- Also we have evolved as clever schemers, polished performers and duplicitous spies, forever engaged in playing complex games of social chess with each other.
- Technology has transformed the speed and range of our access to other minds.
- It has also reduced our privacy, overwhelmed us with too much information, and made us paranoid about our status and popularity.

Intentionality

Theory of mind rests upon a core feature of human cognition and intelligence: intentionality. If I see you reach for your car keys, I know you are about to leave. If you drift around the room randomly, I pay you no attention, but when I detect intention in your actions, an area in my brain is triggered similar to the one which processes language. There has to be meaning in your movement, and method in your madness.

The Mirror of the Mind

The circuit fires with minimal input. When we watch dancers in dark clothing in a blacked-out theatre, performing with small lights on each joint, we don't see random twinkles jiggling across the stage, but the patterns of human forms, animated by feelings and intentions.

We impute intention to every action, real or imagined.

Every action begs a motive, and every question begs an answer, regardless of how it is framed: why did the chicken cross the road, why didn't you phone me, why did you give one to him but not to me? There has to be a *reason*, because we impute intention to every action, real or imagined.

We can take intentionality to extraordinary lengths, layering our thoughts with ifs, buts and maybes at several removes. In what is the triumph of human theory of mind, we can form chains of linked assumptions and entangled intentions, though there is a limit.

See how far you get without losing the thread: 'I hope (1) you don't think (2) you ought not to come (3) just because Joe might be there (4) trying to drown his sorrows (5) after what happened last week (6)'. Animals are barely able to progress beyond stage one, and it remains a dream of AI engineers to gift robopets, sexbots and 'cloud-based voice assistants' in our living rooms with even a modest degree of intentionality.

If this story about Joe were a scene in a play, we could add the motive of the character saying these lines (7) to the manipulation of the audience (8) by the writer. This last stage is vital in understanding irony. Without it we could not 'get inside the head' of Jonathan Swift , who in 1729 advocated in 'A Modest Proposal' that the desperate inhabitants of famine-stricken Ireland should eat their nutritious children in order to satisfy their ravening hunger.

Theory of mind allows us to realise that his true intention was to shame well-fed English politicians into taking action to relieve the suffering and starvation that was devastating the neighbouring island of Ireland. He wasn't really advocating cannibalism.

The Mirror of the Mind

Jonathan Swift
1667-1775
How could such a finely
bewigged gentleman suggest
eating children as a way of
easing hunger? At least he got
our attention. Who would have
listened if he had written a stuffy
pamphlet on the subject?

Multiple layers of intention are enough to keep us busy negotiating the rapids of social intercourse. They also leave plenty of space for paranoia and conspiracy theory: we invent what others might be thinking instead of taking the trouble to find out. We are constantly engaged in a heady mix of social manoeuvring, which forces us to be very devious very quickly. This means we often get it wrong, falsely attributing harmful motives to others, or harbouring unjustified malice towards them. Wars are just as frequently fought over mistaken or wrongly imputed intentions as over properly understood ones.

A theory that works

A theory is a way of seeing, so a theory of mind is a way of seeing how we see into each other's minds, messy though that sometimes is. This sounds a bit circular, not quite what we expect of a scientific theory. We look to scientific theory to account for regular repeatable phenomena such as gravity and evolution, not speculation that is all in the mind, embroiling us in interpersonal disputes and irresolvable culture wars. Why do we need a scientific rationale for something so personal and natural?

Cognitive neuroscientists and evolutionary psychologists nevertheless believe that theory of mind justifies its title, claiming that it is both a powerful neural endowment and an essential foundation of human society. These are bold claims, so does theory of mind have the hallmarks of a good scientific theory?

Yes, in the sense that it is testable and universal. It has firm roots in our evolutionary past, it can be applied to every human interaction, and it explains a great deal about the present. It accounts for why we cannot be narcissists, solipsists or egotists. We are morally implicated social creatures, confirmed as conscious individuals only to the extent that we are recognised by other consciousnesses. Theory of mind helps us to connect our private knowing with our mutual obligations to each other. It is the principle through which we create each other as ends, not consume each other as means.

> *Without theory of mind, life would be lonely,*
> *dull, empty and far more dangerous.*

Another way of looking at the matter is to consider what would be lost from the human life-world without theory of mind. There would be no art (me expressing what is in my mind to you), no espionage (you trying to second-guess what is in my mind), no psychological thrillers (messing with the victim's mind), no trust (I do not suspect your intention towards me), no advertising (let me plant a desire in your mind), no sports psychology (we're trying to psych out the opposition) no politics (lend me your mind for the next five years), no cultural anthropology (we're trying to understand the mind of our ancestors), and no possibility of renewal (you've helped me change my mind on this issue).

In short, without theory of mind, human society, communication, culture and creativity would break down. Life would be lonely, dull, empty and far more dangerous.

When the theory breaks down
And yet theory of mind does face a huge challenge: the fickleness of the very thing it sets out to explain. The physical world is populated by planets, particles and processes that tend to follow fixed laws, but the human mind-world is inhabited by 'giddy things' that keep changing what they mean, believe and hope for. As a result, theory of mind frequently runs into trouble, because it evolved for

seemingly contradictory purposes: to make everything transparent by prising open other minds, while also keeping our thoughts hidden from each other.

This clash of interests comes to a head in our much-valued sense of privacy, on which we base our precious notions of freedom and independence. Consider what would be lost if, in a future society, every thought and desire could be read or known in advance. If the content of our mind were persistently laid bare, our hearts permanently on our sleeves, we would become 'open books' to each other, with no secrets to hide, no charms to reveal, and no surprises to spring.

If our little white lies and true feelings were writ large, human intercourse as we know it would be turned upside down, as the main character Fletcher Reade discovers in the 1997 movie 'Liar Liar'. The film is a comedy, but it highlights the serious implications of being unable to keep our thoughts to ourselves.

Some religions teach that God, 'from whom no secrets are hid', can see into our heart, meaning that merely thinking a bad thought condemns us, regardless of whether we do the deed. Nowadays we balk at the idea of supernatural surveillance, laying bare our secrets, and yet we have replaced it with a million security cameras, treating ourselves as if we are our own enemy, in need of protection from ourselves.

Our public spaces are swept 24/7 with facial recognition technology, which not only scans the negative look in our eyes, but also burdens us with false positives. It's not our fault if we look suspicious, or fit some algorithmic profile of a vagrant, burglar or terrorist. In some dystopian future, our prisons will be either completely full or completely empty, because our faces will openly and unfailingly proclaim our guilt or innocence to the machine intelligence that monitors our every thought and move.

Society works because we keep our thoughts to ourselves.

We dread the idea that our motives might be so see-through that our friends can see what we are *really* thinking. Our privacy and inscrutability are vital psychological defences, explaining why most of the time we keep our thoughts hidden, even from ourselves, if only to save face. We hardly know our own minds, and certainly do not see ourselves as others see us.

The Mirror of the Mind

One of Banksy's images shows a couple checking their phone behind each other's backs while making love. Is each merely distracted, or fantasising about someone else while *in flagrante delicto*? Either way, each is ultimately alone, even in such an intimate moment, sequestered in privacy, not duty-bound to give the game away. If we had to reveal all of our thoughts all of the time, social relations would be strained to breaking point. Sometimes saying 'No you don't look too big in that dress' is the right thing, if only to keep our relationship amicable. Society works *because* we keep our thoughts to ourselves.

Paradoxically, to be an arch-deceiver, we have to be a good self-deceiver first. 'Flat mind' theorists say that this doesn't pose much of a problem, because we hardly know our own minds anyway. What we call our 'self' is a confection of fictions, subterfuges and rationalisations, hidden behind an impenetrable barrier, unknowable and inexpressible in words, to which we have no privileged access.

Worse still, we haven't a clue what goes on in other minds, not just those of strangers, but also those of soul mates, whom we claim to know intimately. We say 'I know what you're thinking', only to blurt out 'If only you had told me' in our next breath, proving that we get it wrong as often as we get it right. We might mirror each other's movements in a conversation, crossing arms and legs in synchrony, or echoing each other's phrases. But we have no window into each other's heart. I never see what you see, but a mirror image in which my right is always your left. Even identical twins struggle to second-guess what the other is thinking

Mind games

Language is the medium through which we conduct our mind games with each other. We tend to assume that words are transparent, but they are laden with subtexts. They are not private symbols but negotiated meanings and fragile bearers of what you mean to say and what I *think* you are saying.

> *We spend an inordinate amount of time trying*
> *to lay a false scent for each other.*

John von Neumann, who applied mathematical principles to human game-playing, which are usually word-games, wrote, 'Real life consists of bluffing, of little tactics of deception, of asking ourselves what the other is going to think I mean to do'. We spend an inordinate amount of time trying to lay a false scent for each other.

John von Neumann
1903-57
One of Neumann's many mathematical legacies is game theory. Life itself is a game, and the bottom line is that, in general, we don't play zero-sum games with each other. In other words, we always expect to get something back.

Since then game theory has become central to international politics, evolutionary studies, conflict resolution, economics and sport psychology. When we place a bet on the races, we go on hunch informed by calculation of probability based on theory of mind. We know that horses have minds of their own, and bookmakers even more so. If not, we are merely leaving things to chance, as in the game 'stone scissors paper'.

Theory of mind, which evolved to help us to second-guess intentions and unmask the unseen, therefore makes poker players of us all. We start by assuming our opponent must think like us, experiencing the same mental states, playing to win with similar strategies. What will be their next call? We have to out-guess the guess that we guess that they are making about what is in our hand. We look for tiny clues in their poker face, mask our own emotional state and randomise our behaviour, trying to make their behaviour predictable and our own unpredictable.

The Mirror of the Mind

Reading faces

Whether we play poker or not, normally we count ourselves very good at reading faces, which have evolved to express more emotion than any other primate. Our facial muscles respond in sympathy to the face before us, and we quickly sense whether we are welcome.

On the savannah, it mattered who was friendly, and who could be trusted, so our brain is smart at distinguishing between a 'social' smile and a genuine one. Each involves a different set of muscles, just as a spontaneous laugh sounds different from a fake one. To the trained eye, tiny involuntary muscle movements give the game away.

Key parts of our brain are dedicated to facial recognition.

The highly social nature of our evolution on the savannah means that facial recognition comes effortlessly to us, even if we can't remember the names of all the owners. We 'log' thousands of different faces, and rightly boast that we never forget one. Both brain hemispheres play a role, the left brain 'clocking' who it is, the right brain giving us our emotional reaction: is it a face we are pleased to see? Key parts of our brain are dedicated to facial recognition, but some who suffer neurological impairment are unable to recognise the face of a loved one, or remember a face from one moment to the next.

We say the face is an open book, but as Shakespeare warned us, 'False face must hide what false heart doth know'. This acknowledgement that the outside can mask what is inside was a considerable advance on the mediaeval science of physiognomy, which claimed that our facial features betray out true nature, hiding in plain sight on our 'fizzog'. A big nose and widely spaced eyes were regarded as signs of greed and sexual appetite.

This was an early version of behaviourism: we can't witness what is inside, so we judge by what we see on the outside. But 'reading' people is much more subtle than this. When we spot a fin in the water, we know that something much bigger lurks beneath, the part signifying the presence of a much greater whole. We never see each other as twitching bodies or facial masks, but as actors with deeper motives and feelings, even if we have to invent what they may be.

The Mirror of the Mind

Charles Darwin believed that there were half a dozen facial expressions instantly recognisable across all cultures, but the great evolutionary theorist underestimated his subject. Recent anthropological studies suggest that facial expressions are infinitely subtle, not universal but locally differentiated. We learn to pull the kind of face that 'works' in our own culture. That tribesman smiling at us might be about to put us into the cooking pot.

This insight was backed up by the work of the film director Lev Kuleshov in the early twentieth century, who showed the importance of context in 'reading' a face. He asked an actor to show the same expression in a variety of scenes. Depending on the juxtaposition of other images in the shot, it was the audience who 'read' love, fear, surprise, hatred or boredom into the actor's face. In similar vein, film-makers compress images to manipulate our expectations, such as cutting suddenly from the seemingly happy faces of a newly married couple to one of their wedding bouquets trampled in the mud as they set off for their honeymoon.

No wonder we invest so much cognitive energy in saving face, and not for nothing is our social media platform named 'Facebook'. We go beyond face value, prepare an appropriate face to take to work in the morning, and hate being called faceless. The one face we never learn to read, because we never see it in action, is of course our own. By the reverse token, in the mind games we play, we are quicker to see faults in others than in ourselves.

Suspicious minds

We spend hours people-watching, not as a vague pastime, but as a subconscious way of internalising their actions and forming a 'generalised other': this is our model of how other people's minds tick. In that sense, we owe the shape of our minds and intellects to our observations of each other.

We are forever caught in a trap of suspicious minds.

This oiling of the wheels of our social life and anticipation of what someone will do next is even more vital in the world of politics and diplomacy. If we can't share the meanings and intentions of the 'other', we cannot understand their beliefs or values. There can be no negotiations, treaties or peaceful co-existence.

41

The Mirror of the Mind

We find ourselves in the position of the lovers in Elvis Presley's song, forever caught in a trap of suspicious minds.

Human relationships are a hall of mirrors reflecting you reflecting me reflecting you, wanting to notice and be noticed. We project an image of our own mind onto the screen of other minds, like a child playing with a doll, which is why social play is vital for children. We base all our dealings with others on how we ourselves feel.

In our daily affairs we are drawn to those who seem to show an interest in us as people, or are sensitive to the world as we see it. We use our emotional intelligence to work out whether other people like us or we want to befriend them. Often we learn more from those who are *not* like ourselves, because they force us to be self-critical, which is never easy.

Keeping tally

We can't make others happy or get them to do our bidding unless we know what makes them tick. We have to stay on our guard, because they might pose a threat. So we keep a tally, below the level of consciousness: where we have been loved we will love in return, but those who have betrayed us must beware.

The feeling is mutual: when I make you a promise I ransom my reputation because I presume you will remember to call in the debt and be angry if I fail to pay. Debts and promises are moral and interpersonal realities that did not exist before we made them, and to which we can be held accountable at a later date, proving that the social realm of our relationships has as great a power over us as any physical or biological imperative.

Reciprocity is a bond but it is also a straitjacket. We carefully keep our tit-for-tat ledger up to date, logging obligations and favours owed, because few of us are able to give and not to count the cost. Some cultures thrive on the principle of the 'gift', which sounds generous, but it is really a way of ensuring future loyalties and allegiances. Why else say 'many happy returns' on our birthday cards?

Revenge is best served cold.

Where reciprocity goes wrong, and great harm has been done, vengeance and blood-debt can erupt centuries after the original offence, as happened in the ethnic

42

cleansing and genocide in the Balkans in the 1990's. This is why gangster-culture, based on loyalties to tight-knit families, is fertile ground for double-crossing, family feuds, blackmail, vendettas and honour killings. You know too much about what I know about you. Pay-back time will come when you least expect it, because revenge is best served cold.

On the plus side, empathy allows us to see ourselves as others see us, and sympathy permits us to share another's misfortune: we know how hurt we would feel if the same happened to us. We think, 'If I had a friend who did to me what I just did to you, I would be upset too'. In anticipation we play out a moving apology scene in our mind's eye. Or we bear a grudge, which means there is no meeting of minds.

In such machinations lie the origins of trust, compassion and empathy, and the avoidance of betrayal, treachery and civil war in the clan. But our instinct for sympathy also teaches us the virtues of torture: we know how to make each other suffer. Psychopaths use empathy to intensify their cruelty, because they know which buttons to press.

Faking it

And then there is fakery. We may pretend to be hurt, rolling in agony like a footballer after a tackle, or we may feint to send the goalkeeper the wrong way when taking a penalty. Some of the greatest stories in myth and history have been acts of deception: Moses in the bulrushes, the Emperor's new clothes, the Trojan Horse, Pearl Harbour, the Twin Towers, Snow White.

The Trojan Horse
Believing it was an unexpected gift from the departing besieging Greek army, the exhausted Trojan soldiers dragged the mighty horse into their city. But that night, as they slept....

The Mirror of the Mind

Theory of mind helped us to survive cunning, trickery, betrayal and deceit long before it brought us closer in understanding. Shakespeare's plays are full of characters like Hamlet who are 'played on' like a flute to someone else's tune, realising too late the evil that is being plotted against them. They caution us to be savvy, to wise up to a world of false smiles, broken promises and double dealings.

This explains why we value sincerity, which literally means 'without wax'. We can trust the bona fides of the sender of the letter, with no other need for proof. Blushing is another indicator of sincerity. Scientists struggle to explain its evolution, since by making our embarrassment plain, it also gives us away. That may however be its point: I have nothing to hide from you. Blushing triggers a different brain reaction from the sensation of being lied to by someone.

Fortunately, we become expert at realpolitik without the need to go into parliament. We grow up as skilful deceivers, keeping our minds hidden, weighing our motives against what others in our group might be thinking, planning against sudden changes of allegiance.

Our ancestors were better at deception than honesty.

It's a depressing thought that we are here today because our ancestors were better at deception than honesty, reflected in the fact that the dictionary contains more adjectives to describe liars than truth-tellers. Crafting a good lie, and the need to detect the same ruse in others, demands more brain cells and cognitive effort than telling a bad truth. Honesty doesn't always pay. Liars also need very good memories if they are to avoid being found out. In that sense, we might say that the need to lie convincingly drove the evolution of our big brain and its cleverness at playing social chess.

Criminal investigators and courts of law invest millions in lie-detecting technology, but it gives so many false positives as to be no better than hunch. Polygraphs easily misinterpret skin conductance as guilt, and the 'truth serum' sodium pentothal reveals no deeper truths than getting drunk down the pub.

Being economical with the truth is as human as wearing our heart on our sleeve. Not for nothing is history littered with charlatans, traitors, hypocrites, turncoats, mountebanks, impostors and confidence tricksters. This reality is reflected in every story we tell or listen to, which must have a plot, not a mere sequence of events. Given a scenario of three unrelated items, a woman, a boy and a broken vase, we will instinctively impute motives and invent a relationship: she is upset with him *because* he knocked the vase over, and then lied about it. Little wonder that, in common parlance, plotting has become synonymous with intrigue, scheming, betrayal and double-crossing.

Throughout history societies have revered the seer and soothsayer who can second-guess the future, but better still is to anticipate the intentions of our enemies so that we can stay one step ahead. In times of war, nations go to extraordinary lengths to deceive. In World War Two, Allied ships were sacrificed in the Atlantic by the Admiralty, which knew that German U-boats were about to strike. They considered it more important not to let the enemy know that their communications code had been broken. This involved a double-deception, of both friendly and enemy captains, in the hope of a greater prize later on.

Arch deceivers

War games are extensions of an essential truth that we learn in the nursery: we can use our mind-reading powers not just to help each other, but also to mess with each other's heads. As we slowly realise that our surface words do not always match our hidden intentions, we learn to lie and dissemble. This is not a moral failing but an essential survival skill. We soon learn that if we tell the truth every time, or say what is really in our minds, we get into trouble.

On the prosocial side, we can work out who to trust, and invent invisible playmates with minds of their own. On the antisocial side, we can tell fibs, bluff and outwit each other. Our new-found theory of mind turns us into arch deceivers and cunning schemers, planting false beliefs in other people's minds, driving a wedge between appearance and reality to suit our own interests. We can be Polonius spying behind the curtain, or Iago spreading gossip and scandal.

Gradually we get the hang of how to play this mind-game lark.

Up to the age of four, we struggle with the idea of keeping a secret, excitedly telling a friend that a surprise birthday party is being planned for them, but they mustn't tell anyone. Gradually we get the hang of how to play this mind-game lark. We can enjoy *schadenfreude*, taking pleasure in someone else's misfortune:

45

The Mirror of the Mind

I've got more sweets than you, so yah boo sucks. We begin to realise that flattery gets better results than whingeing. We become mentalists, clever at working out how to screw with the minds of our mentors, second-guessing their looks of approval or disapproval.

We learn to manage other people's perceptions, even when they are not physically present. When granny phones and wants to see the birthday present she sent us through the post, we can film it with her perspective in mind, giving her a close-up look. But what if we don't like the present? By age eight, we've sussed that it doesn't always pay to be honest. We simulate gratitude, fake a smile to save her feelings, and start to work out how we can make sure that she buys us what we really want for Christmas.

We learn that in order to survive in the group we must not only become skilled in winning friends, but also in keeping them. If we're wise, we heed the Book of Proverbs: 'Faithful are the wounds of a friend, but deceitful are the kisses of an enemy'. But how far can we really trust a friend? We constantly face the Prisoner's Dilemma: if we're both caught and interrogated separately, do we stay loyal to each other and risk a tougher punishment, or spill the beans and get a reduced sentence?

Quandaries like these constantly embroil us in gamesmanship, brinkmanship and one-upmanship, playing one loyalty off against another. And yet we also hate free-riders and cheats. Our first insight into the complexities of justice and morality is our cry 'It's not fair' when we see someone get a bigger share than us, or we are blamed for something they did.

Laughter is a prosocial way of bringing our minds together, but only if we are let in on the joke. If someone we like laughs at us, we can see the funny side, but if it comes from someone who doesn't belong to our 'in' group, we feel mocked. Groups that laugh together and enjoy a similar sense of humour tend to have tighter social bonds and unity of thinking, but there is still a kind of deception involved. To make someone laugh, we must lead thinking in one direction, only to spring a surprise with a contradictory idea.

By getting the humour right, we confirm our membership of the group. If we get it wrong, we risk looking stupid, and may offend local sensibilities. This is more likely to happen with strangers, with whom we lack empathy. This makes theory of mind the cornerstone of shared identity, culture and morality, because without it, we can have no camaraderie, civil society or consensual politics. But our politics is full of machination and chicanery. Why is this?

Macchiavellian schemers

The necessity of political scheming was no surprise to the Renaissance political theorist Niccolo Machiavelli five hundred years ago, whose book 'The Prince' became the bible of strong leadership. His keynote was that, to stay in power, it is not enough to be fair or honest. Ruthlessness and deception serve much better.

It is no coincidence that spies and secret agents proliferated around this time. Everyone became a potential informer, even within families. The really savvy ones hedged their bets by serving as double agents, with the result that no one could be believed about anything.

Machiavelli's ideas resonate loudly in today's vast networks of moles, spooks, cyber-spies, data snoopers, internet trolls, counter-intelligence operatives, narks, whistleblowers and undercover agents. Espionage is big business, essential for national security, because everybody has designs on everyone else. The military invest heavily in psyops (psychological operations), or ways of messing with the heads of their enemy, which means first getting to know how they think.

Niccolo Machiavelli
1469-1527
He looks as if butter wouldn't melt in his mouth, but this is the man who advised his prince that, 'If an injury is to be done to a man, it should be so severe that his vengeance need not be feared'.

Machiavelli set the tone of mutual mistrust by advising princes to befriend everyone but trust no-one, to keep their friends close but their enemies even

47

closer. The US president Lyndon B Johnson expressed this pithily when he said that he would rather have his enemies inside the tent pissing out than outside pissing in.

Never let anyone know what you are thinking.

Sometimes it pays to sleep with snakes: the enemy of my enemy could one day turn out to be my best friend. But it is a mistake to let either party know this. As Don Corleone, the spiritual descendant of Machiavelli, remarks in 'The Godfather', 'Never let anyone know what you are thinking'.

The downside of this kind of politics for those who grab and cling to power, democratically or by force, is rampant corruption, nepotism, decline of the social fabric, a surge in self-seeking, and collapse of trust. They end up surrounded by sycophants, nowadays dubbed 'advisers', who tell them only what they want to hear. Pandered to by courtiers who are afraid to speak truth to power, the Prince never gets to know what is really going on outside his castle walls. The inevitable plot against him succeeds because it comes from those he suspects the least.

We all lose out in this world of pork barrel politics, where coercion displaces open discussion. Friends become enemies, bluffing, lying and talking about us behind our backs. Wary of the villainy lurking beneath, we no longer trust the rhetoric of politicians or the smiles of officials. And yet without trust, our social life becomes, in the words of the seventeenth century political theorist Thomas Hobbes, poor, nasty and brutish. No wonder we become so angry when those placed in positions of trust betray our confidence. They force us not to trust absolutely, and they inflict on us the cancer of cynicism.

And yet we are all Machiavellian schemers, because we oblige each other to be so. Knowing what I know about myself, I wouldn't trust me if I were you. I'm scheming against you, and you would be stupid not to be scheming against me. Survival is premised on knowing who to trust and how to get on in the world, and if we don't finesse our social intelligence, we will get walked over.

Like our primate ancestors, we soon work out that, though we are weak, we can outwit a stronger rival if we can get a few allies onside, even if we have to do a few dirty deals in the meantime. We can always dump these cronies when they have served their purpose, before they have a chance to dump us.

The Mirror of the Mind

Things work out better for us if our default assumption is that everyone in every walk of life is trying to get one over us. That friendly colleague has designs on our place in the hierarchy. Even a friendly greeting of 'hello' needs to be sussed out carefully: it could be a welcome, a threat, a come-on, a warning, even the prelude to being arrested.

If we read too much into the signals that other people give off, we end up neurotic, fretting unnecessarily about imagined slights: why did she say hello in that tone of voice? If we ignore them altogether, we are sociopathic, cut off from the continent of mankind: I don't care whether she greets me or not. If we misinterpret the signals completely, we become paranoid: she's saying hello to me, but really she hates me.

It is a disturbing thought that the crowning glory of theory of mind is to allow us to be successful hypocrites. It makes us worryingly good at lying, or manipulating each other's perceptions, our words saying one thing and our actions another, putting us both in a double bind: at what point do we call each other's bluff?

Given that 'getting on with each other', by hook or by crook, is as great a key to success in life as any academic honour, it is surprising that interpersonal intelligence is barely taught at school, though it was identified by the developmental psychologist Howard Gardner as one of several 'multiple intelligences' that we possess.

Teachers assume that we pick up interpersonal intelligence in the playground, but theory of mind is not an automatic skill or mere telepathy. We have to *learn* how to mind-read, and it is a hard craft, whose complexity we compound with our own machinations. An even more important intelligence, also mentioned by Gardner, is intrapersonal, or getting to know ourselves, which is the most elusive knowledge of all.

Theory of mind meets technology

We tend to think that science equals progress equals a jolly good thing, but the technology revolution presents theory of mind with challenges it has not evolved to meet. It puts us much more frequently in touch with each other, but at a greater remove.

49

The Mirror of the Mind

Even in the days of lengthy hand-written letters, tone of voice was difficult to convey, and just as hard to hear. In a clipped twitter entry, text message or email, even with a smiley attached, the words lie dead on the screen. In reply, we are far more likely to say something inappropriate, hurtful or offensive, not something we would ever say to someone's face, because we are denied the instant response of a raised eyebrow or scowl.

Internet trolls
Originally stupid, ugly and scary creatures from Nordic folklore, modern trolls spread their fear more subtly, hiding their malevolence behind the anonymity of the web.

Online chats don't allow the spontaneity of conversational turn-taking, or alert our ear to the nuances of the voice. In the absence of visual cues and aural clues, and denied mutual gaze, we lay ourselves open to misunderstanding and abuse, not a meeting of minds. The sporty twenty-something guy we meet on the dating site turns out to be fat and fifty, the teenage girl we think we are socialising with might be an adult male paedophile, and the 'true story' about immigrants claiming benefits they are not entitled to might be a fabrication generated by a bot.

Online, we are communing with a faceless machine.

Beware the internet trolls, shadowy saboteurs skulking behind viewless anonymity, telling lies about themselves, hiding their true identity or stirring up hatred. If we are young or inexperienced, we are vulnerable in these situations. Theory of mind is unable to come to our rescue, because we are communing with a faceless machine.

The Mirror of the Mind

It is no surprise that scams and fake news have exploded in the internet age, because without flesh and blood feedback, we struggle to establish that we are not being addressed by an algorithm. Is this really our bank asking for our financial details, and how can we get to the bottom of this conspiracy theory that a secret cabal of child-molesting politicians are hiding behind the chaos caused by Covid 19?

Even on a video-conference or Zoom call, we suffer a degree of face-blindness, because we are denied the tiny 'tells' that inform face to face interaction, not to mention touch and smell. Social cohesion, even success in business, is dependent on our ability to tune into each other's mood and personality. This is a function not of hyper-connectedness, but of social and emotional intelligence, which starts in the playground, and works best around the office water cooler. Those who regularly work from home say they miss the buzz of interacting with colleagues.

Nature gives us a technology-free head start in life. As babies we do not respond to animated robots as we do to a real face, our brain recognising the difference between a machine and a human agent. But then technology enters our tiny world. Psychologists worry that if we spend too much time as children in our formative years texting or on computer games, especially if we are boys, we are particularly at risk of becoming deskilled at reading faces. Without engaging with live playmates, not virtual avatars, we will struggle in later life to learn defences against Machiavellian scheming, which cannot be learned from a machine.

We will not however grow up to be zombies. When we go with a friend to the cinema to watch 'Attack of the Zombies', we cling to each other in the scary bits, then chat afterwards about how scared we felt during the film. In establishing this common space between us, we pass the 'Turing test', proving we are not answer machines giving each other automated responses.

Some philosophers describe the mind as full of 'qualia', or experiences that are unique to each one of us, giving us the 'quality' of what it is like to be me. We can never access each other's qualia directly, but when you say you feel scared in the film, I can empathise with you, because I know *what it is like to feel scared*. By sharing our responses, we go some way to solving the intractable problem of other minds, proving to each other we are not zombies. By using theory of mind to agree objective facts about our feelings, we create a subjective reality between us, which is more than idiosyncratic, because we peer-review it every time we engage with each other.

When we check out in the supermarket, we might be lucky enough to be greeted with a smiling 'Have a nice day'. We don't assume we are being served by a zombie, nor does the cashier assume that the customers are zombies. If we can't use theory of mind to establish personal contact in these real life situations, we won't find it on our Facebook page, where we are nothing but the sum total of our posts, past purchases, likes and data.

The isolated mind: Autism

Mind blindness – MMR vaccine – Kanner and Asperger – the autistic spectrum – savants – high functioning types – acceptance

- Autism is a complex set of symptoms, the most common of which is 'mind blindness', or impaired theory of mind, though 'high functioning' types can be helped to find ways round this, or find their own solutions.
- It starts in the womb, and can manifest as early as the second year, with symptoms such as inability to share attention, follow eye gaze, understand pointing and return smiles.
- Later on there might be hyper-sensitivity to sensory input, delayed language, difficulty relating socially, and fixation with routine.
- It is not a single condition, but manifests along a spectrum, from mild with unusual intellectual abilities at one end, to severe with problematic behaviours at the other.
- It has no known cause, though there is probably a genetic factor at work, and certain environmental factors have been identified.
- There is no known cure, but specialist teaching can address the challenging learning needs of autistic children.
- Medication is of little use as it does not alter the underlying neural structure.
- The term 'autism' was first used in 1911 in relation to symptoms of schizophrenia.
- Leo Kanner was the first to apply it to children with severe learning difficulties in the 1950's, though he mistakenly saw autism as a treatable genetic disorder.
- Around the same time, Hans Asperger recognised that some autistic children possess exceptional intellectual abilities.

- Unfortunately there is evidence that he condemned to death hundreds of less gifted autistic children under Nazi eugenicist policies.
- Autism affects about one in a hundred children, five times as many boys as girls.
- If cases of autism have increased since the 1960's, it is only because there is much better diagnosis with improved awareness.
- Autistic children are no longer labelled 'retarded', because society has become more accepting of neurodiversity.
- Autism was wrongly implicated in an MMR vaccine scare in the late 1990's, leading to an 'anti-vax' movement which unnecessarily exposed a generation of children to dangerous illnesses.
- Autistic individuals are not natural empathisers, but they can learn ways of behaving appropriately in social situations.
- Some possess unusual systemising abilities that allow them to achieve highly in certain high-pressure jobs.
- Many of the great leaders, heroes, iconoclasts and visionaries of the past might have been somewhere on the autistic spectrum.
- Autism is part of someone's identity, which is why those in the autistic community prefer to be referred to as autistic *people*, not by the name of their neurological disorder.

> *You walk into a room. You see faces, but not the people behind them. Someone says to you, 'It's draughty in here', but it doesn't occur to you that they are asking you to close the door behind you. It's a party, but you don't enjoy large gatherings of people. You feel uncomfortable when someone moves too close to you, or looks steadily at you. It hurts your ears when conversation levels get too loud. You see something out of place, and it agitates you until it is put right. You see food on the table, and you take some before it is offered to you. You are asked to remove your coat, which distresses you, because you always wear your coat. You are told to take it into the hall, and say hello to your host on the way out. You take the coat into the hall, because that instruction was given first, which means you don't get to say hello to the host*
>
> *These are some of the symptoms of autism.*

The inwardly focussed mind

Autism, also known as mind-blindness, has no obvious cause, no simple test, and no easy cure. In a further complication, it is not a single condition, but a constellation of symptoms manifesting along a spectrum, hence its acronym ASD, or Autism Spectrum Disorder, making it a different experience for each person. Sensitive understanding from 'neuronormals' and acceptance of the unique mind-world of autistic individuals can however help them to live the best life possible, even with impaired theory of mind.

Slowly the myths are being dispelled.

When we peer into the brain, we see no obvious lesion or neural malformation that 'causes' autism, but if there is a common factor, it is that those on the spectrum process information differently and faster than normal. This can be overwhelming for some, requiring help to cope with life's basics. For others, it can result in extraordinary abilities.

Considerable progress has been made in understanding autism since its identification in the 1950's, and slowly the myths are being dispelled. Autism is a lifelong condition, but not necessarily a learning disability. That said, around half of those on the spectrum do have a learning disability. It is no longer seen as a disease to be cured, but as a cognitive difference. It is unfair to those who are genuinely autistic to stereotype all males as 'slightly autistic': either one has autism or one doesn't. It is far from the case that everyone in the autistic community lacks empathy. It is not contagious, or a mark of bad character.

Levels of Functioning	
Low functioning	High IQ
Low IQ	High functioning

The Autistic Spectrum
Individuals with ASD might be anywhere within this quadrant.

Another damaging myth is that autism is the result of a stressful birth, though there is some evidence that pre-term babies are at greater risk. It cannot be the fault of the mother, because statistically there is a much higher likelihood of autism in children of fathers over the age of fifty.

This suggests that autism, like schizophrenia, is not a breakdown of the relationship between infant and caregiver, but genetically caused, possibly a chromosomal abnormality. As many as a hundred contributory genes have been identified, affecting the anatomy of the brain from early pregnancy onwards.

Searching for causes

Psychologists, psychiatrists and neuroscientists are always keen to locate the cause of a mental condition, if only to identify risk and protective factors. In the case of autism, there are no clear answers. Some point to a deficiency of the empathy-making hormones oxytocin and vasopressin in the womb or during early months, causing a delay in the formation of the connecting axons of white matter throughout the brain. This can result in events being experienced episodically without relation to each other, and a reduced ability to form social connections.

Teasing out cause and effect is almost impossible.

Another prime suspect is disturbed brain-building REM sleep, leading to arrested neurodevelopment, though teasing out cause and effect in these instances is almost impossible, because the condition intertwines with related conditions such as obsessive compulsive disorder (OCD), attention deficit disorder (ADD), and anorexia.

Some point to problems in the messaging loops between the cerebellum and neocortex, affecting the processing of the flow of sensory information. There is a disconnect between top-down executive control and bottom-up messages, resulting in 'noise' which becomes overwhelming, leading to cognitive shutdown or emotional meltdown. Autistic people say that sometimes their ears feel like microphones with no volume control.

Others look to impaired contraflow through the corpus callosum of left and right brain. If one hemisphere overpowers the other, the pathways in the brain are scrambled. Autistic brains are slightly enlarged, so the cause may be lack of neural pruning at the appropriate time, resulting in an excess of activity, not a deficit. Another culprit may be inadequate neurogenesis, or the making of new neurons at key points in the development process.

The upsurge in reported cases of autism since the 1960's is inevitable given better diagnosis and greater public awareness, but some point to the insecticide DDT. It was banned in the 1970's once its harmful genetic effects were realised, but its molecules had entered the food chain, and will take several generations to break down.

Others blame the 'white noise' of modern life for interfering with healthy neural development in babies, affecting the quality of perception, memory and imagination. The list goes on: faulty mirror neurons, undetected hearing problems in the early years, insufficient human touch, lack of vocabulary, harmful bacteria resulting from poor dental hygiene, or a virus that has not yet been identified.

The Mirror of the Mind

These are all speculation, and no single theory covers all angles, which means there can never be a silver bullet cure.

Hunting for cures

Just as experts have struggled to agree on diagnoses, so have they found it difficult to find cures, some insisting that there isn't one, only strategies that mitigate the condition. Hormone injections have helped some autistic people to enjoy better interpersonal relations, and to achieve a more coherent grasp of reality, but the results are not consistent, because the brain operates as a whole organism, not as discrete parts.

Applied Behavioural Analysis is a controversial treatment which aims at extinguishing anti-social autistic traits by confronting them at a young age, perhaps by obliging an autistic child to stay in a room to complete a task with other children. For a brain that is differently wired, finding noise, change and the presence of other people painful, this is like forcing an arachnophobe to handle a spider. If improvement is effected, which is disputed by some, it is at a high personal and emotional cost for the child.

To change our brain is to change who we are.

Transcranial magnetic stimulation (TMS) targets the brain itself, relieving some symptoms, but it also ethically problematic. It is one thing to excise a cancerous tumour to save a person's life, another to reshape a brain. If it is true that we are our brain, then to change our brain is to change who we are. There is some evidence that TMS can activate empathy circuits in brains where they lie dormant, but they cannot instal feelings that are not there.

Some pin their hopes on a pharmacological cure for autism, but teasing out which chemicals react with which genes, synapses and neurotransmitters is like looking for the proverbial needle. Part of the problem is that each case of autism is different, and any improvement, if it happens at all, is slow, difficult to measure, and not necessarily due to the medication.

Whichever approach is taken, the idea of 'curing' autism is not without controversy. Though the condition is hard for those with extreme symptoms (and their carers), and many are unable to find or manage full-time employment, they are who they are, and not all desire to have their consciousness manipulated.

The best and possibly the only 'cure' is for society to become more understanding and tolerant of autistic individuals, not seeing them as outsiders, deviants or miscreants. Though many show aversion to change, acute introversion, weak emotional control and discomfort with human closeness, others possess extraordinary gifts, are capable of empathy, are determined to make a success of their lives, and want to meet others like themselves.

Temple Grandin
Grandin's 1995 book 'Thinking in Pictures' gives valuable insights into living with autism. Her understanding of the minds of farm animals helped to transform abattoirs in America, though she did not find human minds so easy to get on with, remarking 'I can act social, but it's like being in a play'.

It is a mistake however to think that all those on the ASD spectrum are gifted mavericks, cute personalities or autistic savants, like Raymond in the 1989 film 'Rain Man', whose uncanny ability to memorise cards almost broke the casino. Only a few autistics are savants, not all savants are autistic, and many such people are difficult to live with, requiring basic help in negotiating the challenge of getting through the day.

Some, such as Temple Grandin, have learned to adjust to the demands the world makes on them. She has held down a challenging job, pioneering important changes in how animals are treated in abattoirs. She has written her own story and taught the rest of us how to live with difference. Its very title, 'Thinking in Pictures', gives an insight into how the autistic mind processes reality. As if to remind us that we see the world very much through our own eyes, she describes herself as feeling like an anthropologist on Mars. We are the aliens, not her.

The Mirror of the Mind

Others on the autistic spectrum have found their métier in Silicon Valley in California, using their extraordinary ability to see patterns where the rest of us see nothing to design the software that powers the digital revolution. When we look at high achievers such as Grandin, it seems as if their mastery of systems has depended on their ability to look beyond people, if not shut them out completely.

Vaccination scare

Autism hit the news for the wrong reason in 1998 when the medical doctor Andrew Wakefield linked the onset of autism to the MMR (measles, mumps and rubella) vaccine. At the time he was in receipt of a large grant to investigate whether the parents of autistic children had sufficient evidence to bring a case against the makers of the vaccine, so his opinions were hardly impartial. He was also playing on a mistaken fear that an 'outbreak' of autism was going on, as if it could be caught like the common cold. Schools in Silicon Valley were reporting a rise in the number of children with symptoms of autism.

This 'scare' had two probable causes: a better and more inclusive diagnosis, and more autistic children being born to workers in the computer industry. Through assortative mating, parents who were themselves somewhere on the autistic spectrum were bringing together genes which resulted in a higher than the one-in-a-hundred national average for the condition.

Wakefield's research turned out to be poorly executed and based on a conspiracy theory that Big Pharma, by prioritising profits, was putting a generation of children at risk. This led many parents to reject *any* kind of vaccination on the grounds that it exposed their children to the possibility of brain damage. By swallowing this misinformation, bordering on disinformation, they laid their offspring open unnecessarily to potentially debilitating diseases that doctors believed were a thing of the past.

Vaccination is not about individuals, but populations.

Those who refused to allow their children to be vaccinated failed to understand the logic of vaccination. It is not about individuals, but populations. If the scourges of polio and whooping cough are to be eradicated, which have blighted the lives of millions across the world, the coverage has to be total, otherwise the unvaccinated leave a route back for the virus in even more deadly form.

Smallpox was eradicated in the 1970's, and measles was on the way to oblivion, but about sixty thousand still die every year because the protection of the MMR vaccine has been blocked in some communities. Those children who survive a measles infection do not escape scot free: they can experience chronic fertility problems or a depressed immune system for up to ten years after.

Those who refuse to vaccinate their children are therefore committing the ultimate act of selfishness: sacrificing the lives of children they don't know on their anti-science altar, and leaving it to others to carry the torch in the global battle against infectious disease.

Their benighted view goes well beyond complacency, which is harmful enough. It is bolstered by dangerous anti-vaccination scare stories shared uncritically online, even in the case of the Covid 19 pandemic. The 2016 anti-vaccine documentary 'Vaxxed', backed by Hollywood stars who know no more about epidemiology than the guy who takes away their rubbish, is typical of the low level of debate and misdirected concern. The motive was more to do with pursuing irrational science denialism than a rational attempt to get at the truth.

There were glitches with vaccines in the early days, and they do cause occasional harmful side effects, but these are negligible compared to the millions of lives saved. The alleged 'link' between the MMR vaccine and autism remains totally unproven. It doesn't help when doctrinaire conservative clerics insist that vaccines are contrary to the will of God or Allah. This ignorance infuriates the medical profession, and sends many children needlessly to an early grave.

Kanner and Asperger

Autism was identified almost simultaneously by two Austrian doctors working separately in the 1950's, Leo Kanner and Hans Asperger, who took contrasting views of it. Kanner saw it as a rare genetic disability that could be treated, and he pointed the finger of blame at mothers. His work was largely with low-IQ children, whereas Asperger worked with 'high functioning' individuals, whose autism made them capable of remarkable intellectual feats.

Asperger took a much more positive view of the condition than Kanner, calling his subjects 'little professors'. He also believed the condition is much more common than previously believed, perhaps essential for innovation in art and science. He took a more psychological approach than Kanner, pointing to the extraordinary creative qualities of some autistics as the brain compensates in other areas, while not overlooking their social struggles.

To this day Aspergers is considered a milder or 'high functioning' form of autism, some people growing to adulthood without realising they possess some of its symptoms. Parents prefer a diagnosis of Aspergers for their child, as it hints at a touch of genius, but this is not the case for all Asperger diagnoses.

Hans Asperger
1906-1980
Asperger left two totally contrasting legacies. He established that some on the Autistic Spectrum are high achievers, but he also contributed to the extermination of low achievers under Nazi eugenicist policies.

Though Asperger has given his name to this kind of autism, a shocking revelation was made about him early this century. The same logic that selects some for their brilliance can be used to deselect others for their degeneracy. It turned out that Asperger had contributed directly to the Nazi T4 programme, which oversaw the liquidation of three hundred thousand disabled people. He personally condemned eight hundred low-achieving autistic children to death by lethal injection, deeming them unfit to live in a Reich of chosen brains and perfect bodies. By the light of today's standards, those children would have been identified as having special educational needs.

It was Kanner's deficit model of autism that
ruled the roost in education.

The Mirror of the Mind

Before we delete Asperger's name, we must acknowledge that he queried the lines we struggle to draw between giftedness and psychiatric disorder. He also spotted that high functioning autistics possess unique intellectual abilities, and opened the door to the identification of rare genetic conditions such as Williams Syndrome, which sometimes features exceptional musical ability. Unfortunately however, it was Kanner's deficit model of autism that ruled the roost in education until well into the 1980's.

We now understand that, while the cognitive abilities of autistic people can be perfectly normal if not higher than usual, the 'folk psychology' or social module of their brain does not develop normally. Most of us 'suss out' other people effortlessly, but for those on the ASD spectrum the distinctions between pots, pans and people are blurred.

Normally our empathy neurons fire when we see others in pain or showing love to each other, but the emotional responses of autistic people are suppressed, so they struggle to discriminate between types of physical contact, and the feelings they convey, unsure whether they are experiencing a punch, prod, caress or playful nudge.

This does not mean that autistic people are unable to function in a social setting. They may not be able to feel empathy, but they can 'do emotion' by using other thought processes to work out what others may be feeling. They learn to navigate the complex minefield of social relations not by relying on natural sympathy, but as a conscious skill, treating other minds as problems to be solved, and adjusting their behaviour accordingly.

Extraordinary abilities

If theory of mind is to flourish, we need to focus outwards, but in autism (from Greek *autos*, self) the mind is self-focussed to the exclusion of other minds. This frees up under-employed 'social' brain space for types of intelligence that can be extraordinary and unconventional, leading to some unusual cognitive combinations, such as the physicist Paul Dirac, a genius who could unlock the mysteries of matter, but who struggled to understand the art of conversation.

Autistic people are able to focus on one thing
more intently than the rest of us.

63

The Mirror of the Mind

The brain is always keen to colonise under-used neural territory, especially the extensive language-processing region. But robbing Peter to pay Paul has to be compensated for somewhere in the brain. Autistic people find ordinary conversation very challenging. To them a sexual relationship means precisely that: the provision of sex with as little emotional entanglement as possible. A request such as 'can you close the door?' might be met with the answer 'yes' without any follow-up action, because it takes theory of mind to work out that what we really mean is that we are cold.

Mind blindness does have some advantages. Stage fright is caused by what others may think of us, but for autistic individuals, the full auditorium might as well be empty, as there is no awareness of critical minds looking on. They can perform before an audience with no embarrassing self-consciousness. This may be the result of diminished mirror-neuron activity in their brain, and their ability to focus on one thing more intently than the rest of us.

Paul Dirac
1902-84
Dirac was a brilliant physicist, but he was also a loner who struggled with social situations. Like Albert Einstein, he was high on the Autistic Spectrum, though no-one knew or thought like that at the time.

The Mirror of the Mind

At the 'high achieving' end of the autistic spectrum, reduced growth in some brain functions may result in extraordinary abilities in other areas, such as pattern-recognition, spatial awareness, entrepreneurial flair, design skills, memory retention and calculating ability, that eclipse more ordinary but vital 'touchy-feely' social and communication skills. Alan Turing, the genius who broke the Enigma code in World War Two and laid the foundations for modern computing, was on the spectrum, and behaved in a socially awkward manner, though no-one would have understood his symptoms at that time.

In spite of or perhaps because of her autism, Temple Grandin made a name for herself by campaigning for better conditions for farm animals. Though she was unable to empathise with those who ran the meat-packing industry, she could sense the distress of animals about to be slaughtered in the abattoir, and designed systems to reduce their suffering.

Greta Thunberg, who felt isolated from her peers as a young teenager, suffering from difficulties with eating and talking, believes it was her 'laser focus' that enabled her to ask awkward questions, and to force others to provide answers. She was awarded the Gulbenkian Prize for Humanity in 2020 for her work on raising global awareness of climate change, and is able now to address large crowds who are inspired by her example.

Greta presents a challenge to educational systems that are designed to cater for the average and conventional. Teachers identify and try to meet special needs outside the bell curve of normal intelligence, but autistic children present additional challenges and opportunities.

Defining features

Autism is a constellation of symptoms, never reducible to one behaviour. In a further complication, there is a psychological dimension as well as a physical one. Selective autism or mutism for instance involves speaking freely at home but being too anxious to talk at school or in the workplace.

Early intervention is vital.

There are many possible signs of autism, starting around two years old and escalating in the early years. Sometimes these self-resolve by the age of four, but if not, early intervention is vital, because a young child's isolation inevitably compounds into an adult who feels increasingly alienated.

Parents and carers note that communication and social skills are not unfolding to schedule. The child might seem withdrawn and in a world of its own, avoiding eye contact, not returning smiles or engaging in imaginative play. Theory of mind is normally a passport to relatedness, but for the autistic child, the focus is inwards.

They might also observe difficulty in sharing attention, poor conversational skills, detachment from what others in the room are doing, low concentration, fixation on particular things, self-absorption, and discomfort with changes in routine, possibly leading to panic attacks. Autistic children often find it hard to be in the presence of more than one person at a time, preferring the company of animals, especially cats, which do not hold the gaze as dogs do. The message for those working with autistic people is not to stare, or to look them in the eye only briefly.

As they mature, Aspergers children develop some independence and manage social situations well, but only because they gradually learn to mask their awkwardness. At the low-achieving end, one-on-one care might be needed to guide the individual through the day.

The clinical psychologist Simon Baron-Cohen has identified three defining features of normal social engagement, which we owe to the complex Machiavellian manoeuvring that our ancestors had to perform in their evolution as close-knit groups on the African savannah.

The first is an ability which most of us take for granted, an eye direction detector in our brain. We might think it is the pupil of our eye that gives away who we are looking at, but it is the surrounding white sclera that allows others to track our gaze. In our early evolution, knowing when we are being looked at, and when we should look away, played a vital role in establishing our status in the group.

Secondly we possess a shared attention module. When we sit down to read to a child, the book on our lap becomes the focus for a marriage of minds, the gateway to the transmission of human culture. We tune into the way the child sees the world, and the child learns from our understanding. We adapt our adult perspective to accommodate the child's wish to linger over a page, go back to ask questions, talk about things we don't see, and to hear the story all over again.

The Mirror of the Mind

Simon Baron-Cohen
b 1958
The clinical psychologist drew attention to our abilities to detect eye direction, share attention, and practise theory of mind, three key cognitive faculties which autistic people usually find difficult.

Finally, we enjoy theory of mind. If we see someone go into a shop and come out with a bag of goods, it doesn't take us long to work out motive and intention. Our built-in 'intentional stance' ensures that we treat others *as if* they are rational agents, even when they are total strangers to us. We assume that they possess minds like ours, governed by similar beliefs and desires.

The flip side to this, and there always is one, is that we know they are doing the same to us. In many ways, society functions as well as it does because we know we are constantly being watched, or having our minds read. Autistic people lack these social antennae, so to them other people are not fellow minds pursuing personal agendas, but impersonal objects that move around randomly and make the occasional noise.

In addition to social awkwardness, autistic individuals are creatures of fixed habits. They cling to sameness and cannot bear change, often feeling most comfortable in the controlled environment of cyberspace, where face to face interaction is minimal. They find some relief in computer games and virtual reality, where they can explore social spaces without the crushing embarrassment of having to deal with real people. They might be unable to sleep unless the blind is pulled to a precise angle, or they might insist on keeping their coat on even in a heated room. In other words, systems matter more than feelings.

Systemisers and empathisers
This split between systems and feelings may be the echo of a step-change in human thinking a hundred thousand years ago. Palaeontologists note that there was a 'creative explosion' beginning around this time, perhaps the result of a genetic mutation: spotting patterns, predicting outcomes and innovating technically. After a million years of relative standstill, we start to see a greater emphasis on 'systemising': more refined tool-making, jewellery, sewing, musical instrument manufacture and eventually cave painting appearing in the human record. The systemising abilities of autistic individuals might the after-glow of this intellectual 'big bang'.

In the autistic brain, systemising, or preoccupation with patterns, rules over empathising, or reading other minds.

The 'systemising circuit' in the brain was not however the only new feature of human culture. It was accompanied by an equally powerful 'empathy circuit'. Burials around this time start to be accompanied by garlands of flowers, and objects that were held dear by the deceased. A healthy brain holds these two systems in balance, but in the autistic brain, systemising, or preoccupation with patterns, rules over empathising, or reading other minds.

Over-emphasis on systemising has been dubbed 'extreme male brain'. This is misleading, because females suffer from systemising too. Fewer girls are affected than boys, but this may be because they learn social skills faster, and are better at hiding their symptoms, which in any case manifest differently in each sex. Young males are more likely to experience difficulty in handling change, whereas females struggle with facial recognition.

Stereotypes are always dangerous. Men can be sensitive and women obsessive, so it is better to see all of us as somewhere along an autistic spectrum, regardless of our gender, with extreme-male-brain systemisers at one end and extreme-female-brain empathisers at the other. We also need to remember that letting our emotions 'hang out' all the time can be as debilitating as being obsessed with sorting out our sock drawer.

It is not helpful or accurate however to try to console an autistic individual by saying that all men are autistic in one way or another, or that we're all autistic to a degree. We are either on the spectrum or we are not.

The eating disorders bulimia and anorexia, normally associated with young girls, may be part of the autistic spectrum because they involve obsessive calorie counting and inflexible routines, so boys may suffer symptoms of both. The causes of such disorders may not be gender-related at all, but attributable to high cholesterol levels, which give false positive feedback to the brain that the stomach is ravenously empty, or already full. People with eating disorders also report hearing voices in their head which tell them to eat or not eat.

Mr Spock in 'Star Trek', from the planet Vulcan, displays classic symptoms of autism: he is a brilliant systemiser but a poor empathiser, highly rational but void of emotion. He can engage with his fellow human crew members, because he uses logic to second-guess their intentions, not theory of mind. They value him for his ability to provide a dispassionate analysis of any situation, and for his use of words as logical counters, not emotional weapons.

They know that he would never cause harm to them or their mission, because his high-systemising and low-empathising mean that he is always motivated to seek the best outcome, based on reason. In common with autistic individuals, he may not possess theory of mind, and he may lack empathy, but that does not make him a dangerous psychopath. Psychopaths can read minds, and use this knowledge to harm others. Mr Spock sees people as puzzles to be solved, not victims to be exploited.

In real life, autistic people face much more challenging personal problems than surfing the galaxy. Over-intense focus on detail can blind them to the big picture, and fixation on repeated behaviours can turn them into compulsive ritualists. They miss out on the nuances of irony, and the delights of gossip. Their aloofness, lack of tact and inability to tell white lies makes them strangers to love, and vulnerable to bullying, even though they cannot work out the motive for such cruelty.

The Mirror of the Mind

Mr Spock
A Vulcan member of the 'Star Trek' crew, he is valued for his dispassionate rationality and ice cold logic. His intellect spans the universe, but the quirks of the human heart are totally beyond his ken.

Depending where they are on the spectrum, they may have problems with recognising body boundaries, touching other bodies as if they are their own but feeling uncomfortable when touched themselves. Their bodies no longer coincide with where their skin begins and ends, and they do not understand the meaning of pointing to a reality outside themselves. Their senses can be tuned to unbearable levels, making them hyper-sensitive or unable to distinguish input: normal talk can sound like shouting.

Accepting difference

The organic nature of autism cautions us against regarding those who display symptoms as evolutionary abnormalities. They are always individuals, better seen as personality types, not medical statistics. They are capable of giving and receiving love, few of them totally lacking in interpersonal skills and social intelligence.

Many of the great visionaries who have driven forward culture, history, art and thinking have shown autistic traits to some degree, benefiting from some of the insights afforded by being somewhere on the spectrum. One in a thousand of us carries genes associated with autism, and it is possible the condition has survived natural selection because society needs people who can focus single-mindedly on a project to bring about cultural change.

There should be room in an inclusive society for the eccentric,
the unusually gifted and the differently focussed.

Autism might be seen as a high-risk adaptation, but it is more than a mechanical breakdown. It is vital for innovation, diversity, change and charismatic leadership, and there should be room in an inclusive society for the eccentric, the unusually gifted and the differently focussed. After years of exclusion and enforced silence, autistic people, as well as sufferers from the related condition attention deficit disorder, are finally being allowed their own voice, and a say in the kind of lives they want to lead.

After centuries of ignorance, we can now see autism as a natural cognitive variation, no different from having pitch-perfect hearing. Better diagnosis and readiness to accept neurodiversity have in the last half century led to more enlightened attitudes towards those who are at one end of a spectrum whose traits we all recognise.

It's not so long since communities viewed deviants from the norm as cursed by God, leaving them out in the cold to die, or expelling them from the group. Neuroscience and cognitive psychology, not to mention common compassion, have taught us otherwise. Autism is no longer seen as a curse, childhood anomaly or affliction of cold parenting, but a lifelong mind-difference that needs to be understood.

Autism can present children and their carers with many difficulties, but there is growing realisation that autistic individuals view the world in potentially transformative ways, as 'islands of ability', capable of expressing themselves uniquely. They can be helped to learn effective coping strategies, to grow into adults capable of leading fulfilling lives, and to offer the rest of us unique insights.

At school, there are now many creative activities and techniques to integrate autistic children into the mainstream. Appropriate behaviours can be reinforced, and harmful ones extinguished. Consistency of daily routine can shelter them from unexpected emotional disruption. Visual aids, perhaps enhanced by technology,

71

can help them to structure their day and their thinking, as can stories that make feelings explicit, embellished with happy or sad faces serving as emojis. For adults, the autism directory can put them in touch with like minds, and services in their area.

Autism is no longer seen as a disease to be 'cured', but as a natural mind condition, part of the person, to be respected as its own way of being and knowing in the world.

Seeing really

Establishing what is real

Sense and reason – imagination – magical thinking – social reality – reality testing – common sense reality – quantum reality – constructed reality – the reality principle – hyperreality – art and illusion – realism – the Ultimate Real

- We use the word 'real' in so many ways that it is almost impossible to pin it down.
- This is because our mind has evolved as both subject and object, giving us several ways of knowing and being in the world.
- The 'scientific real' shows us a world of physical things, reason gives us realms of thought, and our imagination gives us values and unicorns.
- Our senses access only a fraction of what is 'out there', so they cannot be the sole arbiters of what is real.
- Reason helps us to make sense of things, but without the anchor of the senses, it has no mooring.
- Imagination gives us love, justice, truth and beauty, made real when we live them out, not look for proofs of them.
- 'Reality' is best seen therefore as a finely woven tapestry, created when we mix our mind with the world.
- Our first few years are spent in 'magical thinking', trying to figure out the porous boundaries between appearances, actualities and fantasies, our mind quickly resetting to default.
- At the same time we are inducted into the social reality of friends, how to play together, and what others expect of us.

The Mirror of the Mind

- To help us navigate the complex realities that lie in store, our brain is primed with (usually) failsafe 'reality-testing' circuits.
- These give us what we call our 'common sense' view of reality, bolstered by the scrutiny and correction of other minds.
- Reality is not see-through, or just given to us. It is 'made' by our mind/brain partnership in a 'code' that looks nothing like the thing represented.
- This remarkable feat is best displayed in our ability to probe reality at quantum level, which is 'weird', because it defies our expectations.
- As new technologies transform our 'ways of seeing', we are discovering new realities and mind spaces previously unimagined.
- As well as physical reality, we live in the midst of socially constructed realities, such as language, law, money and our sense of identity.
- These are just as 'real', but in a totally different way, upheld by belief and custom.
- Our social realities are dependent on both time and culture, so they can change, sometimes quite quickly.
- We are primed to want more than we can have, but the 'reality principle' kicks in to keep us grounded.
- This 'reality check' is especially useful in the 'hyperreality' of modernity, where realities shift before our eyes, signs are temporary, images flash by, and style is more than substance.
- To steady the ship, scientists seek the Theory of Everything, or the One True Real that underpins the physical world.
- They follow in a long tradition of religious thinkers and philosophers, who believe there is an Ultimate Reality of 'perfect forms' in a fifth dimension, of which we see only shadows.
- Artists down the ages have given us visions of other realities which are at once illusions, but also glimpses of things unseen.

The Mirror of the Mind

- The most 'realistic' art is only a pale copy of life, but our lives would be much poorer without its exploration of other possibilities.
- We cannot prove the 'existence' of an Ultimate Reality, only commit to it and see what follows.

The real thing

As well as assuming that we can see into other minds, we also suppose that the mirror of the mind gives us an accurate picture of reality. On closer inspection, we realise that we have little evidence for such presumption, and there is more to reality than meets the eye. How, in a puddle of colourless water one inch deep, can we see technicolour clouds reflected eight miles high? How do we know the 'real' colour of a flower, given that it changes with the passing light?

Much depends on the nature of light, our seeing equipment, and the world-making capacity of our brain which, like Dr Who's Tardis, is much bigger on the inside than it looks on the outside. Our eyes contain three types of colour-receptor, red, blue and green, which our brain mixes, but the spectrum of colour we see as a result is a very human palette. Some insects possess up to five or six types of receptor, 'seeing' a very different sort of picture show.

If we add that we cannot see in the dark, like an owl, or pick up sonar, like a bat, we realise that the reality given to us by our eyes is very partial. Without highly specialised equipment, we can't see anything below atomic level, or what is inside a black hole.

Much of what is in our mind is what we realise,
or make real for ourselves.

To complicate things further, as we shall see in this chapter, there are many definitions of 'reality', depending on who is doing the looking, and how. There is an old story about three blind men touching an elephant for the first time. The first feels the wispy tail, the second pats the huge stomach, and the third holds the rough trunk.

The Mirror of the Mind

None of them 'sees' the elephant entire, or understands what kind of thing it is. Each is like a modern photographer who has a case of lenses, from close-up to telephoto, but who uses the same lens for every shot. It is only when we use different lenses, or ask different questions, that we get different pictures of reality.

Defining reality is not therefore straightforward, and perhaps not even possible. In the quantum world, reality turns out to be much queerer than we can imagine, and nothing is as simple as it seems. Much of what is in our mind is what we *realise*, or make real for ourselves. We have to understand how each 'real' gains traction only in relation to all the other 'reals' we live with on a daily basis.

It doesn't help that we use the word 'real' very loosely, revealing more about our attitude to what we are describing than anything objective: she's a real friend, you cook a real curry, I've been told to act like a real man. If we delete the word 'real' in these instances, we take nothing away from the world. All we are doing is expressing and intensifying our feelings.

We also use 'real' to measure something against a perceived gold standard: they've made a real home for the children, I don't think this is in my real interests, that's not real music. These kinds of real are subjective. Someone else might come along and take an entirely different view of them, which poses a philosophical problem. An apple has no taste until its sugar molecules react with our taste buds. Then, having taken a bite, no matter how convinced we are that it tastes lovely, we have no way of knowing what it tastes like to anyone else, or to our horse. The taste is real enough, but it is a private reality, not a public one. It's quite possible to meet someone who absolutely hates the taste of apples, or an apple might taste completely different if we've just eaten a chilli pepper.

The subjective real contrasts strongly with the objective real of the scientist: the real is what can bite back, because it exists independently of our noticing it. We feel the physical reality of a rock when we give it a hard kick. Any pain we might feel is mind-dependent, and will disappear, but the rock is independent of our being mindful of it, and will still be there in ten thousand years' time, even if there is no one to kick it.

The Mirror of the Mind

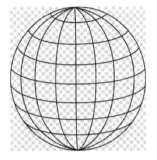

Lines of latitude
These are nowhere to be seen on the earth's surface. They exist in the minds of navigators, 'real' enough to save thousands of lives from a watery death.

The difference between the objective 'real' and subjective 'real' is clear in the two statements 'the fire is hot' and 'I am hot'. In a fusion of the knower and the known, we know that if we back away from the fire, we cool down, while the fire retains its heat. There are therefore two types of heat, one in the fire and one in us, and it makes no sense to say one heat is 'more real' than the other, only to know how and why they differ.

The word real comes from the Latin *res*, a thing with an existence independent of any pain in our toe or our body temperature. In that sense, to advertise a product as the 'real thing' is tautological. A thing is either real or it isn't, it exists or it doesn't exist.

But reality as perceived by the human mind is more subtle than this. We can't step on lines of latitude, but they 'exist' in the atlas, and in the minds of navigators, who have used them to save thousands of sailors from perishing on reefs and rocks.

Intertwined realities

The meaning of a word resides in how we use it, not in its literal derivation. Take feelings and memories. They are not tangible 'things', but we don't doubt their reality, even though they are invisible to others. We can't touch or smell them, but they are 'reals' generated by our mind's ability to create and store images, concepts and symbols.

We must try therefore to define our terms before we set out, difficult though that is, otherwise 'reality' means only what we set out to find in the first place,

The Mirror of the Mind

'leaving a lot to the imagination', as John Lennon quipped. It's too vague to say that reality is 'everything that is'. Nor is it helpful to define reality as 'whatever our brain serves up to us', or 'what the mirror of our mind reflects', because our various 'takes' on it change colour more often than the chameleon. If we're not careful, we end up with Ambrose Bierce's definition of reality as 'the dream of a mad philosopher'.

One way through is to say that reality is how our brain process what it receives through our senses. It is a biological organ and prediction engine, programmed to extract logical consistency from the millions of random electrical signals that assail it every second. This approach does not however get us very far. These signals have to be interpreted within a given life-world, otherwise they remain just that, passive perceptions and bursts of energy with no meaning, no matter how finely ordered.

> *Without subjective response, we get the experience*
> *but miss the meaning.*

As well as possessing a biological brain, we need an existential mind, because we inhabit two realities, an objective one based on our brain's detection of light and sound, and a subjective one grounded in what we see in our mind's eye and hear in our mind's ear. Without the latter, we get the experience but miss the meaning.

We know these two realities are separate and different, because light and sound existed long before human senses evolved to 'realise' or enjoy them, and the Dark side of the Moon remains dark whether we can see it or not. But as well as being different, our objective and subjective realities are inextricably intertwined, and if we are to feel psychologically whole, they need to be integrated.

The reality of rainbows
The Romantic Movement lauded personal insight and flamboyance, leaving brute reality to the scientists, but the split is artificial, unnecessary and dangerous. As we know when we get ill, our mind and body are bound together by hoops of steel.

The Mirror of the Mind

When we are depressed, we may need medication, but a good talk with the doctor or a close friend can help just as much.

The Mind's Reality Show

Empirical reality	The 'hard' reality of sticks and stones, or things that 'bite back', accessible to our senses. It is mind-independent, continuing to exist even when we ignore it.
Rational reality	The 'soft' reality given to us by reason. We cannot see it, but we are born knowing that the opposite of up is down. It is mind-dependent: it doesn't exist unless we think the thought.
Common sense reality	A blend of empirical and rational realities. When we mix our mind with the world, we fuse the knower and the known. This is the default reality we return to after a dream.
Scientific reality	Science challenges common sense reality. We say the sun rises and sets, but we are the ones on the move. Science shows us realities in the quantum world that defy our expectations.
Personal reality	Our private reality beyond the reach of science. No-one else thinks our thoughts, knows our joys, feels our pains, suffers our anxieties or shares our dreams.
Social reality	Our interpersonal reality, outside of which our personal reality has no context or meaning. Other minds shape and nurture us by giving us regular reality-checks. We are because they are.
Constructed reality	Our conscious awareness of how things are *presented* to us. It is shaped by human 'constructions' as 'real' as sticks and stones, such as language, culture, family, law, science, religion and the arts.
Ideological reality	Our 'reality-take' on how things *feel* to us. It is not innocent, but comes wrapped in a bundle of social and political attitudes about gender, race, class, identity and belief. Politically, we see what we want to see.
Moral reality	Our 'Golden Rule' reality, partly instinctive, partly taught to us, but mostly absorbed through our social interactions. All societies have the same sanctions for living selfishly and harming others.
Ultimate Reality	Reality (note the capital R) in the fifth dimension, accessible partly by reason, but mostly by faith, which is driven by feeling. Many deny its existence, or live contentedly without it.
Fantasy reality	Illusions and virtual realities created by our imagination, usually harmless. When they become delusions, fanaticisms or psychoses, they make us much more likely to 'lose touch' with reality, and harm others.

The Mirror of the Mind

*Human reality is what happens when
we mix our mind with the world.*

Rather than pitting science against imagination, we can enjoy the best of both worlds, seeing a real rainbow while appreciating the song as a real artefact of popular culture. We can study light through a prism, which is scientific realism. Or we can go in search of the crock of gold at the end of the rainbow, which is affective realism. The first is 'coloured' by our intellect, the second by our feelings. Human reality is what happens when we mix our mind with the world. It is two realities, neither of which can exist in isolation, or be reduced to the other.

Romantic dreamers wax lyrical about rainbows, blaming scientists for 'unweaving' them with dull theory and explanation. They prefer to seek the crock of gold at the end of each one, an 'imaginary real' that 'exists' as an object of thought. This 'rainbow of the mind' bears little or no relation to the 'scientifically real' rainbow that has weight and volume, can be measured by scientific instruments, and can be accounted for by physical laws.

And yet poets and scientists both rely on the imagination as a picture-making device. Without it scientists cannot probe as yet unseen mysteries of matter. In terms of what can be seen, they want to give us a stripped-down version of nature, free of illusion, to help us understand what we are *really* seeing. To achieve this, they must distance us from our 'common sense' view of the world, with some unsettling results.

Our eyes see a rainbow, but its beginning and end shift as we shift, so although it is fixed in time, it is not fixed in space. Does this make it an optical illusion, the product of neural fireworks in our visual cortex, a pretty trick of the senses? We see seven colours in it, but Isaac Newton revealed that these wavelengths are only part of a much wider spectrum, the rest of which is invisible to our eyes.

In one sense the rainbow is a hallucination, a figment of our visual apparatus. But it is not a delusion, because it is not based on a false belief: we really do believe we see it. Science confirms this, not by appealing to imagination as fantasy, but as fact. It shows us the physical cause of a rainbow, which is even more magical: it is made of photons of light, refracted through raindrops, entering our retina, and processed by our visual cortex.

80

The Mirror of the Mind

These particles, though the fastest things known to nature, have taken eight minutes to get to us from the sun. They may be see-through, but they are nevertheless part of the material world. They can be absorbed, reflected and bent, and when they hit the human eye, they become the colours of the rainbow.

We are helped in our understanding that rainbows are more than random signs from the heavens by the fact that they are always accompanied by other phenomena, such as rain, dark clouds and sunlight. Perhaps most importantly, we know that other people see them too, just as they do the Northern Lights, or a sunset, or a mirage. Otherwise Judy Garland's rendition of 'Somewhere over the Rainbow' would have no more credibility than the sighting of a flying saucer.

The reality of unicorns

We have all seen a rainbow or a sunset, but we have never seen a unicorn, in real life at least. And yet it is real in our imagination. We have seen pictures of one, and 'unicorn' has an entry in the dictionary. Words however are merely signs, and do not necessarily point to anything in the real world.

A unicorn is an imagined entity with no body or substance, so it will never need feeding. If we have a toy unicorn, we can stroke it, possibly get it to make a noise if it has a squeaker, but we can't cuddle the *thought* of a unicorn. Nor will we see one fly around the room under its own steam, except in our mind's eye, or in a Disney movie.

Seeing unicorns
We'll never see a creature like this in nature, but we can blend features from existing animals to create a fantastical beast. Wings were added by later fantasists.

And yet, as a fantasy creature, a unicorn is made from three existing 'reals', a horse, a horn and wings, the last of these added much later, proving it is a mythological beast, not the product of natural selection. It also partakes of the

81

essence of 'horsiness': it has hooves, a mane and a long tail that can be combed. These familiar ingredients make it fairly easy for our brain to create a mash-up of a new 'surreal' creature belonging to the 'real' of the imagination.

Shakespeare appeals to this creative faculty of mind when he asks his audience to 'piece out our imperfections with your thoughts'. He knows that we can suspend our disbelief and toy with reality, enabling us to see things on the stage which we know can't possibly be real, such as ghosts and fairies.

A unicorn is a 'pretended' reality, the fruit of the imagination's ability to make something that was not there before. There is a beast in the bathtub. We need the creative and transformative power of imagination to see beyond the real because, without it, we could never understand ourselves, see into each other's minds, fantasise about the future, or theorise about the world.

Mere thinking cannot make things so.

This doesn't mean that mere thinking can make things so, because that would turn reality into a free-for-all. It does mean that imagination makes our mind plastic enough to embrace new ideas, or to un-imagine ideas we have outgrown, or want to jettison, such as heaven or hell. As John Lennon sang, it's easy if we try. Paradoxically however, when we say 'Bambi is not real', we are attributing a negative existence to an acknowledged fiction, or granting a non-existent entity sufficient existence to dismiss it as a non-entity. No wonder it is so difficult to kill an idea.

The child's reality
We can thank the arrival of the 'big brain' on the human scene about two million years ago for our ability to toggle between fact and fantasy, but we have to spend the majority of our early years learning how to do so.

From the moment of birth we are immersed in reality, experiencing it like a Zen master, with no split between thought and feeling. Peekaboo appeals because it is our first step in distinguishing magic from reality: an object continues to exist, even when we can't see it, and we get excited because we know it is going to pop back up again.

The Mirror of the Mind

To our child's mind, reality *is* magic, related to the word maya, or illusion, but it doesn't stay this way. Our brain is a reality-making machine par excellence, seeing reality as a puzzle to be solved. As our cortex grows, it helps us to map the world in space-time, testing the gaps between physics and fun.

But magical thinking doesn't disappear. It allows us to think and look in both realms, holding contraries in mind: the world is a rational place in which dropped objects always fall to the floor, but our toys can fly through the air, and our puppets can talk, and we can have imaginary friends.

Psychologists have noted strong links between early fantasising,
high intelligence and later intellectual achievement.

These are not delusions but necessary steps in our cognitive development. Psychologists have noted strong links between early fantasising, high intelligence and later intellectual achievement. No culture or childhood is complete without its Arcadia or Middle Earth, and any time we spend there does not weaken our sense of reality, but sharpens our grasp of it. After our foray into the enchanted forest, we return with a heightened sense of the need to tidy up our bedroom and make plans for the future.

Imagination is not a running away from reality, but an enlargement of it. We love it when somebody startles us and then smiles at us: that is how we learn that fear is real but life is a game. What *might* be there matters as much as what *is* there, which explains the strange allure of horror movies.

It takes us a while to get good at discriminating different kinds of appearance. First we must learn to differentiate. Our family pet starts out as a warm bundle of fluff called Joey, not yet singled out as an animal, categorised as a poodle, or analysed as a canine. In the Eden of childhood, our thought is omnipotent: cats can talk and pigs can fly.

Once we've classified the world however, we never quite regain our sense of childlike wonder and oneness with reality, though we can willingly suspend our disbelief by indulging in 'magical realism', a kind of story telling where reality and unreality interweave.

We need the firing of our imagination, because we might be the next Salvador Dali, reclining on a bright red sofa shaped like Mae West's luscious lips, suspended between dream and waking in the subversion of reality that we call surreal art. Or we might be the next Newton, playing on the beach of a vast ocean of undiscovered truth, theorising about black holes, parallel worlds and multiverses at the edge of reality, beyond our current and still-evolving powers of conception.

Social reality

Imagination feeds us only one of the realities we inhabit. During our early years, as well mastering the objective reality of things, we also have to form a subjective reality of self, reaching a point around two years old when we can recognise ourselves in a mirror: this is our own mind reflected back to us. This awareness does not grow in isolation: it needs the interpersonal reality of other people, courtesy of theory of mind. This triple view gives us a three-way mirror of the mind, as displayed in the accompanying table.

Through our delicate relationships with the people who play peekaboo with us, we encounter 'moral realism'. A stern look when we throw a tantrum or hurt someone teaches us that 'being nice to each other' is not optional, or arbitrary. Learning the art of living together is as important as mastering the ability to walk.

Long before we arrive at school, we are thrown into a 'social reality', which goes far beyond the things and thoughts that impinge on our consciousness. We are born into a language, a culture, a set of beliefs, an inventory of values, a world of institutions and expectations. We are fully 'real' only to the extent that we interact not just physically with the hard objects in our world, but emotionally with the soft subjects of other minds, and the life-world into which they socialise us.

Reality is never less therefore than the totality of the immersive, intuitive and interpersonal world we find ourselves thrown into, and how we relate to it. Throughout the course of our life, our social reality will 'really' define us as much as the hardness of any rock, or any pain in our toe.

Our intertwined realities remind us that reality is always plural, never single. This is not a passport to relativism or solipsism, where reality is simply what we believe to be true in glorious isolation. Each 'truth' faces its own form of reality-testing in the presence of other minds, and our job is to get better at it. One of the key criteria for mental illness is an inability to match our perception of the world with what is really there. If we adhere too strongly to a single vision, we become inflexible, perhaps psychotic, our anchor chain too tight. If we have no anchor, we lose our bearings, falling prey to delusion and paranoia.

The Three-Way Mirror of the Mind		
Objective Real Things Quantities Sense data Information	**Subjective Real** Thoughts Qualities Attitudes Interpretations	**Interpersonal Real** Relationships Identities Institutions Social realities
Mind and Brain Scientific experiment Biochemistry The physical body Neural networks	Lived experience Consciousness and self Memories and feelings Mental states	Families and friendships Cultures and languages Group memberships National loyalties
Being and Time Big Bang Cosmic time Fossils and extinctions Evolution	My birth and death 'Me' time The arc of my life My life world	Rites of passage Festivals and fashions My family tree Human history
Belief and Knowledge Empirical facts Physical laws Scientific theories Peer reviews	Personal reasons Private meanings Value judgments Shifting opinions	Political ideologies Religious teachings Academic subjects Philosophies and worldviews

In case it is starting to sound as if reality is beyond the grasp of even the sanest mind, we can be reassured by our capacity to distinguish what is genuine from what is fake. We hate quack doctors, forged bank notes, false smiles, fake masterpieces and paste diamonds, even though they are made of the same molecules as real diamonds, albeit differently arranged. In these cases, 'real' is our guarantee of authenticity in a world bedevilled by imitations, simulations, appearances and 'fake news'.

Our judgement is clouded however by visceral reactions that go back to our evolutionary childhood in Africa. Most of us struggle to put pretend faeces in our mouth, or eat out of a disinfected toilet bowl. Also, our perceptions often overpower the facts of a case. When asked, most of us put crime levels or immigration quotas in our area much higher than they really are, judging what is 'real' by gut feeling, not informed analysis.

The real is something that is not trying to be what it is not.

Then there is the 'real' as determined by the weasel words of lawyers. Bill Clinton, a trained lawyer, felt he could say on oath that he did not 'have sex' with Monica Lewinsky. In his mind, sex was not 'real' if it involved orgasm without penetration. In divorce cases, partners argue whether internet sex amounts to 'real' adultery. In the face of such chicanery, perhaps we can do no better than recall Aristotle's definition of reality, which has never been bettered, and relates to all of our supposed realities: the real is something that is not trying to be what it is not.

Reality-testing

From an evolutionary point of view, the only 'real' that matters is the one that works, or helps us to live another day. Creatures whose inner reality does not correspond to what is out there do not survive long enough to reproduce themselves. One-stop learning is natural selection's gift to longevity. If we attempt to jump a stream but misjudge the distance, fall short and nearly drown, we are stupid to repeat the folly.

Our reality-testing system does not have to be perfect, explain the meaning of life or reveal ultimate reality. In needs only to be good enough for an animal with a nervous system like ours to move about safely and stay clear of predators. Anything else is a bonus.

We are convinced that reality is mind-shaped.

The Mirror of the Mind

But this potentially leaves us in a kind of delusion. Thousands of generations of natural selection have bequeathed us a mind so finely calibrated to fit a specifically human existence that we are convinced that reality is mind-shaped. In what is known as causal realism, we have an animal faith in the truth of our senses and feelings: what is there is what we see and feel, and vice versa.

In fact, the opposite is true. Our feelings are fleeting, and our senses yield only a fraction of what is out there, tuned into a very narrow waveband, to give us what *appears* to be a seamless fit with reality. This is true for every animal that has evolved sensory equipment matched to a particular ecological niche. To our dog, the world appears to be dog-shaped, populated by smells and growls, not thoughts and words.

The reality we see therefore is the one created by our uniquely human brain, which has evolved to fill in any gaps, and to anticipate what lies beyond our ken. Normally this gives us a true enough picture of reality for us to get by, but our 'reality testing' runs into difficulties when vital brain functions are damaged by disease, distorted by hallucinogenic drugs, or lost in a psychotic delusion.

Under normal circumstances, the mirror neurons in our brain tell us the difference between illusion and reality. Hallucinogenic drugs and virtual reality can mess with this system, but they don't show us new realities, only altered perceptions. Real reality reasserts itself when our brain resets to default. There are however no simple on/off switches in our brain that tell us incontrovertibly whether God is real, capitalism is doomed, or America will one day be great again.

Common sense reality

But we do possess common sense, 'common' in a double sense. Firstly it 'communalises' the evidence of our senses and the rigours of our reason. Secondly, it connects to the community of other minds, where our ideas can be tested in the court of public opinion. We haven't really been abducted by aliens.

Not much gets past the quality control of our unshakeable 'common sense' core assumptions: we can trust our senses, other minds are like ours, what is good for me is good for others, the laws of physics are constant, we are free to choose, things don't disappear when we stop looking at them, and we are not dreaming.

The Mirror of the Mind

Some philosophers believe that common sense is a dangerous delusion, built on very fallible assumptions. Its intuitions can indeed be a block to counter-intuitive scientific reasoning, but as 'default reality', it is good enough for a creature with a brain like hours, navigating challenging physical and social environments. Its convictions lie so deep, and are so integral to our psychological integrity, that to waver in one is tantamount to being 'out of touch' with reality, and to doubt the truth of another is to vanish into the pit of scepticism.

Total scepticism of this kind ends in nihilism.

The ancient thinker Gorgias claimed that nothing can be known, and even if it could be, we have no way of sharing it with other minds, because they don't know either. But total scepticism of this kind ends in nihilism. It is true that occasionally we slip up in one of our core beliefs, and social psychologists have shown that we often self-deceive, but the fact that there are seven billion of us on the planet suggests that we get most of them right. Even to argue against them, a sceptic must depend on their being true.

The psychologist William James, immune to scepticism of any kind, took a pragmatic view: reality is that which it is impossible not to know. The trick is not to over-think the problem, forgetting that we have a body as well as a mind. Reality is an affair of our whole body, not just our consciousness. It's all the bits added together.

So, if we want to check that our senses are not disordered, we are not living in The Matrix, we are not a brain in a vat, we are not being deceived by an evil demon, we are not a cipher in someone's computer game, and we are not a stooge in a reality television show, all we need to do is to pinch ourselves.

If we're still not convinced, we can prick ourselves to check that blood comes out, not water or oil. Reality is like a three-legged stool, steady as long as it is supported by the 'stuff' of the physical world, our own observations and the confirmation of other minds. Only if one of these is missing will the stool topple over.

The Mirror of the Mind

> **G E Moore**
> 1873-1958
> Moore felt he could prove the existence of his hands simply by raising them in the air. Seeing is believing. Sceptics remain unconvinced, insisting that we are more likely to believe what we see.

A generation after James, the philosopher G E Moore, agnostic on matters of faith, not a fan of hallucinogens, and also not inclined towards scepticism, took a 'common sense' approach to what can or can't be proven as 'real'. He demonstrated the 'existence' of his hands by raising them in the air: either they were there, or they weren't.

Not only that, he could 'prove' the existence of time by lowering his hands and saying 'I just raised my hands'. By this reasoning, we can reckon that events in the past are real too. Another trick is to give ourselves a mighty whack on the arm. If the bruise is still there tomorrow, we can also be sure that the world didn't suddenly burst into existence two minutes ago.

Resetting to default

Occasionally we mis-perceive, but there are robust reality-testing circuits in our brain to auto-correct and reassert a 'common sense' view of the world. Also, a quarter of our brain is devoted to processing visual signals, which communicate much faster than words and thoughts.

Seeing is not always believing.

The Mirror of the Mind

Misperception for our ancestors was invariably fatal: that sandy-coloured shape in the long grass is a crouching lion, not a boulder. Whatever signals our senses give us, it pays to do a double-take. A baby hesitates when confronted with a 'visual cliff' on a glass floor, and many adults are unnerved by walking over one. Seeing is not always believing, nor can we always assume that 'what you see is what you get'.

Rock and cave paintings from tens of thousands of years ago show human fascination with image-making, to which our limbic brain responds emotionally. Our neocortex is not fooled however: that's only a picture we are looking at. From an early age, our mirror neurons help us distinguish between a real face and a screen face, even one produced by the best digital technology. We do not expect a statue to be warm, even though it is an effigy of a human body.

As we discussed earlier, our mirror neurons are primed to reflect reality as refracted through the minds of other people, reminding us not to overlook the social dimension of evolution. Our urge to look outwards, associating with the truths, attitudes and realities of other minds, is as powerful and highly evolved as any of our inwardly-directed five senses.

We pride ourselves on our sovereign reason, but it is not without flaws. It is the other people in our lives who are our most important 'common sense' reality-testers, fact-checkers and foolishness-exposers. When we pick up our car from the body repair shop after an accident, we might find ourselves arguing with the mechanic over the colour match. She calmly explains that the respray is based on the international standard colour chart, where each colour is identified according to the vibration of its spectral waves, not personal opinion.

Unless of course we are a member of a weird cult that has decided that black is white. In that case, our only hope of reconnecting with 'real' reality and resetting to default is to escape its clutches and re-enter society, the only place where our ideas can be exposed to the sharp edges of other minds, and our judgments can be confirmed.

What mind adds to reality

It isn't just our brain or natural selection that shapes our reality. Our mind acts as a powerful filter and interpreter. But it doesn't operate in a vacuum: it needs constant sensory input. In fact, it disintegrates without it. Prisoners kept in isolation in padded cells become seriously disorientated, if not deranged.

The reality we inhabit is never pure and unmediated.

Once our mind is fed sensory data, it becomes the measure of what we see. This is initially a question of cognitive perception: a coin is always a coin, whether we see it spinning, side on, twenty feet away, in a picture, or lying at our feet. Then it becomes a question of judgment: are we so destitute that we need to pick it up? Either way, the reality we inhabit is never pure and unmediated.

In a peculiar way, each new experience limits as well as expands our mind world. Our first sunset or love affair shapes our perception of all those that come after, and cannot be over-written. Our photograph album becomes our memory of the past, because we have deselected all rival images in order to make it. The lyrics of our favourite song become the tracks of our years, along which our feelings travel. The scientific laws we are taught at school determine how we look at and understand the rainbow.

And yet, without our mind's mediation of incoming sense-data, adding value to perception, reality would be, in the words of the philosopher A N Whitehead, 'a dull affair, soundless, scentless, colourless, merely the hurrying of material, endlessly, meaninglessly'. It is our mind that 'makes' the beauty of a sunset, or the harmony of a love ballad.

It is a disconcerting thought that the fabric of reality is woven from colourless and formless 'bits', transformed into a habitable life-world. Objective reality is 'realised' by a subjective observer, suggesting that an out and out materialist approach is inadequate. Our mind is not an evolutionary add-on or afterthought, but the principal architect of the reality we see. It is our model-maker and theory-generator. The pioneers of particle physics could not have 'seen' something as abstract as an electron unless they had first 'seen' it as a possible feature of the invisible world in their mind's eye.

The model can't be the same as the reality, but without the model, we don't know what we are looking for. In fact we can't even see it. It is as if we wear a pair of goggles that give us a uniquely human 'take' on reality. This might sound like a circular argument: what we 'see' as real is what we set out to seek in the first place.

The Mirror of the Mind

But we have no other way of turning the figments and fragments of 'stuff' into a human world of experience and understanding.

This insight also explains how we are able to 'see differently', from age to age, culture to culture and person to person. Reality might stay the same, but we 'adjust our set' according to the spirit of the age, the latest theory, the prevailing mindset, and what those around us are saying. This is especially the case with the discovery of quantum reality, an idea that simply didn't exist until about a century ago. We shall discuss this shortly, but first we need to spend a few minutes contemplating how our mind helps us to see the unseeable.

Phenomenal reality

Phenomenology is the study of how our mind pulls off this astonishing feat. 'Phenomenon' derives from a Greek word meaning what is shown to the mind. Unravelling this process requires some bewildering psychology to explain how the mind needs to be more than a mirror reflecting what is there. It is more like an artist creating reality from nothing.

Consider vision, to which our brain devotes huge resources. Outside us is a world of objects, but we don't have a gallery of little pictures of everything we see inside our head. There simply isn't room. Instead, our mind makes a representation, in a neural code that looks nothing like the thing itself. There is a map, but it cannot be a like-for-like copy of the territory.

Compare this thought with how we 'see' what is on the screen of our laptop. If we peel back the user-friendly interface of its 'what you see is what you get' screen, we reveal impenetrable coding and complicated electronics. This is what the inside of our mind looks like. When we recall a memory, we are calling up not pictures of the past, but strings of code. How our brain achieves this miracle of conversion is the Holy Grail for the designers of artificial minds.

What we see is not 'things' but the signals they give off, which have to be received, interpreted, processed and stored. This has led some philosophers to insist that we never see the 'thing as it is', only 'the thing as it appears to our senses'. David Hume concluded that all we ever come up against is our own ideas of what is there, never what is really there.

The Mirror of the Mind

The Dalai Lama
b 1935
Philosophers east and west have taken pains to explain how it is not reality that we see, but a picture of it made by our mind.

The Dalai Lama relates this insight of Western philosophy to the Buddhist doctrine of *ten del*, or dependent origination, which covers our emotions as well as our thoughts. 'Everything we perceive and experience arises as a result of an indefinite series of interrelated causes and conditions'. That anger we feel, or joy, or despair, exists not in the real world, but in our reaction to 'stuff'. We feel overwhelmed at the time, and the feeling lingers, but when we look for the cause, it has already gone, or was never there in the first place. What we experience as suffering is in fact illusory and fleeting impressions generated by our restless senses.

Reality is not what happens to us, but how
we set our face to the world.

The Stoic philosophers of the ancient world understood this as well as anyone: reality is not what happens to us, but how we set our face to the world. Our psychological reality is fluid, moving with us as we change and age, like a halo around our head which we can't remove. For the analytical psychologist Carl Jung, reality cannot be anything but phenomenological, like gazing in the mirror and seeing our own mind staring back: 'The world becomes the phenomenal world, for without conscious reflection it would not be'.

We know the fleetingness of our take on the world from the simplest of observations. When we feel hungry, we bite into an apple, and our hunger is gone. So is the apple, which we don't see for what it is. Instead we bring to it all our previous experiences and expectations: its firmness, texture, roundness, colour and sweetness. We don't see its trillions of atoms, or miles of DNA, even though, at the micro-level of reality, that is what it is made of. At the macro-level, which is the world in which we have evolved to operate, we always see a Cox's Pippin or a Granny Smith.

When we bite into the apple, its taste and texture feel real enough, until we realise we are simply experiencing sugar molecules reacting with our taste buds. If we eat a chilli pepper first, the apple will taste completely different. Taste is therefore a private reality, nothing 'in' the apple itself, as we realise when we meet someone who can't stand the taste or texture of apples. Welcome to 'affective realism', or the realisation that our reality is always coloured by our feelings. Eve did not see the apple as Adam saw it. An apple is an apple, whichever angle we view it from, but our relationship with what we see, whether it's an apple or a conviction about the presence of evil in the world, is much more volatile.

Quantum reality

When we enter the quantum world, or try to define reality in quantum terms, things become even less stable. Quantum reality plays by different rules, making it weird, even to physicists. We judge reality by our physical size. When we put a plate of food down to eat a meal, we don't expect it to fall through the gaps between the atoms that the table is made of. And yet, at the fundamental level, of the very small, the table comprises vastly more empty space than solid. We live in the Goldilocks zone, where there is a surplus of matter to anti-matter, which allows us to lean on the table without falling through it.

Democritus theorised over two thousand years ago that matter is made of tiny particles which he called atoms, meaning they cannot be cut up any further. This was mere speculation, because without a powerful electron microscope, he had no way of seeing an atom.

Scepticism about the existence of atoms continued until the nineteenth century, when the physicist Ernst Mach remarked 'I don't believe atoms exist'. In 1919 however, in a series of ingenious experiments, Ernest Rutherford not only 'found' the atom, he also showed that Democritus had not gone far enough. As well as atoms having a real existence, they can be split into ever diminishing particles, worlds within worlds. They are not solid little balls, but full of acres of empty space. With the invention of the electron microscope in 1931, scientists could finally begin to 'see' the new reality of the infinitesimally small.

We inhabit one golf-ball sized galaxy.

At the centre of the atom sits a nucleus, around which whizz protons, electrons and neutrons. These are so vanishingly tiny that they are beyond our humble powers of comprehension. It we think of the nucleus as a golf ball, the nearest electron, also no bigger than a golf ball, is a mile away. The same is true at the other end of the scale of magnitude, in outer space. We inhabit one golf-ball sized galaxy, but all around us, miles away in every direction, more galaxies are being formed, cosmic golf balls speeding off down the fairways of eternity.

These are not realities that any of us will ever see: they are theoretical models, the nearest we can get to understand what makes matter 'work', not just on our level of apprehension, but in the range of the infinitesimally small and unimaginably large. We do well to remember the words of the quantum theorist Niels Bohr: 'Everything we consider to be real consists of things that cannot be regarded as real'. We can never know subatomic particles or white dwarfs as they 'really' are. And yet we make them real by our powers of conception.

In everyday reality, we don't need to fret about nano, micro, macro and giga worlds, because the scale of things is 'just right' for embodied creatures like ourselves, with our sensory apparatus. Our dining table allows radio waves and internet signals to pass through its gaping holes at the atomic level, but it won't collapse under the weight of our spaghetti bolognaise.

New realities
It's an exciting thought that there are new realities out there waiting to be stumbled across, or created by the human intellect and imagination. Our particle colliders are smashing particles into a seemingly endless array of quarks. In addition to up, down, strange, charm, bottom and top quarks, theoretical physicists are discovering pentaquarks, heptaquarks and octaquarks, ad infinitum, in a world they describe as elegant and beautiful. Meanwhile, astrophysicists are discovering new 'rogue planets' and opening up 'out of this world' realities inside massive black holes.

The Mirror of the Mind

Reality in this sense is what is revealed to us by our scientific instruments, not our eyes. It is a reflection of the kinds of question we ask of nature, the quality of our theories of what might be, and our ability to envisage the hypothetical existence of theoretical phenomena beyond our perception.

Even if we can get our head round levels of reality that are beneath and beyond our feeble senses, and scientists testify to how mind-bendingly difficult this is, the 'real' inside the quantum world shreds the rules of everyday reality to the point that, if we're not shocked by this revelation, we should be.

And yet we're not shocked, because in our daily routine, at our level of magnitude, we simply don't notice quantum effects. We rely heavily on Newton's dependable physical laws of the universe, enabling us to prophesy solar eclipses centuries ahead. To him we owe the predictability of the snooker table, and the classical physics of balls colliding.

Armed with the right mathematical formulae, we can calculate the trajectory of every shot, because the angle of incidence always equals the angle of refraction. There's an element of human skill in playing the shot, and the idiosyncrasies of the baize, but once the ball has left the cue, the laws of physics take over. Albert Einstein introduced a few bumps and curves into the game with his theory of relativity, but at our level of awareness, we don't notice. In fact we're so sure that we often bet on the outcome.

Once we get inside the quantum world however, things are very different, and it's impossible to predict the winner of any game. At the quantum level, the red we've just cannoned into the bottom corner might go straight through the pocket, suddenly veer to the left, bounce back as strongly as we struck it, or take every possible route to the pocket, including doubling back in a loop. At any second, it could be potentially in two places, here or there, but not both, its final position being fixed only after we have interacted with it by striking it.

Einstein was unhappy with this level of uncertainty, insisting that God does not 'play dice' with the universe. Gradually however, ingenious experiments showed that he does precisely that. It had been known for some time that a photon of light can travel as a particle or a wave, but the ingenious 1972 'double-slit experiment' showed the mechanism that decides which it is: the human mind, in the act of observing. If we 'see' the particle, we can't see the wave, and vice versa. We experience this phenomenon in the faces/vase optical puzzle. We can switch our perception between the two, but the important point is, we can't see both at once.

The faces/vase illusion
Do we see two faces or one vase? We can't see both at once. Our looking makes the decision for us. We are like King Midas: we turn reality to gold by touching or perceiving it.

Seen this way, matter is not fixed or solid, but more like music, a composition of our mind. It is not an object but an event, not static but dynamic, not a 'thing' but a fluctuating field, continuous and indivisible, like a child growing before our eyes. Our act of looking fixes the wave/particle duality in something called 'a collapse of the wave function'. When we flip our visual receptors between faces and vases, *we* are deciding the outcome, or creating a fraction of quantum reality. Reality is not just what is shown to us, but how, from all the possible permutations, the outcome is determined by our observation of it.

Things are as they are for us, because
we are part of the reality we gaze at.

In a conclusion that is anathema to materialists, consciousness is shown to be a fundamental property of matter. There is no pure reality, only reality as experienced by partial human minds. There is no aboriginal reality, only our relationship to what we create after we have perceived. As well as things as they are in themselves, there are things as they are for us, because we are part of the reality we gaze at.

The Mirror of the Mind

Quantum uncertainty

Quantum mechanics is an exciting field for physicists, though they are occasionally accused of multiplying entities beyond what is necessary to make their theory work, or of making reality more exotic and mystifying than it really is, causing it to dissolve before their eyes. They become like the dreamer who disturbs the nature of the dream in the very act of waking, unable to predict any outcome because they don't have a way of measuring that doesn't change with the thing it is measuring, or with the person doing the looking.

They have reason to be cautious. As the physicist Richard Feynman remarked, 'If you think you understand quantum mechanics, you don't understand quantum mechanics'. It shreds our normal understanding of what is 'real'. How for instance, in what is known as 'spooky action at a distance' or 'entanglement', can we explain that events in one region of space-time can be instantaneously affected by events many light years away?

One day we might have answers to such questions. Meanwhile we don't have to abandon all hope of reality, or dismiss reality as a fantasy we make inside our brain. Quantum uncertainty is not an invitation to regard truth as a free-for-all, nor can mere wishing change how things work in the 'real world'. We are implicated knowers, part of what we see, creating our experience of the world by participating in it, but things don't simply disappear when we are not there to see them.

Stars are made of 'bits' until we make them 'its' of our awareness when we gaze up into the night sky, bringing the universe into being by our act of looking. But they do not vanish when we close our eyes. If all humans became extinct, the stars would cease to exist in terms of human conscious awareness, but they would continue to shine into eternity.

The piece of crockery knocked off the table and heading for the tiled floor has only one future ahead of it.

Although there is quantum uncertainty at the microlevel, a cosmos of complexity constantly slipping into chaos, even catastrophe, when scaled up massively to the human world, we get consistency. Billions of random 'superpositions' of particles that could topple either way when they stop spinning give us a 'probability cloud': that piece of crockery knocked off the table and heading for the tiled floor has only one future ahead of it.

There is indeed indeterminacy at the quantum level, but that gives us no cause to jettison free will. It is true that when an electron passes between two locations, it makes use of all possible trajectories. In its wave form, like water crashing onto rocks, it is capable of being everywhere at once, moving in all directions simultaneously, seemingly passing through solid objects.

When it comes to making a decision 'up top' however, we are not faced with making an arbitrary decision driven by chance. 'We' are so removed from events at the quantum level that our 'self' is able to power along as a free agent at the top of a hierarchy of causes, never reducible to events at the subatomic level. Our thoughts move like a flock of starlings, neutralising any sense of randomness. When one moves, all move. We can't point to any single bird as leader, only the reaching of a tipping point.

Aspects of quantum uncertainty do however unsettle our notion of free will, as Erwin Schrödinger demonstrated in his satirical cat-in-a-box thought experiment. A cat is placed in a box with some uranium. There is no known way of predicting when a radioactive uranium atom will emit an alpha particle, killing the cat with radiation poisoning, but when it does, the cat will die. Or it might not.

This is a feline demonstration of quantum uncertainty: we don't know whether the cat is dead or alive until we look. It has to be one or the other, because it can't be both at the same time, but until we look, we don't know which. By looking, we seal the fate of the cat.

Or perhaps the cat dies in our world, but lives in another. Welcome to the 'Many Worlds Hypothesis'. From billions of possible universes, this is the galactic road we have chosen, and the planetary path that has chosen us. Given that particles are infinitely crashing into, around and through each other, capable of being everywhere at once, or nowhere, there is almost certainly someone just like us out there beyond infinity, maybe with a slightly longer nose, opening a very similar box, perhaps slightly bigger, determining the fate of another cat, perhaps slightly smaller. Or it might be a hamster.

It gets weirder still. The philosopher Nick Bostrom says we have no way of knowing whether the one out of the billions of possible worlds that we inhabit is in fact a computer simulation. We are the ciphers in the video game of some teenager of the future, playing 'dead or alive' with us too.

He arrives at this conclusion by reverse thinking. Given that, here on our planet, Artificial Intelligence engineers are investing millions in creating conscious beings like ourselves in virtual worlds, there has for some time almost certainly been a civilisation out there much more intelligent than we are, amusing themselves by 'playing' us in their online simulations. We are in The Matrix, but we don't know it, and even if we did, we can't disprove it.

Speculation about 'superintelligences' in parallel worlds aside, quantum uncertainty is not merely an intriguing intellectual puzzle that keeps physicists busy, or a moral challenge to our sovereignty as individuals. It is at the heart of both the physical and biological worlds. Without it, our phones could not carry messages, we would have no sense of smell, our computers would grind to a halt, plants could not photosynthesise, birds could not find their way on their long migrations, and tadpoles could not turn into frogs.

Consciousness, intelligence and creativity might also be the results of quantum effects. Our brain may possess causal mechanisms and powers we have yet to explain, such as telekinesis and other aspects of the paranormal. These are phenomena currently outside the realm of classical physics, but if we develop the science to understand the brain as a quantum engine, we can open an exciting new frontier of knowledge.

Constructed reality

Before we disappear into loops of our own minding, we need to come back down to earth for a while. Living in the material world reminds us every day of the reality of hard objects. But it doesn't take much thought to realise that we also live in 'soft' social realities constructed by human minds, such as the words this text is made of.

These socially constructed realities have evolved over thousands of years, passed on by culture. This is further evidence, if we need it, that our mind does not merely reflect the world: it forms powerful alliances that build superstructures that do not exist in nature, and were not there before. With the help of technology and mutuality, it creates realities that were not in our consciousness before, such as social justice, global heating and internet banking.

The Mirror of the Mind

Vast sums of money exchange hands online every second, but 'cash' has gradually departed from physical reality, like the grin of the Cheshire cat. Our ancestors needed actual goods to barter with, but today we can trade in bitcoin and traffic in crypto-currencies, allowing us to drift into the red or the black without even knowing. We can be a billionaire without ever coming into contact with filthy lucre.

Money as social reality
We can be rich without possessing any coins or notes. We can lose a fortune overnight if the stock market crashes. Our stash of notes under the mattress can be rendered worthless by hyper-inflation. So where does the worth of money reside?

Gradually money progressed from material goods to symbolic tokens of wealth: cowries (shelling out money), animal hides (lend me a buck) and salt (I want a rise in salary). Modern economies trade in 'futures' which don't yet exist: I'll pay you a fixed price now for the corn you promise to give me, and only me, when the harvest is ready.

Coins originally were worth their weight in gold and silver, stamped proudly with the imprimatur of the supreme ruler, but now they are made of baser metals. The paper that our banknotes are made of has practically no value at all. It is the chief cashier's signature alongside the 'trust me' look on the face of the head of state which enables us to buy lunch with it. When this trust vanishes, as happened in 1930's Germany, the bank note with its 'notional' value becomes worthless. We notice the value of money most when we haven't got any, or when the wad in our pocket turns out to be forged.

The Mirror of the Mind

When we're locked in a cell, it's not just the prison walls
that restrict our freedom.

The law is also a social construct, honed over centuries of carefully argued and painstakingly drawn up legislation. We dismiss it as a bundle of scrolls gathering dust in legal chambers at our peril. When we're locked in a cell, it's not just the prison walls that restrict our freedom: it's the law of the land, and the constitution of the citizenry, road-tested over hundreds of generations in thousands of court rooms. These social and moral pacts against zero-sum antisocial behaviour are as strong as any iron bars.

The law can be criticised for cementing existing power structures in place, but at its best it upholds principles of justice and fairness for the underdog, which are also unseen but powerful overarching moral constructs. On one level, these ideals are mere human inventions, but as Aristotle pointed out, society could not exist without them as living ideals. We arrive at them not by mathematical proof, but by collective wisdom, and we keep them alive not by force of arms, but by sustained belief.

Even something as ephemeral as a popular song is a social construct. Its reality does not reside in its lyrics, harmonies, performances, number of covers, or the radio waves that carry it into the ether. It is an artefact of all the minds that know it and hum along with it, keeping it alive in popular memory by repeat listening.

Reality, science and progress

Science is an adventure in human thinking, and the development of scientific method is an extraordinary feat of the intellect. Barely two millennia old, it was driven by gifted pioneers who took great risks to peel the scales from our eyes to reveal the 'scientific real' of how things 'really are' in the natural world, without recourse to myth or miracle. Our primary mode of thinking is storytelling, so persuading us to think analytically has been an uphill task. Galileo observed that the world is made of numbers, but what we *perceive* is sunsets, smiles and sausages.

Science's triumph is to advance its knowledge by constant testing and revision of its theories, not because they are wrong, but because of a determination to make them more right. This explains why science appears to go through certain 'paradigms', marking major shifts of understanding. This is a sign of strength, not weakness. Just as we wear the clothes of our day, so do scientists think the thoughts of their era. Newton remarked that he stood on the shoulders of giants, acknowledging that all scientists are not only in debt to their predecessors, but also limited in how high they can climb.

This means there are inevitable shifts of dogma, disagreements, wrong turnings, rivalries and heretical schisms, but this must be the case as they lift their gaze to see and interpret a view that no-one has seen before. In what is a sign of strength, not weakness, scientists are constantly changing their minds in the light of new knowledge, which human beings generally find difficult to do. The excitement of science is that, even after two millennia of probing, there is still so much to discover. Each breakthrough reveals another twenty panoramas.

Science is not therefore simply driven by the search for 'pure' knowledge. It is a human pursuit, so it too, alongside art and religion, is a social construct. It comprises the whole scientific establishment, the priorities set by government, the battle for funding, the profits that accrue, how and to whom the subject is taught. As the philosopher Ludwig Wittgenstein noted, the meaning of a system must lie outside the system. If science has any meaning, function or purpose, it emanates from the minds that pursue it, and perceive its worth.

Science is a great force for good, but its value is determined by the insights, ambitions and ideals of its practitioners. Politicians can task scientists with finding data to prove a point, and some scientists use science to pursue a private agenda, meaning the phrase 'follow the science' always needs to be heavily scrutinised.

Intelligence testing for instance is regularly carried out, but it is not without controversy. Is IQ a real thing, can it be measured, and what are its implications for how children are taught in schools? Is our genome a blueprint with predetermined outcomes, or an invitation to an open future? Studies of identical twins have been used to 'prove' whether nature or nurture has the upper hand.

In these debates, science is the servant, but in the Soviet Union in 1928, it became the master. The biologist Trofim Lysenko instructed that vast areas of subarctic Siberia be planted with temperate corn seed, on the assumption that it would defy its genetic programming and conform to party propaganda as surely as serfs and kulaks. Millions starved to death as a result.

The social sciences are particularly vulnerable to the egos of academics keen to make a name for themselves. For over a generation, Stanley Milgram's 'obedience

The Mirror of the Mind

experiment' of 1961 and Philip Zimbardo's 'prison experiment' of 1971 were taken as 'gospel' in their disciplines, establishing the 'reality' of human conformity, selfishness and nastiness. Closer investigation years later, when the full circumstances became known, has showed how each study was manipulated from the outset to reach a predetermined conclusion.

Even as 'pure' knowledge, science doesn't follow a simple progress towards unchallengeable truth or total understanding. Biology, chemistry and physics are presented to us at school as fixed bodies of knowledge based on unarguable truths, but to fathom the mysteries of the cosmos, life and human intelligence, they are increasingly having to try on each other's clothes, and gaining much from the experience.

Without political will, science by itself cannot guarantee progress.

Ironically, science's advances in all fields of human endeavour have partly created the problems we face. Pessimists worry that, although we've made huge strides in our knowledge and technology, we're morally stranded somewhere in the Stone Age. Optimists see only an upward curve to reduced violence, wider compassion and diminished suffering, in a gradual shift to 'non zero sum' mutuality.

They are both right, but for different reasons. For the first time in human history, the future of civilisation, or indeed its demise, is entirely in our own hands. We can pull together to protect our fragile blue planet and colonise space, or we can stumble into the sixth mass extinction, taking ourselves down with it. We can make such momentous decisions only by bringing deeper values into play, which science alone cannot provide. Without political will, science by itself cannot guarantee progress.

Meme theory is the study of how ideas like these are generated, and which ones get passed on. From an evolutionary perspective, we might expect a community that shares its resources to flourish better than a death or suicide cult, and by and large this is overwhelmingly the case, so we can claim that progress towards a more humane world is 'real' in many areas.

But not all memes are life-enhancing. They come in all shapes and sizes, by no means all of them 'scientific' in motivation, or good for us. Nazism and democracy

104

are both memes, but only one was the winner in 1945. Nazism was grounded in very dubious eugenic thinking, which was in turn based on very questionable science, much of it emanating from the democratic west. What matters is to understand why eugenic thinking flourished, and how it was put to flight, not just by better science, but also by stronger values.

A meme becomes a permanent and widely shared social reality only if it passes the 'hundredth monkey' test, and even then, it may do more harm than good, until a better or more other-regarding meme replaces it. Two people worshipping a holy book or revered relic every second Thursday are not going to change the world, but when thousands do it, and their children inherit the practice, their beliefs become 'causally relevant', infusing every element of daily life. We end up with sacred texts, state religions, soaring temples and choral anthems. These can cross international borders, survive for millennia, and adapt in each generation.

These cultural realities are generally impervious to the counter-prevailing techno-scientific culture, because they are swept along by passion and tradition, not reason and modernity. Nations invent their identities in a similar manner, writing stirring foundation myths, creating inspirational folk heroes, and writing their own history from the standpoint of the victor. Science, if it is to flourish, must distance itself as far as possible from such distractions. It cannot be responsible for the uses or abuses that society puts it to.

The reality principle

We are all dreamers, otherwise we have no incentive to improve ourselves, or build a better world. Without dreams, tomorrow will be just the same as today. Our dreams might involve idealising the material world by fighting for causes bigger than ourselves. But our dreams won't come true unless we also materialise our ideals. If our dream is to make a difference, it has to be given shape. We set our politicians a tough task, expecting them to give us a vision of something better, while also staying 'real' enough to protect what we already have.

Humankind cannot bear too much reality.

Being a dreamer, or having a vision, is not the same as being escapist. We need occasional relief from dull grind and stark truth because, as T S Eliot reminded us,

105

The Mirror of the Mind

'Humankind cannot bear too much reality'. Visionaries and poets inspire us to lift our eyes unto the hills, or follow the sacred river to Xanadu. Love and marriage, which amount to no less than the future of humankind, would wither away without our belief that we can turn tedium and appearance into something beautiful and fulfilling.

Imagination is a great release, but we are also highly conscious of the need to 'get real', and stay there. Sigmund Freud framed this in psychological terms. When we are babies, we feel omnipotent, because we are given all the breast we want, when we want it. Then, one day, the breast is empty, or not offered on demand.

Welcome to the disappointment and frustration of the reality principle. The real world has a habit of not going away, because things get broken, people get hurt, and dreams disappoint. We won't all grow up to be princesses and superheroes. In what Freud saw as our greatest psychological challenge, we quickly learn that the wish is not father to the thought: we cannot bend reality to our wishes, nor is it ever perfect. If we don't learn to defer gratification, we're in for a tough time as an adult.

He also knew however that we never give up on wish-fulfilment, finding substitute nipples in consumerist indulgences, character defences and hidden yearnings well into adulthood. The pleasure principle is so much more appealing than the reality principle. His solution was not to chide us for our constant cravings, but to encourage us to be honest about them, on the basis that forewarned is forearmed.

It's not all our fault, as falseness and fakery abound. Advertisements for tobacco sell us Marlboro Man breathing the clean air of the Western Plains, not the lung cancer he will eventually die of. Our parents tell us we are wonderful or fantastic, when really we are average at most things. They would do better to praise our effort, not our achievement, because nothing valuable or fulfilling comes to us without sacrifice of some kind, facing down pain, frustration and setback. Life doesn't always say yes to us, and we often have to say no.

If we are to develop what the Ancients called character, it will be through resilience, or how we react to adversity, not our easy passage through the false promises of consumer culture, which urges us to 'take the waiting out of wanting'. Nor does celebrity culture do us any favours, merely masking the suffering behind the lip gloss. Between 2005 and 2015, over twenty 'reality tv' stars committed suicide, representing just the tip of the iceberg of failed dreams.

Hyperreality

Our social real is not like the real of our physical world. It shifts with the times, and as we increasingly see in our politics and digital culture, its 'realities' are highly contested, less certain than the behaviour of quarks at the quantum level. Chief among those who have exposed the fragility of our constructed realities have been literary, critical and postmodern theorists, especially the French sociologist Jean Baudrillard (1929-2007), who coined the term hyperreality.

Jean Baudrillard
1929-2007
Here is a picture of Jean Baudrillard. But it's only a picture, not the man himself. The cigarette is just part of his image. Welcome to the world of the hyperreal. Nothing is what it seems, and what it seems is merely symbolic.

Increasingly we live our lives not through the non-negotiable realities of pain, hunger and death, but through the flickering neon signs of popular culture. These are highly seductive, but point to nothing substantial behind them. In the media-fest of the hyperreal, we increasingly judge by appearances, 'sold' to us as logos, brands, slogans, soundbites and icons.

We are no longer 'real' people, but the sum total of our catchphrases, fads, latest purchases, pet hates, selfies and facile 'likes' on social media. Alternatively, everything is real but empty, with no way of knowing which is authentic or synthetic, stranding us in a 'desert of the real'.

The Mirror of the Mind

'Reality as entertainment' infects every aspect of our lives. 'Rolling news' gives us a manipulated version of reality, usually with a cheesy story on the end to send us happily on our way. Baudrillard was particularly critical of the media presentation of the 1990 Gulf War, tightly controlled by the Coalition Forces for public 'consumption'. Tens of thousands of Iraqis were killed, mainly civilians, but on screen it looked like a computer game, with bloodless surgical strikes from the air, so 'movie-like' so that some doubted it had taken place at all.

When death was shown in all its grizzliness, some objected that it spoilt their Sunday lunch. The voyeur in us wants to see, but the wimp doesn't want to be upset. Most of us have never seen a corpse on our quiet suburban street, and death is merely an attitude we take to the movies, part of the hyperreal.

Cocooned inside the auditorium, we can be stern critics of how 'real' the blood looks, or how convincingly the actors convey pain. Screen deaths conform to a series of conventions: short gasps, sweating brows, last words, drooping eyelids. When we are finally confronted with real death, we're shocked that dying doesn't look like this at all.

Horror movies appeal because they offer us unconventional images of death, which are far more scary because they defy our expectations. Guts emerge from mouths, heads rotate, flesh peels off like clothing, a replicant picks up a severed limb and sticks it back on. Our right brain wallows in fear in pity, but our left brain knows the gore and mayhem are not real. If we find the scenes too 'psychologically real', we just need to close our eyes.

Politics has similarly become a media game show, in which reality, cast adrift from facts, is merely what the pantomime performers believe. Whatever the challenges, a 'great' or 'fantastic' future is promised in some Disneyfied Neverland, where all we need to do is keep on believing.

Literary theorists have attempted to debunk this shallow view of reality by depicting the 'individual', even in the works of 'great' writers, as a construct of the ruling ideas of the age, tarred with sexist, classist and racist prejudices. The reader is deconstructed and decentred even further, as a shadow puppet dreamed in someone else's dream. Even before the digital age arrived, with its sowing of division and dissent, there was no single vision, stable reality, cohesive message or shared value, only a million televisions tuned to a million different channels.

The mind's processing of reality	
Apple **Hammer**	Particular **real objects** capable of being eaten or used to exert force, accessible to more than one sense, corroborated by more than one observer.
Red apple **Black hammer**	A particular **empirical thing** (apple) qualified by a universal **rational category** (redness). The mind makes and understands a new reality by mixing sensory data with experience.
Fruit **Labour**	Universal umbrella **concept**, open to imagery, association and metaphor, such as the apple of my eye, the fruit of my labours, a labour of love, made real through the social pact of language.
Cider **Steam hammer**	**Inventions** that bring about material changes in the world, whether through the work of human hands or as mechanical extensions of muscle power.
Atom **Electron** **Gravity** **Rainbow**	**Necessary hypotheses** to explain other phenomena in the natural world. We need special instruments to 'see' them or, in the case of the rainbow, to understand the true nature and cause of what we are seeing.
2 + 2 = 4 **E = mc²**	**Logical abstractions** arrived at by powers of reason, never experienced directly but always true. There is no reality in numbers, but they determine the shape of the cosmos, and how our brain works.
Truth **Falsity** **Justice** **Goodness**	**Ideals** rooted in social practice, or intuitions turned into 'objects of thought' by frequent use. There could be no discourse, science, culture, art or morality without them.
Money **Law**	**'Real'** by virtue of being social constructs subscribed to by millions. We notice their importance most when they go missing.
Red Riding Hood **James Bond** **Unicorn**	**Fictions** based on real-world characters, made from known objects (unicorn = horse plus horn) or imagined as fantasy creatures known (by most) not to be real, but enjoyed as play, switched on or off by suspension of belief.
The love of God **Human rights**	**Collective beliefs** grounded in tradition, faith and group solidarity, making them social realities, lived out through individual lives. They remain true as long as they are sustained by a community of believers.
God **Brahman** **Nirvana** **The Tao**	**Spiritual phenomena** in the fifth dimension, neither conventionally verifiable nor falsifiable but made real for the faithful by private experience, shared religious practice and openness to the transcendent.

The Mirror of the Mind

We often allow our brain, or our unconscious,
to do our thinking for us.

It's too facile to blame the destabilisation of the self, reality and truthfulness on trendy theorists, wacky entertainers or populist politicians. They are giving us what we want, and the fault lies in us. Cognitive neuroscientists have shown how, in its pursuit of a non-existent entity, our brain often deceives us. Social psychologists have steadily whittled down the notion of a sovereign self, showing how we often allow our brain, or our unconscious, to do our thinking for us.

Dual realities

So what or where is our backstop reality? To an empiricist or materialist, the evidence of our senses is all we have to go on. Seeing is believing. The true real is the cupboard door we bang our head on, and the pain we feel after. A rationalist or idealist disagrees: what we see is not all there is. A stick looks bent in water, but our reason assures us that it isn't.

To our brain, this is not a real conflict. It doesn't fret about integrating sense and reason, because it has evolved to cope with the duality of appearances. The faculty of reason doesn't mysteriously appear in adulthood, but is primed by years of childhood learning. When we study geometry, it seems we call on innate knowledge about shapes and intuitive insights into mathematics, but in fact we are building on hours of experience in the nursery and sandpit.

Either way, we end up with more than one way of knowing. Without being given explicit knowledge in a science lesson on how water 'bends' light rays, we have implicit knowledge: we just 'know' it's the same stick, seen through two different elements.

The faltering progress of Homo sapiens offers clear evidence that the mind sees more than the eye, or that reason enhances the reach of our senses. The 'net' of our sensory apparatus doesn't capture every fish out there, and there are fish we will never get to see unless we are shown them, or know what we are looking for. This is especially true of science. Think of all the 'truths' that no one had seen before Galileo, Newton, Darwin, Einstein and Hawking fished them out of the water.

Plato toyed with the idea of a reality beyond appearances in his parable of the cave. He asks us to imagine some cave dwellers sitting by their fire, by which he means us. They have never been out of their cave, so they assume in their ignorance that the shadows of their bodies cast onto the cave wall by their flickering fire are the true reflection of reality. In their 'unenlightened' mind, their tiny flame is the 'real' source of light.

One day, one of them ventures to leave the cave, only to be blinded by the true source of light, the sun. When he goes back into the cave to tell the others, they don't believe him, suspecting he has had some sort of weird vision. He is disappointed by this reaction, but realises that they will never believe in the Real that he has seen until they see it with their own eyes.

All we see is a shadow reality.

According to Plato, many of us never get to leave the cave to discover what lies outside it. Consider the case of Mary, the subject of a modern thought experiment. She has been brought up in a black and white house, but has read every book about colour. She 'knows' about red, but she has never seen a red object. So she doesn't know red at all, or what it is like for her visual cortex to be flooded by redness. She can't say she has left the cave of ignorance until she goes out and sees red in all its glory.

Plato might have been familiar with the ancient teachings of Hinduism. Our lives down here are Atman, brief episodes in the much greater reality of Brahman, from which we come, and to which we shall return. Brahman is everywhere, like the sun reflected in every puddle of water.

Hinduism has many gods, but the reality they represent is One. In the Abrahamic traditions, the idea of monotheism, or one God to rule them all, emerged slowly, firstly in Babylonian and Egyptian religion, then most powerfully in the Hebrew prophets.

The urge to find a single cause for everything that exists is strong in the human mind, for things above and below. When the first Greek thinkers turned their thoughts to identifying the core organising principle behind the material world, they variously suggested water (Thales), air (Anaximenes), fire (Heraclitus), earth (Anaxagoras), or the four elements acting together (Empedocles). Other options for the 'logos' that transforms chaos into cosmos were eternal motion (Anaximander), atoms (Democritus), or simply The One (Parmenides).

111

The Mirror of the Mind

Modern physicists are still driven by the lure of discovering The Theory of Everything in their particle colliders. They do not however imagine that science alone can show us the true nature of reality, and certainly not the meaning of life, if only because particle physics is beyond the intellects of most of us.

This raises the problem of knowledge as a secret revelation or hidden gnosis, (linked to the word diagnosis), whether of things earthly or spiritual, attainable only by the initiated few. This is a dangerous idea, because it is exclusive and elitist. In a parallel to Plato's cave, Hindu 'shadow puppets' made of paper are worked by sticks from below against a transparent screen. The higher caste are privileged to sit in the front, so they can see the brightly lit colours. The lower caste are not so lucky. They are made to sit behind the screen, so like Mary, they never see get to see red. All they 'know' is a shadow reality of black and white silhouettes.

Hindu shadow puppets
If we're enlightened, or privileged, we get to see the show from the front. But how do we know we're not stuck behind the screen, seeing only a shadow play of reality?

The early Christian Church Fathers embraced Plato's notion of God as the Real light behind creation, though they took great pains to explain the mystery of the Incarnation to everyone, and not to deny the reality of this world. Jesus was deemed to be fully God and fully man, speaking to our whole being, sensible to both reason and feeling. What use is a veiled reality in some timeless and perfect zone if no one can see or feel it? Charity is pointless unless it reaches down to those who need it most, in the mud and the grime.

The Mirror of the Mind

Higher reality

Regardless of whether we feel a religious or spiritual presence in our lives, we are all Platonists to a degree. From being party to countless small acts of fairness and justness, we form an overarching concept of justice, to which we appeal when we feel wronged. Justice, law and order are social constructs that arise from this-worldly consensus, but they are also underpinned by other-worldly ideals which guide our expectations of each other.

As a philosophy, idealism tends to get pushed aside by our predominantly materialist 'take' on reality, encapsulated in the scientific conception of the world. But materialism is very tied to a world of things. Idealism's core principle is that consciousness is made of thoughts. For something to exist, it must be realised in our mind. Think of all the things we don't know, because we haven't had thoughts about them. They exist, but not to us, not yet.

This is not the same as saying that the world is a fabrication, vanishing as soon as we imagine it. On the contrary, our ability to create mental realities is pivotal to how we think, live together and generate values. If we couldn't hold things in mind for longer than five seconds, we would be creatures of the moment, with no reason not to believe that the world wasn't created two minutes ago, or that it's okay to help ourselves to other people's property.

We are all idealists at heart.

When we stamp our feet and cry 'That's not *fair!*' in the nursery because someone has stolen our toy, we are extrapolating a sense of what *essentially* makes behaviour just or moral. We are all idealists at heart, because we are primed to create universal truths from fleeting particulars.

Some reject idealism and essentialism, insisting that the law is a compendium of particular and practical judgments, based on custom and shifting with the times. In the case of common law this is true, but 'Thou shalt not kill' has a Platonic universality to it which rings down the ages.

The ideals we live by are 'higher' in the sense that they guide our actions, but Plato took the idea of a 'higher reality' to an even more elevated plane. The difficulty is that this creates a higher/lower split in reality. He was a rationalist who believed that the ultimate destiny of our soul is to rise 'above' our body.

113

The Mirror of the Mind

Matter is a distracting mess of the senses 'down below', impeding the 'ascent' of reason towards understanding the true Real. If we are to discover Reality at all, it must be through our powers of reason. It won't be found in the dirt at our feet.

His pupil Aristotle took a different tack altogether. He was quite content to look at the real dirt at his feet, full of plants and insects that he could observe and anatomise. He was at heart an empiricist, prefiguring modern scientific attitudes to matter as 'real' stuff. He wasn't an idealist like Plato. Instead of a cold ideal of beauty, he preferred a real warm pretty face to look at.

No, replied Plato: don't be deceived by changeable appearances, or place your trust in them. The youthful bloom on this girl's face will wither. Better to look on this statue of Aphrodite, whose beauty, captured in cool marble, is beyond earthly corruption and passing desire. Think of her as a goddess of the mind, and of her beauty as a timeless ideal and ageless essence. No mortal has ever met Aphrodite, but her eternal summer shall not fade.

Their dispute over the true nature of the real seeped into their politics too. Plato saw the ideal state as a utopia that flawed citizens must aspire to. Aristotle was much more pragmatic, a forerunner of Machiavelli: to stay in power, leaders have to crack a few heads and tell a few lies. With so many minds arriving at their own opinions, there can never be one Ideal State to please them all. No two minds will ever see eye to eye, so we have to find ways of accommodating our differences, however messy.

Plato is criticised by some as the forerunner of totalitarianism. In his dialogue 'The Republic', he suggests that a handful of 'philosopher kings', sound of character and trained in the art of statecraft, make better rulers than might arise from the rabble of democracy. Aristotle disagreed: the people have a right to choose their leaders. He did not however believe in extending the vote to slaves and women.

The debate about the 'ideal' versus the 'real' distribution of power was a lively one in ancient times, a matter of life and death for warring states. The Spartans had a strong vision of the state, fortified by strict training of the young and military valour on the battlefield. They scoffed at the Athenians for their wishy-washy political ideals. But it was Athenian democratic ideas that survived, and Spartan arms that were buried by history.

The Mirror of the Mind

In an age of populism, it remains an open question which is the better option: Plato's neat utopia overseen by potentates, or Aristotle's messy democratic freedom. On both sides of the argument, demagogues, airy-headed system-builders and happiness-engineers have made millions suffer in the present in the name of some future unattainable ideal.

The illusion of art

Plato's notion of the changeless Ideal behind fleeting Appearances influenced his views not just on politics, but also on art. He was suspicious of paintings and statues, because as faulty copies of our flawed sensory apparatus, they are illusions of an illusion. A painter can depict fruit so realistically that birds try to eat it.

Such visual deception distances us from the truth behind the image, or makes fools of us. The sculptor Pygmalion made such a beautiful ivory carving of a maiden that he fell in love with her. He even named her Galatea or 'milk white' after the colour of the stone he carved her from.

It was antipathy to the dangers of worshipping idols that motivated the Hebrew prophets to forbid graven images of God, Muslims to outlaw pictures of Allah, and Puritans to deface representations of Christ in church buildings. Iconoclasts want to wean us off earthly images, so that we can dwell on the eternal verities that lie just out of sight beyond them, otherwise we end up bowing down before plaster saints.

We want our reality to be instant and virtual,
no matter how temporary and shallow.

Before we scoff at such superstitious notions, we need to recall Baudrillard's theory of how, in one way or another, we find ourselves worshipping the hyperreal. If Plato were to visit our image-laden culture, he would be aghast at our reliance on the flickering visual image. We obsess about looks, appearances, youth and shiny newness. We want our reality to be instant and virtual, no matter how temporary and shallow. When we stand in front of the Taj Mahal, we're more intent on taking a selfie to prove we've been there, rather than marvelling at the monument's ethereal beauty. The photograph we take home is 'truer' than being there in the moment.

Our imagination, which is essentially an image-making machine, doesn't mind either way. It hijacks long-evolved brain processes to activate the same neurons as the really real, hence our expectation in the cinema to see 'realistic' action with 'real' effects. Computer-generated imagery (CGI) allows us to see stunts that make real-life daredevilry look tame.

Even before the invention of photography, artists strove for centuries to give us reality as they saw it. But the artist is not a photographer, the eye is not a camera, and 'realism' is a slippery term which bears little relation to how our eyes actually see. A Dutch painter of a still-life vase of tulips goes to great lengths to show us the striations on every petal, and yet when we look at tulips in real life, we focus on only one petal at a time. If we switch to a second petal, the first petal becomes a blur. Impressionist painters such as Turner or Monet apply this principle to our whole field of vision, softening edges to give us a shimmering, half-seen 'reality' that hints at what lies beyond the sunset or the water lilies.

Whatever 'school' they belong to, artists play a double game, promising to help us to escape reality on one hand, and trying to make their work as 'realistic' as possible on the other. They offer us artifice, but they also try to hide their trickery. Painters attend 'life classes' to sharpen their perception, actors devote their careers to making their characters as convincing as possible, and directors try to stitch us into a seamless narrative.

Some film directors take a contrary approach to being 'realistic', breaking the spell by using montage or juxtaposition as an anti-realist tactic to remind us that we are watching a performance, not eavesdropping on reality. The dramatist Brecht deliberately 'alienated' his audience by shattering the illusion of the 'fourth wall' in the theatre. He wanted to remind us to focus on the political ideas in his plays instead of being sucked in by the emotion of the story.

The reality of art
'Realism' in art is a matter of degree. We don't see the muscles rippling under the skin of the Pharaoh in an Egyptian tomb painting, but we have no doubt what we are looking at. 'Flat' presentation in Egyptian painting is a convention, and conventions shift with the times. Plato said that art cannot hold up a mirror to

The Mirror of the Mind

nature, because the artist shows us only a limited view of the world, which we see through particular eyes. Even *cinema verité*, which is committed to showing reality 'as it is', must edit out a hundred images for each one that it includes, as must a news bulletin or a documentary news-reel.

Mediaeval paintings give us 'icons', flattened discs of faces with little inner psychology to animate them, and even less individuality. But when change started, it happened quickly. Paintings of the High Renaissance begin to give us hints of a smile, as in Leonardo Da Vinci's portrait of the young and comfortable Mona Lisa of 1503. Only three years later, Giorgione's painted an old woman. There are blemishes on her face, she comes from a lower class, and we can feel her fear of dying.

Perhaps realism is just a reflection of the subject matter. In 1866 Gustave Courbet painted 'The Origin of the World', a close-up view of the female genitals. For some, this was too 'real', an offence to decency, too pornographic to hang in an art gallery. For others, the image points to a Platonic eternal truth beyond itself, captured in the title. If 'real' images of the human body are all we seek, they are abundantly available on the internet.

Cycladic art
Heavily stylised, recognisably human, angular but graceful, Cycladic figures influenced Picasso's portrayal of the human form five thousand years later.

117

The Mirror of the Mind

Nowadays we can ogle any body part in intimate detail, but it took artists a long time to learn how to represent the human form. Five thousand years ago, the beautiful Cycladic islands in the Aegean Sea produced a type of statuary that stylised the human form into graceful curves and angular poses, and the first figures on Archaic Greek vases almost look like stick insects, hardly people at all.

Egyptian figures look odd to the modern eye, with their side-on noses and forward-facing eyes. We are given a frontal view of the upper body, but shown the legs walking sideways. The faces are always the same, gazing impassively into the afterlife. But the Pharaoh's painters and sculptors were not aiming for realism, only a representation of what they saw as important in the human form. It was not until Classical Greece that sculptors showed us 'real' perspectives and proportions of the human body, with veins and muscles on view.

In the Renaissance, human figures were placed in three-dimensional landscapes, 'rounded' by the new art of perspective to provide a greater sense of realism, even though this is not how the eye 'sees' normally. Since then, modernist painters have returned to primitive forms, focusing on the materials that art is made of, giving us only hints at the human form, veering on abstraction.

In a nod to Plato, abstract and non-figurative artists urge us to see the higher reality beyond the forms themselves. The coloured squares of Mark Rothko's canvases, dulling eventually to black, abandon us to our own ideas. Installation art goes a step further, leaving our mind to make sense of an unfamiliar space.

Art is by definition artificial, a recreation,
not a slavish copying of nature.

Such distancing from the anchor of the visual image is in stark contrast to photography. The advent of the camera in the 1860's challenged art's monopoly of the visual image. Art is by definition artificial, a recreation, not a slavish copying of nature. Photography forced artists to question the very process of seeing, and to diversify into presentations of reality that the camera could *not* achieve.

118

The Mirror of the Mind

But even the realism of the photograph has its limits. As the mere click of a shutter, it is artless, merely freezing a moment that normally vanishes from the retina as soon as it is seen. A photojournalist might claim that a timely snap documents a scene for posterity, but like any work of art, it still needs the informed eye of the beholder to make sense of it. The fine-art photographer might win a prize for composition and technical ability, in which case we are not being given reality at all, but a dressed-up version as seen through the lens of someone else's vision.

In both these instances, contrary to the popular saying, the camera *does* lie, or can be made to manipulate our perception of reality. Most of us hate our passport photograph, because it shows us as we really are. Our social media shots by comparison are cropped, airbrushed and doctored. The Victorians, not yet wise to the tricks of the developing room, were taken in by photographs that purported to show fairies at the bottom of their garden. Today, 'deep fake' software can depict the most celibate and abstemious politician having drunken sex with a goat.

The cultural critic Walter Benjamin had further concerns about the effects of living in an age of unlimited mechanical production of images. When everything is presented as spectacle, we become more careless in our looking, not more observant. When instant and endless replications are automatically available, we become tourists of reality, losing the dexterity of drawing and making for ourselves. Everything starts to look the same, originality is devalued, and privacy is lost.

Life as it really is
We tend to see new things in the light of our previous experience, so one of the roles of art is to present us with alternative realities, challenging us to see the familiar in unfamiliar ways. Artists are not photo-journalists or omniscient narrators holding up a mirror to reality. They are tightly focussed lenses which narrow our looking, and we the viewers are shifting and partial voyeurs.

It is no use criticising Jane Austen for showing us status-obsessed middle class mothers in a country mansion fretting over finding the perfect catch for their daughters, while ignoring the gore of the Napoleonic Wars, the stink of the city slums and the threat of cholera. She gave us reality as she saw it, and within her small canvas, it has the ring of truth.

119

The Mirror of the Mind

We might prefer the naturalism of Emile Zola, who was alert to the class injustices identified by Karl Marx, and the cruel animal struggle to survive described by Charles Darwin. He set out to give us the nitty-gritty reality of life in a working class mining community. But reading his novels doesn't give us a more 'scientific' take on reality, or a truer picture of the human heart than Jane Austen. It doesn't show us what it was *really like* to work exhausting shifts underground, breathe toxic dust, or go hungry when times are hard. The only people who know what it is like to hew coal are coal miners, because the only true realism is to live the real life.

'Life as it really is' can never therefore be captured raw, whatever social level we are snooping at, because art is never artless, but always an artifice, a creative selection. The best we can hope from such writers is to get a truthful *feeling* about their subject. All art is mimesis, an imitation of reality, caught between showing us how things really are, and how they could be. It is highly selective, because art that shows us everything, unfiltered, is tantamount to living twenty four hours in the uneventful day of Mrs Average.

Many of us turn to art *because* it is different from the daily grind, and the more different the better. It enables us to feel what life is like inside someone else's skin. Often this is fantasy, but if we want 'kitchen sink' realism, we can turn to television soap operas which feature 'real issues' in their plots, such as redundancy, poverty, divorce, depression, addiction, rape, gambling and sexual discrimination. For most of us, living on the breadline, feeling suicidal or being desperate for the next fix are fictions, but for many they are facts.

Even the news bulletin is not an open window
onto a transparent reality.

When the credits roll, we exit from the scriptwriter's dream and go back to our own reality, or segue into the next programme. Even when the news bulletin arrives, it is not an open window onto a transparent reality. It is part of someone else's carefully filtered and edited narrative.

So why should we bother with art at all, if it can't give us the real thing? The answer lies very deep, both personally and socially. No known society has existed without expressing itself through art. If it is well made and authentic, and we are

120

open to its challenge, it can redeem the time for us, shake our prejudices, and take us to new places of the mind.

Ultimate reality

Regardless of whether art captures life as it is really lived, it often tries to portray a reality beyond the one we see, or point to an Ultimate Reality beyond temporary appearances. There is no room here to discuss whether the Ultimate Real has always existed, or whether it is an idea-complex that has grown with the human imagination. It could be either, because 'proof' either way is under-determined, we can't settle the matter by logic, and we can't recreate the mindset of our ancestors.

Some argue that the Ultimate Real must exist because we can imagine it, but that is a difficult argument to sustain. We can't realise a physical entity by thinking it into being. The twelfth century theologian Anselm wrestled with this problem, maintaining that by believing in something, we make it real by giving physical substance to a non-physical essence.

He is right in the sense that the real is what we realise. If we commit ourselves to a particular worldview as a matter of faith, we will make it real for us. If we subscribe to a justice-based model of reality, we will campaign tirelessly until it comes about.

We can't believe in something however without first understanding its essence, or the greater whole to which it belongs, the universal shape into which particular things fit, which Plato called a 'form'. A twig is nothing outside the greater 'form' of a tree, and love is mere biology without seeing it as an ideal to which we are prepared to devote our life. In that sense, much of our everyday thinking, and all religious thinking, partakes of Plato's forms.

We are all essentialists at heart. Few of us would feel happy throwing darts at a photograph of a loved one. It's only an image, but we can't detach our feelings from the person represented. This superstitious thinking also applies to words, which is why we set great store by vows and oaths. At his presidential inauguration in 2008, Barack Obama mis-spoke some of the wording of the swearing-in ceremony. His team were so concerned that his enemies would use this as proof that he wasn't 'really' the president that they persuaded him to take the oath again in front of a smaller audience the following morning.

The Mirror of the Mind

We might be tempted to think that essentialism is an abstruse philosophical sideshow, but it lies at the heart of many of our 'culture wars'. Essentialists for instance do not support transgender issues, or believe that sex-change operations are right. Either we conform to what a woman essentially is, or we don't, and this is determined by the presence or absence of female biological and reproductive organs. That's what *essentially* makes a *real* woman.

Marriage and abortion are also clear-cut for essentialists. Marriage is the sanctified union of a man and a woman, which rules out same-sex weddings. Without the magic words 'I do', couples are merely cohabiting, conducting serial monogamy, or being promiscuous. In the eyes of the law, even married couples are not *really* married until they consummate the union by having sex. Sex is for pleasure, but only within marriage. It is also for procreation, so once an embryo is conceived, it is essentially a human being from that moment. Termination of a pregnancy is therefore murder.

We become who we are through our own choices.

Essentialists tend to be absolutists: gender, marriage and abortion are non-negotiable. Constructivists are relativists: the essence of a person is who or what we make of ourselves. If we feel we are a woman trapped in a man's body, or we love our partner regardless of gender, or we wish to be in control of our reproductive biology, that is for us to decide, as part of our identity.

Existentialist thinking challenges essentialism. Jean Paul Sartre famously said that existence precedes essence. We are not just born into a set of rules, or a preconceived notion of what it is to be a person. We become who we are through the choices we make. Rocks and trees merely exist, but we must exercise our freedom to act in the world.

Essential truths

By worshipping together in a consecrated building, modern Christians believe they are earthly proof *in substance* of the One True Church *in essence*. They make God 'more real' by intensifying their absorption through music, prayer, ritual and incense in a community of believers. They nevertheless argue over whether the bread and wine in Holy Communion become 'essentially' the body and blood of Christ, or remain 'substantially' what they are.

Anselm lived in a pre-scientific age, in which God was the default 'Theory of Everything'. Even if God is not physically among us, he is in us as an ideal. When we draw a circle, we sketch out an imperfect copy of the perfect circle in our mind. Anselm argued that our conception of the perfect circle emanates from God, who is the 'necessary' embodiment of perfection.

It follows therefore (says Anselm) that our ability to conceive the perfect circle, or contemplate God's eternity, is proof that he exists. How otherwise could we conceive such greatness, or think of a thing that isn't there? Quite easily, replied the monk Gaunilo: we can think of a lovely large island, but that doesn't mean we can go on a holiday there.

This kind of logic-chopping about the 'existence' of God does not trouble true believers, who put faith before reason. They seek the God of Abraham, not the God of the Philosophers. They 'know' God not as a noun, but as a verb, a way of being, experienced in the spirit, not in the intellect. Their 'evidence' comes only after a leap of faith, in the form of miracles, redemption and life after death.

Atheist and agnostics accept that God exists as an object of thought, no less than Bambi or Father Christmas, but merely giving him a name proves nothing. In Samuel Becket's 1953 play 'Waiting for Godot', the Godot of the title is conspicuous by his absence. Two men wait patiently for him, but they don't know who he is, what he looks like, whether he is coming, or when. The one thing they seem least inclined to do is to give up their belief in him. In fact the more elusive he is, the stronger their belief.

Even the most devout faith does not justify the claim 'God exists', if by existence we mean his being is an objective reality. Saying 'God is real' or even 'God is love' really means 'I *believe* these things', which is an assertion, not a fact.

We don't say 'my head exists' because its existence is self-evident.

At this point we run up against the ambiguity and imprecision of language, which takes us back to logic-chopping. We don't prove the existence of the thing that is pointed to by a noun by simply adding 'exists' to it. We don't say 'my head

The Mirror of the Mind

exists' because its existence is self-evident. We demand proof only for claims that lie outside our normal range of empirical confirmation. Think for instance of the proofs a scientist would have to provide to back up the claim 'Life exists on Mars'.

Then there is the copula, or the little word *is* that often slips by unnoticed. We need to pay attention to it, because it shapes our thinking subconsciously. Aristotle identified as many as ten uses of it, including identity (this is a stone), quality (this is stony), condition (this stone is hard) and quantity (this stone is enough). What is the copula doing, or what claims about 'reality' are being made, in sentences such as 'London *is* in England', 'It *is* raining', 'Coal *is* black', 'Oliver Twist *is* an orphan' and 'Murder *is* wrong'?

If we're not careful, the copula can narrow our understanding. What do we mean for instance when we say 'she *is* a teacher'? Who or what is she when she is not teaching, or after retirement? At all times, she is also a mother, a citizen, a music lover and a tennis player. Words can objectify things, making us think we understand them merely by pigeon-holing them. When we say 'the sun *is* red' to describe a beautiful sunset, it can get in the way of our seeing the whole sky light up with fire and blood. Such cavilling doesn't bother religious believers when they declare 'God *is* Love'. Their measure of reality is its ability to transform people's lives.

Imagining what is there

Illusions – delusions – hallucinations – hearing voices – prayer – angels – inspirations and revelations – transient states

- Optical illusions remind us that seeing is done by our brain, not our eyes.
- Illusions are a normal feature of a brain trying to make the best sense of what it is given.
- Illusions are correctable errors of perception, but delusions are errors of belief, clung to despite evidence to the contrary.
- We all are in the grip of at least one delusion about ourselves or the world, but we can't be certified 'mad' if we keep it private.
- Illusions and delusions are misapprehensions of what comes into the brain from outside, but hallucinations are generated by events inside the brain.
- Some psychologists see reality as a 'controlled hallucination', but that short-changes our brain's ability to present us with a reliable version of what is out there.
- A common hallucination is hearing voices. As a core feature of human imagination and intellect, it is not necessarily a sign of psychosis.
- Without it, we would have no prophecies, stories, art, innovation, and possibly no science.

- Hearing internally generated voices marked the beginning of a sense of self for our ancestors about twenty thousand years ago.
- It led to consciousness, our awareness of the moment during which we regularly talk to ourselves and think aloud.
- It gave rise to conscience, the voice in our head that tells us off when we stray from the group norm, or fall short of a personal standard.
- Many of the world's religions began with a lone visionary whose ideas became 'social facts' in a community of believers bound together by ritual and belief. Only then could a sense of the transcendent flourish.
- Religion and prayer are not evidence of a deranged mind. They are echoes of a much older spiritual sensibility, or natural desire to experience the world as a unity.
- The voices of revelation and reason, or religion and science, are complementary ways of knowing and 'right seeing', with no necessary contradiction between them.
- We undergo many transient states caused by happiness, sadness, anxiety or inspiration in which we might hear voices.
- The Hearing Voices Network helps voice-hearers to understand their internal dialogue, and not to see themselves as abnormal or cursed.

Illusions

We assume our senses give us an accurate version of what is there, but we know from experience how often we can be mistaken. 'How easy is a bush supposed a bear', wrote Shakespeare. Optical illusions make it clear how we frequently have to do a double-take to establish some context, before we can work out what it is we are looking at. Is it a bird, a plane, a UFO, Superman, or a leaf blown in the wind?

Our eyes do not give us an exact photograph of reality. They transmit to the brain information extracted from light, from which the brain selects as much or as little as it needs to make sense of what it is seeing. Its main concern is to make a seamless approximation of its surroundings, which means it often cuts corners, misses things and inserts them if they are not there. It also distorts some aspects of reality, suggesting that things are not always what they seem, as revealed in the 'two table' illusion.

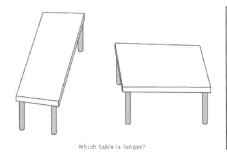

Which table is longer?

Believing is seeing
When asked which table is longer, most of us say the one on the left because, to the brain, verticals appear longer than horizontals. They are in fact the same size. Measure them and see. If you want to look taller, wear vertical stripes.

The world is full of illusions, which are disordered perceptions. We don't see things that are there, walking into a sliding glass door, having forgotten that we had closed it earlier. We see things that aren't there, mistaking a mirage of shimmering air in the desert for the cool water of an oasis. When we get closer, we realise it is no such thing. We have failed to triangulate our senses. We are the victim of a false perception, which has generated a false belief. The mirage will look even more like water if we are dying of thirst, because what we see is usually a projection of our psychological state at the time.

In an orchard in autumn, we assume that a round yellow-greenish thing lying under one of the trees is a ripe apple. We bring previous experience to bear, and see things within our frame of expectation: apples are that colour, about the size of a tennis ball, and they fall off apple trees at this time of year. When we pick it up, we discover it *is* a tennis ball, the one we hit over the hedge several weeks earlier and failed to find in the long grass of the orchard. Mistaking a tennis ball for an apple sounds like a simple error to make, but it takes a quarter of our brain's visual processing capacity to sort it out.

Illusions are temporary blips of a brain trying to make sense of the world, seldom interfering with our daily functioning, but they require constant vigilance. We detect a stimulus, which we might misinterpret if we are in a hurry, preoccupied, careless or in a bad mood. Our mistake is short-lived, so long as we apply critical reason. We auto-correct by triangulating reality through our other senses: we can eat an apple, but not a tennis ball.

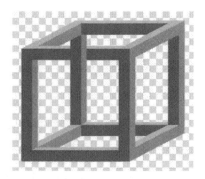

Illusion or Impossibility
Drawn by Louis Albert Necker in 1832, the Necker Cube makes us look twice. Is reality at fault, or our visual apparatus?

What is remarkable about our reality-testing is how often we get it right. We evaluate the improbable and eliminate the impossible, until we arrive at a fair grasp of what is actually happening. We just *know* we are not dreaming. With no facility to separate appearance and reality, everything would appear to us as an illusion, which is not a sustainable ploy in a world of hard objects with sharp edges. When we watch a murder in the theatre, we don't jump onto the stage to grab the dagger, or run out of the auditorium in fear.

Evolutionary psychologists point out that our brain is an automatic inference engine, bubbling with intuitions but often jumping to the wrong conclusion. When we are young, our brain bristles with possibilities, and we retain our flexibility of response to a stimulus throughout adulthood. This is a vital asset, not a failure to mature.

Throughout our lifespan we need to be able to think associatively, handle symbols and generate novelty. We owe such flexibility of response to our doughty ancestors. Life was much less certain for them, in a world constantly shifting before their eyes and in their ears. It made sense to react to a creak in the dark as a potential intruder or predator, not a branch blown in the wind.

The Mirror of the Mind

Our futures are far less unpredictable than theirs, allowing us ample time to appeal to experience and reason to confirm what we see. Descartes prided himself on his cogito: I think therefore I am. Most of us make a much more modest claim: I'm thinking, therefore I can't be mad. We adjust the dial on our reality-testing equipment, operating as proto-scientists, testing out hypotheses about what we think our senses are telling us. The problem is, we're not very good scientists, or consistent in our method. Was that the door bell, have I seen this face before, is the ball heading for the back of the net, did I see my purse on the table in the other room, or was that yesterday?

The difficulties begin when we *think* we've seen what's there, or what we expect to be there, and fail to look again, or to contemplate a different response. Some automatic responses are justified and necessary. We might act charitably because we subconsciously hear our mother's voice from years ago urging us to be kind, our conscience acting as a long-lost voice in our head. The stimulus is not present, but that doesn't mean that the memory is an illusion.

> *We have to think our way out of our bubble,*
> *which involves seeing what is really there.*

It may however become an unthinking habit. Our brain's instinct is to take a short cut where it can, which makes for speed, but lacks the freshness of perception we experience when we see something for the first time. We need to be awake to those moments when a stock response that has served us well all our life will not do this time. This is a new situation we are facing, demanding a moral response that pushes us beyond our comfort zone. We have to think our way out of our bubble, which involves seeing what is really there, which may be different from what we saw yesterday, what we presume to be there, or what we want to be the case.

Magicians are mentalists, 'illuding' us deliberately, using sleight of hand and distraction techniques so that we don't see how the magic is done. They reduce our brain to a state of 'under-knowing', so that it leaps to conclusions, or attributes what it cannot understand to 'magic'. This is better than 'over-knowing', where we are convinced we've seen everything, with no need to double-check.

For our knowing to be 'just right', we need to be on our guard against illusion. One of the cornerstones of Buddhist teaching is 'right perception'. Some of this is

129

given to us: we are born knowing that where our body ends, the world begins, otherwise we might find ourselves biting our fingers as well as our sandwich. Some of it we arrive at through the reality principle: those fairies at the bottom of our garden are actually glow-worms. Right perception matters, because it is the foundation of right action, which keeps us alive: that hill is too steep to skate down without breaking our neck at the bottom.

Illusions might however be an inescapable aspect of human perception, and by no means exclusively visual. Einstein believed that something as fundamental as our sense of time is a trick of the brain, describing our sense of past, present and future as a 'stubborn persistent illusion'. All we see is succession of events, not time passing. The cosmos rolls on and on without us, but here on Earth it's only five hundred years since we invented mechanical clocks.

Delusions
Illusions are mistaken sensory impressions, correctable by thinking again, but delusions are errors of belief, clung to against the weight of reason and evidence to the contrary: we cannot 'see' that our persecution complex has no basis in reality, and that no-one is out to get us.

It's one thing to claim that we have seen a flying saucer in the night sky, then to admit in the cold morning light, in a calmer emotional state and with more information to hand, that it was probably a satellite. It's another thing to insist that we were specially sought out by aliens, taken for a ride in their spaceship, and shown a different future for mankind.

There may be many reasons why we don't auto-correct to the default on such occasions. We haven't had enough quality sleep, or we have been under great stress. We might have a psychological need to be singled out for special treatment. We might be bored with real reality. We might have been 'under the influence' after a party. We might have read too many comics or seen too many films about alien abductions. We might have been abused as a child, and this is our way of being noticed, or of forging an other-worldly identity that is safe from our earthly abusers. We might be suffering from a medically diagnosed psychosis.

We might have 'seen' the apparition in the company of several others, and now we find ourselves caught up in a mass delusion. The more we are questioned and challenged, the more convinced we become about our extraterrestrial encounter, and the more tightly we close ranks.

One person harbouring a delusion is a crank, but when someone else joins in, this is the start of a conspiracy theory. 'They' are out to get us, and only 'we' know the truth. Mobile phones cause brain cancer, a cabal of Jewish financiers is plotting to overtake the world, the 'deep state' is intent on exploiting our ignorance.

We must be wary however of attributing delusions to everyone except ourselves. We are all dreamers. Which little girl doesn't dream of being a ballerina? Gradually her delusions of grandeur will be exposed to some harsh realities: she possesses neither the physique nor the discipline to glide her body across the stage like a swan. But she can still dream.

From an evolutionary perspective, it may be the case that we are simply a deluded species, a truth played out in myth and history. The story of Pandora's box relates how, after all the evils have been released into the world by a vengeful god, hope is cruelly left locked inside, denying us even that consolation. Ever since, pessimists decry our belief in progress as our greatest delusion.

History in many ways bears this out. We regularly afflict ourselves with economic bubbles, witch hunts, popular follies, utopian killing fields, moral panics, gold rushes, fervent crusades and bloody revolutions, abandoning not just hope, but reason too. It's almost as if, every so often, the group brain implodes, overwhelmed by information, or deluded by wishful thinking. Our neocortex outstrips our limbic brain's ability to cope, making hallucination and delusion inescapable design faults.

Psychologists reckon that most of us nurse at least one or two delusions. We consult astrologers, go to prayer meetings, get remarried and support football teams that can't possibly win the championship. When we call someone deluded, we usually mean they believe something different from us.

We are not likely to imagine that we may be mistaken.

The Peters Delusion Inventory measures the strength of our delusions. 'Low' delusions such as religious and political beliefs are more likely to bolster our ego and help us make sense of the world. They cause us and others no particular harm, so long as we leave others to their own delusions. This is important, because

131

whatever our faith or political persuasion, we are not likely to imagine that we may be mistaken. It doesn't occur to us that, when two sides are totally convinced the other is wrong, only one can be right.

'High' delusions such as a Messiah Complex and erotomania (being convinced that someone we idolise but who doesn't know us is in love with us) have clear potential to work out badly. Worst of all are mass delusions, such as the cult mentality that allowed Jim Jones to persuade over nine hundred 'believers' to commit mass suicide at the 'Jonestown massacre' in Guyana in 1978. This is the ultimate rebuttal of a delusion carried to extreme lengths, winning a Darwin Award for eliminating large numbers from the gene pool.

Not all delusions are psychogenic. The somatic delusion results from an organic malfunction in the part of our brain that 'recognises' body boundaries. We are so convinced that one of our limbs does not belong to our body that the 'offending' limb has to be amputated.

Social delusions can be just as bad for our health. Most of our deepest fears emanate from what we imagine other people may be saying about us, or thinking of doing to us. This allows paranoia and persecution complexes to imprison us as effectively as any brick wall. We perceive only the threat to our safety, and our brain becomes locked in, as if our captor is always standing just outside our cell door. We persuade ourselves that we are unjustly imprisoned by a cruel world, or that we deserve everything we get. Either way, we become our own jailers, lacking the will or the wit to liberate ourselves.

We might be tempted to label those suffering delusion as mad. We cannot however pronounce anyone mad unless and until their delusion becomes public, manifesting itself in speech and action which endangers the lives of others. In law, we can be judged only on what we do, not what we think.

Our next door neighbour might believe Jesus is waiting to welcome her into the kingdom, but if she doesn't tell us, her madness is her own affair, in the private sanctuary of her own mind. She can *be* mad while living what appears to everyone else as an ordinary everyday life. If her delusion generates no conflict in her outward behaviour, it attracts no attention. We cannot accuse her of *going* mad until her delusion shows itself in public, perhaps causing her to stand for hours on a street corner singing hymns to the sky, while ignoring the needs of her children on the ground. Only at that point might a social worker accuse her of neglecting her family.

Occasionally one of our delusions might be true: our partner really is two-timing us. What matters is the foundation of our knowing, not our insecurity or jealousy. Without any grounding in fact, our suspicion remains no more than that, a fabrication that only coincidentally accords with reality, not a justified true belief.

Finally, delusions might be necessary to make society work, or to make it governable. Plato wrote about the Noble Lie, or the myth that governments of all stripes propagate to keep their populace biddable and in line. We are told we are free, our nation is special, we are all in it together, the future is bright, technology is good for us, surveillance cameras are for our protection, immigration is under control, the law is fair. No government admits that it has little control over events, or that its manifesto is a string of unrealisable promises which can be ditched when the wind changes direction.

Hallucinations

Illusions and delusions are generated by signals that come from outside the brain, regardless of how accurately they are processed, or corrected if wrong. This is not the case with hallucinations, both visual and auditory, which arise from signals generated inside the brain. As such, they are much harder to auto-correct, or submit to the correction of other minds.

*Our thinking is seldom as reasonable or
evidence-based as we like to think.*

This is because the 'dividing walls' in our brain are very porous, and our thinking is seldom as reasonable or evidence-based as we like to think. Our emotions colour our perceptions, for good or ill. If we really desire something, we will see what we want to see, and overlook the absence of proof, which is why horoscopes are so convincing. If we are afraid of something, we will see only the negative, which merely confirms our phobia.

An illusion starts with a real sensory input, but in a hallucination our brain *invents* the sensory input. There is something there that is not really there. We can give ourselves a hallucination by pressing on our eyelids. We 'see' activity in our visual cortex, but there are no light signals from outside. Or we can take a hallucinogenic drug that activates our synapses, triggering images that relate to nothing in the real world. In these instances we are changing our brain internally, but external reality stays the same.

Hallucinations are features of normal brain activity. Our brain craves input, as we discover in the Ganzfeld effect. When we sit alone in an empty and silent room, our brain begins to 'invent' stimuli to keep itself busy. Normally we quickly reset to default when something 'real' happens to disturb our reverie, so any hallucination is at best temporary.

Some psychologists go as far as describing reality as a 'controlled hallucination': everything is unreal until proven real. This does little credit to how our brain normally gives us a pretty reliable version of what is 'there'. If it didn't, everything could be anything, and reality would become a masquerade.

We realise how well a healthy brain gives its owner its best shot at reality when something goes wrong, perhaps after a stroke, or in Charles Bonnet syndrome. This is a condition that affects people whose vision deteriorates, especially later in life. Desperate for information, their brain starts to 'see things', creating false knowledge of what is 'out there'. This can be distressing for sufferers, because they know these hallucinations are not real, but they see them nevertheless.

A dagger of the mind
Macbeth hallucinates a dagger, though he knows that his senses are deceiving him. More serious is his delusion that he can murder his king, and get away with it.

The Mirror of the Mind

The character of Macbeth hallucinates a vision of a dagger on the night he is 'psyching himself up' to kill the king lying asleep as a guest in his castle. His mental state is a curious mix of hallucination and delusion, the difference between them laid bare by Shakespeare's psychological insight. Macbeth knows that the dagger before him is not real because, though he can see it, he cannot clutch it: it is a 'dagger of the mind', generated by his tortured conscience. He is hallucinating, but aware that he is doing so.

Delusion is not so easily shaken off. He is sane enough to realise his perception is at fault, but deluded enough to believe he can kill a king and get away with it. He is not psychotic, merely ruthless. We watch the play in appalled fascination because we all walk the line between metaphor and reality: we 'look daggers' at each other, and make back-stabbing remarks. The Bible says it is a crime merely to think such thoughts, but fortunately we can't be arrested for our fantasies, however violent.

The neurology of hallucinating is complex. If we think of the brain as a series of compartments with dividing walls, it is usually good at partitioning incoming signals from internally generated activity, not sending a message to conscious awareness until it has solved this puzzle. In an important operation called source monitoring, involving the speech areas of our brain, it works out where a 'voice' has come from: are we thinking to ourselves, or has someone just spoken to us?

Fortunately it is very rare for our brain to 'flip' unexpectedly, though our mind is constantly on a bio-chemical knife-edge. If we define psychosis as being out of touch with reality, of doing un-understandable things, we all come close to it sometimes. Ebenezer Scrooge thought his hallucination of Jacob Marley's ghost was due to an undigested piece of potato, while psychotics may suffer delusions that they actually *are* a piece of potato.

The lifebelt thrown to us by our brain is that illusions, delusions and hallucinations share one important feature: they cannot be universalised. We cannot drive anywhere in an illusory car to a deluded destination running on hallucinated fuel. Back on the African savannah, if all of our ancestors' blips of perception had been possibly true, with no way of double-checking fairly quickly, they could not have survived their harsh encounters with reality. Those who did were the ones who passed on to us their uncompromising reality-testing genes.

The Mirror of the Mind

Hearing voices

'Hearing voices' is usually associated with paranoid schizophrenia, but the flimsy walls between compartments in our brain make us all prone to the phenomenon. We seldom act on what they tell us, and what they tell us isn't necessarily good or bad. In their extreme form, they may urge us to kill ourselves, or to kill someone else. If we are anorexic, a beast in our head persistently tells us to starve ourselves to death. If we are a convert to a faith, the voice is a compelling call to a life of service and sacrifice. Only when the voices threaten our very existence do we need medication.

To the brain, the voices are just electrical signals, which can be randomly generated, as the neurosurgeon Wilder Penfield showed in his work with epileptic patients in the 1950's. While they were still conscious, he stimulated parts of their right hemisphere with an electrode to test which parts he should excise to cure the epilepsy. In the process he discovered that he could induce 'voices'. In other words, if certain neural buttons are pressed, any brain can be made to hallucinate, or 'hear voices'.

Without an electrode in sight, we frequently experience moments of heightened awareness or sudden insight, during which our perception is inexplicably and subtly altered for a while. One in thirty of us will experience a 'schizophrenic episode' at some stage in our life, seeing things, hearing voices or harbouring strange beliefs, so we are all potentially somewhere along a schizophrenic spectrum, struggling to adjust our private perception to hard-nosed reality.

Highly imaginative children who are alert to their
inner voices often go on to be especially creative in adult life.

We often talk to ourselves, communing with our own voice. This starts in childhood play, when we give our toys voices and converse with imaginary friends. These young fantasies are benign and normal features of a growing brain, going through over-active spurts. At this age our brain boundaries are still porous, and counterfactuals have not clipped the wings of imagination: our neurons haven't yet been pruned back to the solid wood of the 'reality principle'. This is a sign of intelligence and self-awareness, not delusion or insanity. Highly

136

imaginative children who are alert to their inner voices often go on to be especially creative in adult life.

These inner voices are what make up our consciousness, or being-in-the-moment, so they never go away, getting even louder in adulthood. We hear a constant inner dialogue, by turns supportive, critical, manipulative or straight-dealing. We are encouraged and bullied by a persistent voice urging us not to give up, or telling us to buck up our ideas. We argue with ourselves over difficult decisions or choices, feeling the prick of conscience, as if a good angel is perched on one shoulder and an evil one on the other.

Some of us are more sensitive to our inner dialogue than others, finding inspiration in it, or being tormented by it. We occasionally have a sudden epiphany, or a 'bee in our bonnet' that won't go away, unable to say whether we invited the idea into our head, or it forced itself on us. Novelists live for months with characters they have created in their head, sports stars talk themselves through their routines at critical moments, and Beethoven was still hearing whole musical compositions in his head during the last ten years of his life, even though he became totally deaf.

Listening to our inner voices

Hearing voices is not therefore freakish, but written deep in the human condition, recorded in history and culture. Many of us regard our job as a 'vocation', which derives from a sense of a voice calling to something within us, bringing out the best in us, guiding us to a particular life of service beyond financial remuneration.

We learn which voices to suppress, and which ones to listen to. When we nag at ourselves, it is only because we believe we have the power to 'pull ourselves together'. Our grip on reality is not threatened, because we possess the inner resources to soften the conflicts between our fragile self and the demands the world makes on us.

We are all fragmented to some extent. Consciousness is seldom unitary, but comprises lots of subsystems, each with its own mouthpiece and agenda. On New Year's Eve, one part of our brain makes a firm promise, but by the middle of January, another part of our brain has gone back to its old ways.

Perhaps our very sense of consciousness owes itself to the mutant genes which 'play' the voices in our head. At first they came from outside. The earliest

The Mirror of the Mind

literature from the Ancient World shows its characters responding to voices from the clouds, their thoughts put into their minds by the gods, with no strong sense of 'I' to resist their commands. Achilles and Hector felt motivated by a force outside them, not their own passions. The Old Testament prophets believed they had a hotline to Jehovah, who channelled his divine commands directly to them.

Around the same time however, we start to meet characters who realise that they are not hearing 'a' voice, but listening to their own voice, emanating from their own mind. The psychologist Julian Jaynes attributed this step change in human consciousness to the 'breakdown of the bicameral mind': the two sides of our brain started 'talking' to each other, or our inner voices became just as loud as those outside us. This internal dialogue between 'us' and 'other' slowly turned us into creatures that created art, mourned our dead, and asked questions about the meaning of life.

Harvey
As children we often have secret friends, or talk to our fluffy toys. The 1950 film 'Harvey', about a man who is convinced he has a giant white rabbit friend, asks how worried we should be if we're still doing this as adults.

Some argue that we need our silly delusions and imaginary companions, an idea playfully explored in the 1950 film 'Harvey'. The main character Elwood P Dowd insists that he is followed everywhere by a large white rabbit, which the audience never gets to see. Initially his family thinks Elwood needs to be institutionalised, but by the end of the film, others become convinced that they too can see the rabbit.

We judge our strength of character by our relationship with the voices we hear. We are 'individual' to the extent that we can find a voice of our own, helping us to establish an agentive 'I' to kick back against circumstances. Such self-assertion and resistance has a long pedigree. Pythagoras, St Augustine and Galileo claimed to hear voices. Their brilliance was to stay this side of madness by letting the rest of us in on what they were thinking. Hamlet's soliloquy 'To be or not to be' fascinates us because it is as if we are eavesdropping on our own thoughts being played back to us.

We can afford to listen to our inner voices,
because not all of them are harmful.

The 2010 film 'Shutter Island' teasingly explores what it feels like when we lose our ability to discriminate between our inner and outer voices. Ordinarily however we don't inhabit a film set or fantasy island with strange voices in the air: we live in and on the mainland of human reality. We can afford to listen to our inner voices, and learn how to interrogate them, because not all of them are harmful, and our imagination is porous. When we have creative ideas, we can make them productive by grounding them in practicality.

Socrates claimed to hear the voice of his daimon, or presiding spirit. He would stand transfixed for hours through the night, then fall to the ground dumbstruck. His enemies took these self-induced trances as proof of a dangerous mania, accusing him of being a corrupter of the youth of the city. Unperturbed, he listened to his inner voice as a guide to rational action and truth. His accusers mistook him: he was not too mad, but too sane. He saw through their hypocrisy and foolishness, their lesser minds unable to live with his wit and wisdom. They sentenced him to death.

Demons all around us
Unsurprisingly, cultures have generally been ambivalent in their attitude to voices in the wind. Do they emanate from angels or demons, reasons or revelations, truths or deceptions, certainties or distractions? Are they generated by transcendent realities, buried neuroses or faulty genes? Psychologists describe us as natural born believers, as if to alert us against believing six impossible things before breakfast.

The Mirror of the Mind

Most religions invent gods in their own image, as if to say that they are hearing an idealised version of their own voice reflected back to them. Gods have no mouths or vocal cords, so if we are to hear their words, it can only be through human ears, tongues, hands and languages.

The great religions of the world began with lone souls going off into the wilderness, fasting to the point of starvation, waking from a dream, meditating under a tree or scaling a mountain. During social isolation and physical extremity, voices get much louder and more frequent. In their seclusion they heard a message from beyond the visible world, or in the case of the Buddha and Lao Tzu, possibly their own thoughts amplified back to them.

Materialists scoff at such ideas of revelation and transcendence, suggesting that Mahavira, Zoroaster, John the Baptist, Jesus of Nazareth, Augustine of Hippo, Muhammad, Francis of Assisi, Joan of Arc, Guru Nanak, Ignatius Loyola, Francis Xavier, George Fox and all such visionaries were either mentally ill or experiencing seizures in their temporal lobes, as likely to hear a devil as a god.

We all dream and talk to ourselves, especially when faced with a big decision, but whose voice was Abraham obeying as he raised his sacrificial knife over his son Isaac, and why was he being tested in this way? Who was Moses listening to beside the burning bush? What apparition did Saul (later Paul) of Tarsus see on the road to Damascus? What special quality did Muhammad possess that drew the Archangel Gabriel to him?

The interesting point of all these characters is that, centuries after their death, we are still talking about them, and feeling their influence. Whether or not their inspiration came from a source beyond them, or within them, or both, they changed the cultural, moral and political landscape of their times by exposing hypocrisy, urging repentance, instigating social reform, encouraging compassion, and inspiring a devoted following.

We have no grounds for diagnosing them all as schizophrenic, deluded or irrational. They dared to be different, took personal risks, and within the context of their time and culture, their actions were embedded in the beliefs and practices of their community.

It is significant that the great world faiths originated at a formative time in the history of modern consciousness. For millennia, our ancestors felt one with their surroundings. Private spirituality, the precursor of organised religion, emerged as a sense of deep connection with the natural world, combined with a greater awareness of the different 'voices' emanating from the self, the group, the ancestors, the animal kingdom and the life forces that animated the wind and the waves.

The Gnostics, writing soon after the death of Jesus, believed not in a deluded voice in our head, but in an Inner Light that is present from birth. Each of us is a shard of light surrounded by darkness, and the purpose of the spiritual life is to rediscover the illumination we once all enjoyed, but have long since lost.

In accordance with this tradition, mystics, sufis and gurus devote their lives to becoming channels of the divine voice, isolating themselves in a desert cave, declaring celibacy and spending hours in prayer to avoid mundane distraction. Orthodox religion is unnerved however by arcane and private knowledge, relying on public ritual and approved dogma to keep the faithful in line.

Anthropologists and evolutionary psychologists trace our penchant for generating and hearing voices all the way back to the explosion in size of our big brain. As it became increasingly stuffed with extra modules to process incoming information, so it grew more prone to creating entities beyond mere sensory input. Sensing that the earth is peopled with spirits is a natural by product of a busy brain keen to second-guess other minds, intuit causes, attribute agency, stay ahead of predators and make sense of chance.

If this is so, attempts to divide human cognition neatly into the sacred and the secular are misdirected. Our mind remains deeply ambivalent about the 'truth' of the voices of spirituality and the verdicts of science even in the digital age, as likely to revert to primitive superstition as to embrace new technology. Organised religion, doctrinal purity and paganism are alive and well. Hindu nationalists, the Christian right and Islamic fundamentalists, for better or worse, influence our politics as much as any secular ideology.

Our 'culture wars' are not resolved however by pitting faith against reason. Despite the ire of militant atheists, there is no conflict in someone being a 'person of faith' while having a job as a writer of medical research papers. Nor is our democracy put under strain if we accord each other the freedom of religious belief in private, while publicly adhering to a secular moral code that owes no allegiance to any particular divine revelation.

The Mirror of the Mind

Instead of dismissing religion as an evolutionary wrong turning, we do better to accept it as a natural cognitive habit of a large-brained creature eager to unite earth and sky. For religious believers and adherents, their faith is not a childish or sub-rational opt-out, but a taxing spiritual discipline, challenging call to sacrifice, and vital organising life principle.

Faith answers an existential need for reassurance,
not a rational calculation of risk.

Faith, as in belief in a possibility that we cannot prove is a probability, also emanates from our emotional yearning to feel at home in an otherwise soulless cosmos. It answers an existential need for reassurance, not a rational calculation of risk. For Blaise Pascal in the seventeenth century, it was not the promise of eternal life that motivated him, or a yearning to hear the voice of God, but consolation for the fear he felt when he contemplated the eternal silence of the infinite spaces.

We crave togetherness and meaning, but the 'voices' of spirituality do not necessarily manifest themselves as transcendent in origin. Reality comprises a series of symbolic orders that we move between freely, in a science laboratory one moment, in a place of worship the next. We live out a series of fictions, or different modes of story-telling about ourselves, each a work of the imagination, which we freely step into and out of.

On days when our favourite team is playing, we might hear the tribal chants, accompanied by colourful insignia and stirring rituals. In these situations, it's not the single voice that calls us to belief and action. It is our 'oceanic' sense of belonging to all the voices around us.

Angels on our shoulders

Whether or not we believe in benevolent beings that speak to us, or angels that look out especially for us, millions attest to the power of 'talking back' through prayer. This involves more than clasping our hands, falling to our knees, 'telling' our beads or looking skywards with our eyes closed. For Tibetan Buddhists, it means writing sacred messages on prayer flags, to be blown into the ether by the wind.

142

The Mirror of the Mind

We can feel transformed, calmed and encouraged
when we become part of something larger.

A prayer can be prompted by a deep yearning, a memory of an ancestor, a concern for someone living, or a search for an answer to an imponderable question, with no fixed expectation of response. Those who pray regularly say they feel they are self-communing within an established spiritual tradition that is greater than the self. We are solitary creatures who can feel alone, rootless and confused, but we are also deeply social, which is why we can feel transformed, calmed and encouraged when we become part of something larger, or visit a place where we know many have dreamed, prayed or been uplifted before us.

Guardian angel
Some of us feel we are protected by an angel on our shoulder, who might occasionally speak to us. But how do we know we are not hearing our own voice reflected back to us, or the voice of a demon?

Prayer has a secular role too. Research shows that it acts as a kind of emotional and psychological therapy, stimulating our immune system and healing ourselves as much as those we intercede for. The poet W H Auden believed that prayer helps us to concentrate our attention on something other than our own ego. It puts us in touch with the best in ourselves, as well as with the needs of others. When we give ourselves up to prayer, we tend to find what we are looking for, fulfilling the biblical promise 'Seek, and you will find'.

Thinkers such as Marx, Nietzsche and Freud dismissed prayer as self delusion riddled with issues of class oppression, moral weakness, sensory distortion and hallucination. They may be right in the sense that the formula 'I pray the Lord my soul to keep' is merely a string of words that, though sounding comforting, relate to nothing in the real world. That is however to miss the point that language performs a number of roles for us, expressive and social, not just literal and functional. If our words were limited to their face-value, our life world would be much the poorer.

Rationalists insist that superstitious prayers cannot effect any change in the real world. In the nineteenth century, Francis Galton put this to the test empirically. He reasoned that the royal family of the day had more prayers lifted up every Sunday for their health and wellbeing than the rest of the nation put together. Disappointingly, these same blue-blooded monarchs on average had shorter life spans than the majority of their subjects.

This is not however a killer argument for or against prayer. Galton was investigating prayer as intercession, which is the only form that can be subjected to science. He was too obsessed with measuring everything in sight to appreciate that much of human behaviour is infused with values and beliefs that defy calculation. Prayer does not yield to utilitarian analysis, because its ends exceed its means.

In the evolution of human consciousness however, prayer might have played a practical role in the steady enlargement of the human psyche, and the growth of altruism. When we consider what motivated the founders of the world religions, it was a desire to realise the good, not to boost their ego or control the masses. That came later, when religions organised themselves as kingdoms of this world, not the next. Mediaeval bishops were powerful political princes, their thrones rivalling those of earthly kings.

No matter what political or economic system we espouse, or whether we accept that we have flourished in spite of religion, not because of it, prayer has played a vital role in ensuring that the moral intuitions of mutual aid, sharing and fairness, inherited from our ancestors and evident even in small children, have been formalised and universalised as the 'Golden Rule'. We owe each other a duty of care, and the rights of the poorest matter as much as the privileges of the most powerful.

Our understanding of what is good is based not on what the gods declare to be so. On the contrary, our moral intuitions and laws have shaped the kind of gods we worship, which explains why there are striking similarities in the moral codes that sustain communities across the world, whether religious or secular. Given this triumph of rationality, prayer may well have become irrelevant, if not defunct, little better than 'hearing things' or 'talking to ourselves'.

But we must not be too hasty in our dismissal of prayer. It remains a potent tool for self knowledge and mutual understanding. For all our technological advances, our lives still regularly confront us with uncertainty, loss, loneliness, disappointment, injustice, disease and death.

Some worry that we have no way of knowing whether the angels on our shoulders that we hear in prayer are in fact demons. René Descartes fretted that his view of reality might be little more than the whispering of a demon in his ear. He rescued his sanity through honest doubt: the mere fact that he was asking the question suggested that his reason was intact.

Mother Teresa
1910-1997
Now Saint Teresa, she was canonised not just for listening to the better angels of her nature, but also for converting them into charitable acts. Some say she was deluded, but a better measure of her vision might be the amount of suffering she helped to relieve in the Indian subcontinent.

Descartes was a rationalist, but he conceded that those who listen out for the call of a higher voice have not lost their reason. Nor do they seek a mask for their personal failure, or a stick to beat others with. They are motivated by a duty of care towards their fellows, not fanatical self-promotion. Francis of Assisi, Mother Teresa, Dietrich Bonhoeffer and Martin Luther King listened to the better angels of their nature, not their demons. They were not delusory, because they kept in view the reality test of the greater good.

We must not therefore become deaf to our inner voices, or regard them as irrational. Our intuitions often come to us as quiet whispers that we initially

145

ignore, only to realise that they are telling us something important. Many bereaved people say they still feel the presence of their loved ones, or hear their voices, but this does not mean they are mentally ill. Our consciousness is frequently liminal, or on the edge. If all those who testify to a 'felt presence' at key moments in their life are certified, there won't be many left to run the asylum.

Religious voices

In today's techno-scientific climate, those who profess a religious faith or sense a 'calling' to a life of service are dismissed by some as victims of a mass delusion, or helpless carriers of a parasitic meme. This is far too simplistic. They are not being controlled by a mind virus, but carefully choosing a path to follow. They are also testimony to religion as a social reality which cannot be detached from cultural tradition, historical context or public practice. Religious beliefs are persistent and shared by many, giving them collective force and legitimacy.

Those who worship in a temple, synagogue, mosque, vihara, church or coven are not in the grip of a grand hallucination, if only because brain scans reveal real events going on inside the heads of the faithful. These in turn determine their daily routine, thought patterns, sense of wellbeing and actions towards their neighbours.

If spirituality can be dismissed as a delusion, so can art, progress and even our trust in scientific method. All are human constructions, each calibrated to different aspects of reality and activated to match the situation. Alchemy raises a smile these days, but its practitioners heating their alembics and mixing their elixirs were not just wizards, wyrds, warlocks and wiseacres. As they discovered which of their wild experiments produced consistent results, they were converting magic to science. In a similar way, religious mystics are explorers of the spiritual realm, opening up new frontiers of the mind.

Faith can be as rational as science can be irrational.

Seen this way, spirituality is not a hallucination, and religious belief is not irrational. Like science, they are natural expressions of the human mind, and intrinsic aspects of our cognitive evolution. Faith can be as rational as science can be irrational. Religion has inflicted its share of suffering on mankind, but science

146

has also deceived with false idols of racial superiority, genetic determinism and eugenic utopia.

Was it a perversion of religion or science that was being worshipped at Auschwitz, where operations without anaesthetics were performed as 'experiments' to see how much pain the human body could bear? The choice before us lies not between reason and unreason, atheism or theism, materialism or idealism, science or religion. It lies in negotiating shared values based on all of our ways of knowing, without which human flourishing can never be complete.

It is true that some fanatically kill and maim in the name of religion, using the command of their god as cover for much more mundane ambitions of power and resentment. This is a universal human failing, not a particularly religious one. If we strip the robes and sacred texts from theocrats and ayatollahs, we find they are common bullies and dictators underneath.

Religion has no monopoly over hatred, bigotry or cruelty. Most of the atrocities of the twentieth century, including the horrors of Stalinism, Nazism and the Red Guards, had no religious motivation at all, nor did the Killing Fields of Cambodia. Violence is human, not divine. Religion is not the villain of the piece: there is something in the human psyche that makes us do appalling things when the normal safeguards of civilised behaviour collapse, and the barriers to barbarism break down.

Behaving morally, expressing religious feeling, making art and practising science are human group activities that make sense only as part of a unified view of what makes us tick, and what helps society to work. They achieve traction by force of tradition, weight of numbers, long-term efficacy and personal engagement. They may be answers to a deep need of the human mind to see something rather than nothing.

Occasionally this yearning can result in cognitive dissonance: our brain's internal models no longer match the external world. We experience this phenomenon when we dream, but this does not mean that religion, or any foray of the imagination, is a dream we cannot wake from, or the sign of a deranged sensibility. Our motor system is deactivated when we dream, so sleep-walking aside, we can't act on or in our dreams. When we wake however, we return to full normal brain service. Whether we sense realities in the fifth dimension or believe that what we see is what we get, our beliefs are not like a tap that we can switch on or off. They inform every moment of our waking life.

Transient states

As our understanding of the mind has deepened in recent years, psychiatrists have become much more subtle in their appreciation of when and why we hear voices in our head. It has long been known that victims of multiple personality disorder (MPD) create other identities to help them cope with deep stress or trauma, but there are many 'transient states' of voice-hearing during which we are by no means suffering from a psychiatric condition.

These include liminal states between sleep and waking, idle daydreaming or hypnotic trances, which we encounter every day, and after which we quickly reset to default. Much rarer 'one-off' epiphanies might involve artistic or scientific inspiration, religious conversion, moments of joy or ecstasy, falling in love, or episodes of mathematical insight.

Against these positive experiences there are many negatives, such as sleep deprivation, sustained stress, illness, alienation and bereavement, even the disorientation caused by space flight. Trauma is often a catalyst, whether remembered from childhood, or following a bad experience such as witnessing a disaster, or being deeply frightened.

The voices we hear might be trying to guide us
or tell us something important about ourselves.

The Hearing Voices Network, first established in 1987, provides an international forum for those who hear voices, but do not regard them as signs of illness, failure or curse. They want to integrate their voices as part of who they are, and accept them as coming from their own bodies, without being controlled or stigmatised by them. Carl Jung believed the voices we hear might be trying to guide us or tell us something important about ourselves, not to destroy us. In neurological terms, they might be our brain's way of getting us through a crisis.

Whether or not we occasionally catch ourselves thinking aloud, we can all learn from this advice. David Bowie spoke for all of us when he said, 'I'm just a collection of other people's voices'. In many cultures, young men are expected to

148

spend a time apart in order see visions of the spirit world or hear the voices of the ancestors, perhaps under the tutelage of a shaman and a dose of hallucinogen. They are not considered 'initiated' or ready to assume the responsibilities of adulthood until they return to share what they have seen and heard.

It seems idle to speculate whether the voices heard in these heightened situations are biologically or psychologically caused, because they are real phenomena to the people who hear them. This includes spiritualist attempts to communicate with the dead, via self-proclaimed mediums or ouija boards.

There is no scientific evidence for anything in the paranormal realm, and claims to be 'psychic' are usually hoaxes when investigated, faring no better than guesswork, but this does not stop people from hoping. In the late nineteenth century, many educated Victorians became obsessed with death, believing they could commune with their deceased loved ones. Even Arthur Conan Doyle, creator of the apogee and embodiment of logical deduction, Sherlock Holmes, attended séances. There was much charlatanry about, but also much spiritual anguish.

A similar phenomenon occurred a generation later, when so many millions of young lives were snuffed out in the trenches, or by the Spanish flu pandemic. Thousands were desperate to cling to the memories of those they had lost. If they did hear their voices, this was to answer a deep emotional need. It does not mean they were suffering the auditory hallucinations of paranoid schizophrenia, which we consider next.

The shattered mind: Schizophrenia

Schizotypy – symptoms - causes and cures - paranoia – source monitoring - propensity to violence - visions

- After centuries of portraying schizophrenia as demon possession or madness, we now have a much better understanding of it as distorted perception with organic causes, not disturbed emotion.
- Its causes are difficult to pin down, and the condition is complex, but the symptoms are consistent, with clear genetic markers.
- They are not always triggered, and many of us are schizotypal to some degree without developing full-blown symptoms.
- Cures have proved to be as elusive as causes.
- Paranoid schizophrenia is the type usually associated with hallucinations and hearing voices.
- It is principally an organic disorder which requires carefully targeted medication, but appropriate therapy can also help.
- The disease can start in childhood, but usually manifests by the mid-teens to early twenties, earlier in boys than in girls.
- Asylums run like prisons are a thing of the past, but some untreatable cases who may be a danger to themselves or others need care in institutions or secure units.
- Modern drugs allow less severe cases to manage their symptoms and live in the community, which imposes a burden of care on all of us.
- We are statistically more likely to suffer violence at the hands of 'sane' members of the public than schizophrenics.
- Schizophrenics are much more likely to self-harm or be the victims of violence than its perpetrators.

The Mirror of the Mind

You can tickle yourself, because your body feels under alien control, not part of you. You constantly hear a voice, possibly several, but you don't know whether they belong to someone else, or are an amplification of your own. They are sometimes friendly, often critical, and occasionally tell you to do something you don't want to do, even to kill someone. Other people seem to be collections of molecules, on the bad side in a cosmic struggle between good and evil, anything but real persons. You possess secret knowledge that can save the world, but you can't trust anyone. Every helicopter flying overhead, or anyone approaching you wearing a white jacket, is part of a conspiracy to steal your secret from you. You are not in control of events, but witnessing your own slow disintegration.

This is what it is like to suffer from paranoid schizophrenia.

The shattered mirror

Schizophrenia means 'split mind', but that is misleading. The disease does indeed undermine the sufferer's sense of identity and self-monitoring, but not through disintegration of emotion, character and personality. It is a disorder of cognition, perception and thought, which can reduce overall IQ by as much as five per cent, affecting memory, speech, executive function, and most crucially, the sense of agency, or being in control.

Inputs that the brain usually deals with straightforwardly are blown out of proportion. Irrelevant information is given significance it does not merit, patterns are perceived where they don't exist, friendly greetings are imbued with threatening intent, and conspiracies against the self are fabricated out of thin air.

Schizophrenia is what happens when the
mirror of the mind is shattered.

The Mirror of the Mind

As a disease of the intellect, schizophrenia is not to be confused with a 'Jekyll and Hyde' split between night and day, multiple personality disorder, or the mood disorder of bipolar depression. The challenge that sufferers have to deal with is not warring egos, but what happens when the mirror of the mind is shattered. The fragile coalition of senses, memory and other people that we rely on for our reality testing is dissolved, with no way of stopping reality and imagination, or self and world, from 'bleeding' into each other.

The disease, affecting twenty five million sufferers worldwide, is one of many pathologies of the self which are part of the human condition, or 'come with' our genome. It accounts for as much as fifty per cent of admissions to psychiatric hospitals, with probably an equal number walking the streets at any time.

It is not a single disease but a complex constellation of overlapping brain conditions that are difficult to diagnose and even harder to treat. As there are no visible scars on or in the body, doctors have to go by what patients tell them, which by definition is highly subjective.

Like autism, the condition runs along a spectrum, one in a hundred crossing the threshold into full-blown schizophrenia. At the extreme end, distorted perceptions and hallucinations create an inner conflict between the figments of an overactive imagination and the facts of an unforgiving reality.

Because the mirror of their mind is shattered, schizophrenics struggle to keep their imagination in bounds, not 'reality-testing' in the ways that the rest of us take for granted. They tune into realities the rest of us don't or can't see, inundating their brain with messages that seep into the wrong compartment, without the benefit of blocks or filters.

As a result, their brain draws all-inclusive and over-generalised conclusions which the rest of us would judge as mere coincidence: that's the second time I've seen that red car this morning. This is insufficient grounds for arriving at a deduction that correlates to nothing in the real world: I am under surveillance and my life is under threat. Such anxieties are the seeds of paranoia. They sound irrational to the rest of us, until we remember that 'reality' is a creation of our whole psyche, not just our reason. Our emotions play as important a role as our cognition in establishing who we are.

The Mirror of the Mind

This explains why, when challenged, schizophrenics can become agitated that their construction of reality is being called into question, because it is part of their identity. They become impervious to argument, considering any evidence to the contrary as an attack on their person, and proof that they are right, serving only to strengthen their delusion.

If we are convinced that the prime minister is the Great Satan who must be executed, that every report of a dangerous virus on the loose is a government hoax, or that every offer of help is a part of a plot to steal our mind, and we can't reconnect with the corrective mainstream of human discourse, we are in the grip of a terrifying paranoia.

Being schizotypal

Paranoid schizophrenia is a full-blown psychosis: we either have it or we don't. As so often with genes however, they operate along a continuum. In other words, it's not simply a case of whether we've 'got' schizophrenia, more an issue of whether we are schizotypal, or at greater risk than others.

This explains how the genes for schizophrenia have survived: the symptoms are not always severe or disabling, which has allowed many schizotypes high on the spectrum to use their visionary 'gift' to go on to become great leaders, artists and parents. They might have reproduced before their symptoms intensified, so their schizotypal genes were not deselected.

Paranoid schizophrenia is the legacy of 'voices'
that cannot be contained.

One theory is that there was a breakthrough in human intelligence about sixty thousand years ago, when one side of our brain 'invaded' the other. Anthropologists note the appearance around this time of an increasing capacity to think expansively, innovate technically, and extend territorial range. Those able to control their 'voices' were the ones who commanded allegiance, making their genes more attractive to female partners in the process. Paranoid schizophrenia is the legacy of 'voices' that cannot be contained.

Even if we carry schizotypal genes, they may never be triggered, and if they are, their worst effects can be moderated by those who care for us. The genes for schizophrenia seem to belong to a complex genetic 'package' which includes Parkinson's, Huntington's, Alzheimer's, multiple sclerosis and major depression, though the biological links between them, and their psychosocial risk factors, are as yet poorly understood.

Also the disease takes different forms, with a positive or negative manifestation which can't be predicted from a DNA readout. Type 1 schizophrenics are generally intellectually bright, exhibiting positive attitude, with transient symptoms that can be treated. With therapy, the voices they hear can be resisted and even disobeyed. Type 2 tend to be intellectually challenged and withdrawn, with chronic symptoms that do not respond to treatment, such as persistent voices, flat emotion and difficulty coping with social situations, leaving the sufferer feeling guilty and helpless.

Even with identical twins who inherit the condition, the disease's trajectory can be influenced through a phenomenon called epigenetics. Nature decides our biology, and is irreversible, but nurture, or the life-world we are born into and the events that befall us on our journey, are much more malleable, and can strongly influence which genes are expressed.

Madness and the law
Schizophrenia used to be dismissed as 'madness', a term so imprecise as to be useless. Until fairly recent times, asylums were full of people monotonously rocking in chairs or aimlessly walking the corridors, their mental condition undiagnosed and their symptoms untreated. Some by any other measure would have been sane, but many would have been in various stages of paranoid schizophrenia.

Not all would have been unhappy. Some schizophrenics testify to grandiose feelings and extraordinary visions, admitting them to higher planes of euphoria, spirituality and insight. Others are not so lucky, falling prey to apathy, joylessness and loss of pleasure in anything, not even wanting to get out of bed in the morning.

For those suffering full-blown paranoia, madness defines its own reality, leaving them unsure whether they intend themselves harm, or others are conspiring to harm them. In London in 1843, the M'Naghten rules were drawn up after Daniel M'Naghten, who had come to the attention of the police two years earlier, fired a shot at the prime minister Robert Peel. He felt that he was being 'persecuted by the Tories', and that the PM was trying to kill him. He ended up mistaking his target, killing a secretary instead.

He was possessed of a false belief which put him in a dangerous relation to reality, and a fatal one for his victim. He was arrested and put on trial, but his legal counsel pleaded insanity on his behalf, arguing that he was 'labouring under a defect of reason', not in possession of his right mind when he pulled the trigger.

Daniel M'Naghten
Judged insane at the time of shooting dead the prime minister's secretary in 1843, M'Naghten was sent to an asylum, not prison. In what was a breakthrough for the new science of psychiatry, he was judged to be mentally ill, not a common murderer.

The jury decided that, at the time of the shooting, McNaghten was suffering impaired or diminished responsibility: he was deluded, and did not know he was doing wrong. He was acquitted of murder, his insanity proclaiming a kind of innocence. He was not judged to be a criminal, so he avoided prison, but he spent the rest of his life in an asylum.

Insanity is a legal term meaning not being *mens rea*, or in our right mind when we perform an action. In psychiatric parlance, our default reality testing device is not functioning effectively, and our cognitive faculties are not keeping us 'in touch' with our neighbour. M'Naghten's case was a breakthrough in understanding complex psychiatric conditions: it is treatment that the patient needs, not punishment. With hindsight, we can say that M'Naghten was displaying classic symptoms of paranoid schizophrenia, but it was to be another hundred years before the disease was given a name.

Lawyers can prosecute or defend only on the basis
of what has actually been done.

The law nevertheless is placed in a real predicament with the likes of M'Naghten. It cannot determine guilt in advance, based on what harm someone might be capable of doing. In the film 'Minority Report', the hero is arrested on the basis of what crimes he *might* commit. But the law does not work like this. Lawyers can prosecute or defend only on the basis of what has actually been done, leaving it to psychiatrists to advise on mental state at the time, to judges to determine fair trial, and to juries to decide guilt.

The philosopher Friedrich Nietzsche might have been schizophrenic. He suffered a psychotic breakdown at the age of forty four, leaving him dependent on care until his death aged fifty five. It used to be believed his descent into madness was caused by late-stage syphilis, but it is now put down to a manic-depressive psychosis giving way to paranoid schizophrenia.

The signs of a mind divided against itself were present in his first book, in which he polarised the cult of the primitive wine-god Dionysus and the worship of the refined sun-god Apollo. This imagined schism between darkness and light, instinct and reason, slave and hero, festered in the German psyche for two generations, erupting eventually in the perverted Nazi dream of the Reich of a Thousand Years.

Types of schizophrenia
Madness and insanity are descriptions of behaviour, revealing nothing of what is going on inside. To this end, five subtypes of schizophrenia have been identified, the most common of which is paranoid schizophrenia, characterised by hallucinations. There is also disorganised schizophrenia, manifesting confused speech and behaviour, and catatonic schizophrenia, a deadness to the outside world, though modern drug treatment has made this very rare. Schizo-affective disorder is technically not a type of schizophrenia, but a compound condition in

which hallucinations may be involved, but exaggerated swings of mood are the bigger problem.

Diagnostic symptoms are difficult to isolate.

To be classified with the disease, sufferers must show at least three identified symptoms. They must experience bouts of sustained delusion, hallucination and incoherence lasting at least four weeks, which in turn impair their ability to function normally without help. They must also be free of substance abuse and other medical conditions. Diagnostic symptoms are difficult to isolate, because the disease often associates with ongoing conditions such as depression, obsessive compulsive disorder and alcoholism. It is also exacerbated by nicotine addiction.

Emil Kraepelin
1856-1926
Kraepelin was the first psychiatrist to distinguish between two different psychoses, what we now call manic depression and schizophrenia. It was Eugen Bleuler who coined the name schizophrenia in 1908, by which he meant a dissociation between thought and volition.

Schizophrenia was first recognised as a specific psychosis by Emil Kraepelin at the end of the nineteenth century. He called it *dementia praecox*, or premature dementia. Unlike senile dementia, schizophrenia attacks young people in their twenties, with warning signs in the teens, preventing the sufferer from functioning safely in normal society.

He was convinced it was a disease of the mind/brain with organic causes, as identifiable as a broken leg, manifesting as a disorientation of the internal reality checks most of us manage effortlessly. He noticed it progresses in four stages, which clinicians still accept today: slow withdrawal from the world, increasing paranoia, unsettled speech and thought patterns, and eventually catatonia or a state of frozen immobility.

Paranoia strikes here

Given the advances in our understanding of schizophrenia since Kraepelin's day, and its constantly shifting diagnoses, pity the psychiatrist trying to make fine diagnostic distinctions between schizomania, schizothymia, schizonoia, and various closely related depressive states. She must differentiate between negative symptoms that flatten the emotions, and positive symptoms which generate hallucinations. She must separate out schizoid personality disorder, schizoaffective disorder and paranoid schizophrenia.

Paranoid schizophrenia, the form we are most familiar with, or hear about the most, affects about one per cent of the population, so it is as much a part of our genome as genius, possibly its flip side. What is lacking in paranoid schizophrenia is a unitary sense of 'I' operating as a responsible agent, explaining why sufferers may break into smiles or giggles without knowing why.

The neurological cause may be a case of left and right hemispheres failing to cohere, so that conversation is not a unified experience but a bewildering cacophany of different voices, each too loud. Sufferers complain of an absence of a locus of control, as if it is no longer they who think, but their thoughts that think them. They lose their sense of agency, speaking of themselves in the third person. Their ego feels fragile and porous, like a city divided against itself, fantasy breaking into reality unhindered.

For paranoid schizophrenics, the split is not so much between warring selves as a disconnect between self and the outside world, leading to confusion between what is self-generated, and therefore *feels* true, and what is externally given to the senses, and therefore much more likely to *be* true.

158

The Mirror of the Mind

We don't have to be schizophrenic to suffer paranoia, which means being 'beside our own mind', as in being beside ourselves with fear. Paranoia is not necessarily irrational, and may even be constructive. After all, in a storm, branches *do* occasionally snap and kill someone below, so we are wise to take sensible precautions.

The logic is good, but our behaviour becomes paranoid if we over-react to a perceived threat. Paranoia becomes our jailer when we become so afraid that we never go into the woods again. We have succumbed to 'catastrophe thinking', rushing to conclusions that bear little or no relation to the real risk. Statistically, we're far more likely to die falling down the stairs at home (seven hundred a year in England) than be struck dead by a falling tree (six a year).

Paranoid about trees
Every year a few people are killed by falling trees or branches, but statistically we are far more likely to die falling down the stairs at home.

Paranoia may be an emotional cry to be noticed. Many older people who live alone phone the police regularly because they believe someone has been in their house while they have been out, perhaps even trying to kill them. In these cases, the possibility of police attention is more bearable than the certainty of being alone and ignored.

There is a strong sense of the 'other' invading our psychic reality.

For those who suffer from clinically diagnosed paranoia, being 'paranoid' is a severe and frightening condition, involving far more than baseless anxiety. Most of us have a clearly defined sense of self, allowing us to be sure where 'we' end and 'they' begin. In acute paranoia, this distinction breaks down, and there is a

159

strong sense of the 'other' invading our psychic reality. Irrational mistrust of others leads to an overwhelming feeling of being persecuted.

Paranoid schizophrenics speak of this experience in surprisingly logical and rational terms. It starts with feeling a hole at the centre of their lives, or lack of explanation for social rejection and the denial of love, resulting in a strong sense of abandonment and isolation. Even the healthiest mind/brain struggles to cope with unexpected setback, trauma or absence of meaning.

Ordinarily we have psychological defence mechanisms to get us through a hard time, such as finding a scapegoat when things go wrong, or inventing a story that the world is against us. The problem for the schizophrenic mind is when the 'solution' is solidified into an elaborate set of beliefs, and given permanency.

Aliens have abducted me, then returned me to earth as the only person capable of saving the planet. The only problem is, anyone with a beard or dressed in black is out to thwart me. This may sound irrational to you, but it gives me a sense of control: I know what our mission is, and what my enemy looks like.

Source monitoring

And then there are the voices, which never stop. As children we gradually internalise the words we hear as 'inner speech', taking command of 'our' voice when we realise we can say 'no' when our parents expect us to say 'yes'. We learn to think to ourselves, quite sure it is 'our' voice we are hearing.

But what if voices emanate unbidden from the 'talking' area of our brain while simultaneously popping up in our 'hearing' compartment, so that we don't know if it's our own voice or that of an alien? Our 'source monitoring' is compromised, and we can no longer tell the difference.

Unwanted and unfounded messages are predominantly auditory, not visual, though a few paranoid schizophrenics also see faces that are not there. Sufferers are more likely to hear voices than see ghosts, often complaining of someone inserting unwanted thoughts into their heads.

The voices force their way in uninvited.

The overwhelming feeling that these inputs come from an external source means that there is no reason *not* to believe that the voices are real. Deaf

The Mirror of the Mind

schizophrenics suffer hallucinations too, not auditory but as signs that come to them through different sensory channels. What matters is that, however sensed, these voices deny schizophrenics volition or first refusal: they force their way in uninvited.

The hallucinations may well be prompted by the unconscious, arising from trauma or anxiety. The sufferer might be driven by an intense wish to escape a bad situation, be in a safer place or be a different person. When the voices come however, they obliterate any links to the real world, or make it hard to go back there.

While hearing voices, cause and effect are hard to disentangle: do we become aroused because we hear voices, or do we hear voices because we are aroused? For the schizophrenic in the grip of an 'episode', there is no time for such musing: the auditory hallucination is mistaken for the reality, and the belief in an external controlling force creates a sense of paranoia. The voices may be accompanied by characteristic eye movements, and take on a menacing quality.

Natural causes

Various theories have been put forward for the causes of schizophrenia. There may be fixed biological or physical factors present from birth, that will 'out' one way or another. To this end, researchers use neuro-imaging to find tell-tale genetic, biological or organic 'markers' in the brains of sufferers, and to identify unusual patterns of activity.

There might for instance be a blip in a particular neural network, such as our inter-hemispherical messaging system, source-monitoring module or Bayesian prediction engine. These functional mechanisms enable us to self-interrogate, identify where messages are coming from, and second-guess what is coming next. These are activities which determine the essence of reality for normal brains, but can be problematic for schizophrenics.

No two schizophrenic brains are alike.

Sophisticated imaging technology also throws up organic abnormalities in the schizophrenic brain, without fingering particular culprits. Scans reveal larger cerebral ventricles or hollows in the middle of the brain, a smaller hippocampus,

161

decreased activity in the frontal cortex, frontal lobe lesions, overactive Von Economo neurons, and reduced activity in the insula. No two schizophrenic brains are alike, but any combination of these abnormalities has the potential to impair executive function.

Neuroscientists devote themselves to understanding how one neurotransmitter might block the release of another, or interfere with specific neuroreceptors. An imbalance or misfeed may distort perception and reality-processing, which has a high existential cost for the sufferer: raw feeling and delusion are ramped up to full volume with no on/off switch.

Neurotransmitters such as dopamine, serotonin, GABA and glutamate not only lubricate the brain but also regulate it, their release calibrated by genes. An excess of dopamine might over-stimulate the brain to the point where it cannot reconcile what is going on inside with the facts of the case outside. In recent years however, the theory of dopamine overdose has been tempered with the possibility that the condition might have more to do with the right number of dopamine receptors in the brain which put it to best use, rather than with the supply of dopamine itself, though there is little understanding of the link between blocking dopamine receptors and reducing hallucination.

The role of nurture
Some experts, unconvinced that the disease is purely genetic, point out that it is much more likely to be triggered by life experiences and cultural factors, regardless of the underlying biology. Before the modern age, spiritual crisis and divine curse were favourites. Psychoanalysts came up with a flurry of possibilities: blocked energy flows, ego depletion, castration anxiety, cold mothering, weak fathering, a hostile sibling, sexual abuse as a child, or a sense of alienation caused by a threatening modern world.

Most psychiatrists and therapists now accept that childhood abuse and social alienation, though not causing the disease, can contribute to its severity, but most of the other psychoanalytic theories have been debunked. Many schizophrenics come from loving homes, where parenting has been more than adequate. Also, the disease is by no means limited to the affluent West, or modern times. It exists in all cultures, so it has been in our genome since our ancestors left Africa.

The Mirror of the Mind

Whatever the biology, the trigger for the condition is likely to be developmental, a one-off or ongoing blip at a crucial point in the growth cycle, leading to lifelong complications. There may be a problem with the placenta during pregnancy, abnormal synaptic pruning in childhood, a bout of temporal lobe epilepsy, a virus which inflames the brain, prompting a misfiring of the autoimmune system, or heavy use of cannabis, mescalin or LSD while the brain is undergoing its delicate reorganisation during adolescence.

Schizophrenics generally sleep poorly, and have shorter life spans.

Lack of quality deep sleep in the early years, during which the brain sets its house in order, might compromise the healthy growth of the brain's 'reality checking' systems, leaving us feeling we are dreaming while awake, unable to tell the difference between what the world is doing to us, and what we are doing to ourselves. Schizophrenics generally sleep poorly, and have shorter life spans.

Whether we look to nature or nurture for an explanation, there is agreement on one important point: schizophrenia is not a lifestyle choice, cultural fad, flight from reality or gateway to a higher realm. There may be a quirk of the mind we have yet to discover, hidden deep in our evolutionary past, but the modern consensus is that the answer lies in our genome, manifesting in the brain and expressed in the mind. With the right medication and therapy, it can be treated, or its symptoms alleviated, though they never go away completely.

Experts have come to accept that, while the social situation of the patient must always be taken into account, the disease also needs to be treated at the level of brain cells with appropriate medication. In a re-run of the age-old nature/nurture debate, the causes of the disease are multi-factorial, both an inherited brain condition, and neurochemistry shaped by experience.

This consensus doesn't mean that treatment is straightforward. Pharmaceutics can give quick relief, but drugs merely mask the symptoms temporarily. Psychotherapy takes much longer, and is therefore more expensive, but by getting to the root cause, perhaps a complicated series of psychological crises and triggers years earlier, it holds out the chance of deeper healing, though never a complete cure.

The Mirror of the Mind

The role of the genes

Up to three hundred genes have been identified in association with schizophrenia, manifesting as a cluster of symptoms that form a syndrome. No single gene controls the disease, because it is polygenic, operating on a spectrum, controlled by the expression of genes, a bit like our height. We cannot 'catch' schizophrenia unless we've inherited specific genes, and even then the disease's intensity and progress will be variable, depending on other accidents of life, such as our season of birth, which may expose us to winter viruses.

Schizophrenia can skip a generation or leave one
identical twin untouched while the other succumbs.

The condition seems always to have been part of our genome, found in all cultures, with a high degree of heritability. It tends to run in families, but how the genetic chips fall can never be predicted. It can skip a generation or leave one identical twin untouched while the other succumbs.

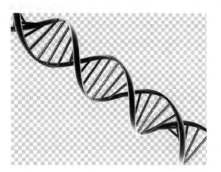

Genetic causes
There is a strong link between genes, DNA and schizophrenia, but they are poorly understood. There are many other factors at work, because genes are neither inert nor lone operators.

Only one in a hundred carries these genes, so the risk level is quite low. If we have one parent carrying the genes for schizophrenia, we have a ten per cent chance of inheriting the condition. If both parents carry the gene, that rises to fifty per cent.

The Mirror of the Mind

We need to remember that for every schizophrenic in the family, there will probably be someone who flourishes in the creative professions. Who gets what appears to be a lottery. For the lucky, it manifests as giftedness; for the unlucky, as a 'formal thought disorder'. In between are many who display schizophrenic tendencies which do not develop into full-blown symptoms, so the penetrance of the genes is not complete or predictable. One sibling might be normal, one touched with genius, and one destined to develop full-blown schizophrenia.

Even when necessary causes are found in the neurome or genome, they are not sufficient, because symptoms manifest themselves differently in individual lives, societies, environments and historical circumstances. In the Dutch famine of 1944, pregnant mothers were forced to survive on less than a thousand calories a day. When the babies who survived were tracked into adulthood, they were found to be twice as likely to suffer schizophrenic symptoms. Sexually abused children are three times more likely.

Even if scientists crack the genetic puzzle of schizophrenia, the disease might never disappear from the human story. In a sad coda to the work done by Kraepelin, the Nazis decided that the 'bad genes' he identified needed to be purged. In their eugenic fervour, they sterilised or murdered up to a quarter of a million people diagnosed with schizophrenic symptoms. The puzzle is that, in the post-war generation, schizophrenia levels returned to pre-war levels, suggesting that genes alone cannot explain the prevalence of schizophrenia. It might be intrinsic to the human condition, always lurking in the wings.

Early warning signs

It used to be thought that schizophrenia was an adult phenomenon, but the Dunedin Study, begun in 1972, tracking children in New Zealand through to adulthood, established that there are early warning signs of the failure of the mind to integrate all its processes in childhood. Occasionally schizophrenia manifests before the age of thirteen, so the disease is not necessarily the degeneration of an adult brain.

Children who claim to 'hear voices' beyond the normal fantasising
of childhood are much more likely to develop schizophrenia as adults.

The Mirror of the Mind

Childhood is when full powers of symbolisation and imagination develop. For most this is an exciting expansion of their cognitive world, and they manage to keep fact and fantasy in balance. For a few however, the boundaries between reality and hallucination begin to blur. Children who claim to 'hear voices' beyond the normal fantasising of childhood, but are unable to integrate them with their own thoughts, are much more likely to develop schizophrenia as adults, leading to the conclusion that early treatment and intervention are essential.

An early warning sign of control by an 'other' in children is the absence or gradual disappearance in their speech or writing of self-oriented words such as my, believe, think and feel. There is now a phone app that can detect early warning signs by scanning language patterns, vocal pitch and facial expression. Another sign is a steady distancing from family and friends into a private world. The victim might be unable or unwilling to articulate the thought, but increasingly feels under surveillance, another reason for withdrawal.

It is in our psychological nature to veer between opposites, such as our desire for attachment and our urge to be alone. Normally we solve this tension creatively, but in the young schizophrenic brain, opposites are not so easily reconciled. The two sides of the brain do not mesh, the moody and inventive right often dominating, with the result that the language-processing left starts to malfunction, misinterpreting its own inner speech. Puns are taken literally, and alien voices are generated.

Following these early warning signs, and without intervention, the disease will strike fully between the ages of seventeen and twenty five, rarely after thirty. It usually appears around the age of eighteen, after the brain has undergone the major re-organisation of the teenage years, later than other developmental conditions such as ADHD, dyslexia, autism and mood disorder. Men and women suffer in equal numbers, but boys tend to succumb up to five years earlier than girls.

Seeking a cure

For centuries the disease that came to be called schizophrenia was shrouded in mystery, generally feared as evidence of possession by demons. As recently as two hundred years ago, if physicians couldn't cure it by bleeding the patient or

The Mirror of the Mind

making them sick, they pretended to cure it by removing a stone from the head, if only to act as a placebo.

Our journey towards a deeper understanding of schizophrenia is a remarkable tale of the triumph of science over superstition, medicine over mystery and psychiatry over pseudoscience. We have learned to be more compassionate towards those with mental disorders, not viewing them as fairground freaks. Based on a more subtle understanding of how our brain negotiates the different realities we inhabit, we have become more accepting of those who are neuro-divergent, from left-handers and homosexuals to sufferers of autism and schizophrenia.

Gone are the days of blaming the 'refrigerator mother' for inflicting the illness on her child by weakening its ego and creating conflicting voices in the head. According to this theory, by starving affection the emotionally cold and manipulative mother creates a 'double bind' of contradictory messages. She assures the child of her love, but exercises coercive control by imposing conditions. I love you, but not unconditionally. If you do not do as I wish, I cannot love you in return. This leaves the child feeling confused, guilty and 'split': I cannot stop being bad, therefore I do not deserve love.

This line of thinking did more harm than good, especially for struggling mothers. It produced a generation of parents who had their suffering unnecessarily doubled: a schizophrenic child (usually male) and the guilt of being a bad mother. The disease is biological, not psychological. By the same token, we cannot blame schizophrenia on the Oedipus complex, because our risk of developing the disease is determined in the womb, not by our later wish to sleep with our mother.

Without intervention and treatment, schizophrenia leads
to a steady deterioration of grey matter.

Schizophrenia is an organic disease first, and a psychological affliction second, though there are still psychoanalysts and psychotherapists who see it as unresolved trauma or suppressed memories that have not been properly dealt with. Cognitive therapists help some sufferers to disengage from the tyranny of the voices they hear by training their conscious thoughts to fight back against them. Behavioural therapists provide practical strategies for living with schizophrenia, or use virtual reality to 'accompany' their patients on a non-threatening journey to recovery. Most sufferers are best helped however by an evidence-based psycho-neuro-pharmacological approach which embraces the whole of their condition.

Whatever the causes, origins, diagnoses, symptoms or cures, the key challenge is how to prevent or block the progress of the disease, because without intervention and treatment, it leads to a steady deterioration of grey matter in the brain. There are pharmacological cures which do more than sedate or tranquilise without becoming addictive, but it has not been easy to find the optimum biochemical cocktail or antipsychotic medication to calm a disordered mind, because each sufferer hallucinates differently and for different reasons.

The drug chlorpromazine, discovered by accident in the chemical dye-making industry and legalised in 1953, mitigates some of the symptoms by blocking the action of certain neurotransmitters, or serving as a dimmer switch. It is a suppressant, not a cure, helping those with severe negative symptoms to manage what would otherwise be life-destroying mind-controlling hallucinations.

It doesn't work for all sufferers, and there are long-term effects such as jerky movements, but pharmocologists are constantly developing second-generation antipsychotics, more carefully targeted and with fewer side effects, often discovered through trial and error.

Treatment does not have to be drug-based. Non-invasive transcranial magnetic stimulation (TMS) provides relief for some plagued by hallucinations, but most commonly, minimal drugs allied with careful therapy prove to be the best form of treatment. Most effective of all is drug-based self-management, because it gives the patient a sense of control over their condition. Some accuse drugs of coercing patients, or shrinking their brain, but although a small number die from their medication every year, far more are saved by them from misery, incarceration and suicide.

Caring for schizophrenics

It is easy to talk about schizophrenics in the third person, forgetting that they are also people like you and me who are very confused about what is happening to their mind. They know they are ill, and many show great courage in coming to terms with their diagnosis, recovering sufficiently to lead as near to normal a life as possible, including holding down a job.

The Mirror of the Mind

They say that they are greatly helped when their symptoms are explained to them, they are given a treatment plan, they receive support in sticking to it, they are prescribed the right medication and therapy, and they are assured they are not alone. It also helps that the public are educated in the everyday challenges faced by schizophrenics.

Sufferers would like to engage with the wider world on level terms, but with no concept of 'I' or 'you', hearing the question 'can I help you?' can be confusing, even threatening: are we being offered food, criticism or sexual favours? Without a steady sense of self, social intercourse becomes all but impossible, and losing our sense of self is our greatest existential threat.

Psychiatrists focus on what schizophrenics *feel*: sufferers believe persecution is real because the same part of the brain is activated, whether persecution has happened or not. That said, many schizophrenics live in difficult family situations where the rejection they feel might be only too real. Also, some feel so socially isolated that they regard their inner voices as their only friends.

This raises difficult issues for carers, many of whom selflessly devote themselves to family members with schizophrenia. Research shows that sufferers are more likely to relapse if they live in a critical family environment, or experience a stressful event after recovery.

A wide public understanding of the problems of living with schizophrenia makes a great difference.

Also, the symptoms of schizophrenia can be exacerbated by a feeling of social exclusion, especially for those living alone or in deprived areas. Sufferers express their feelings in many different ways, not always intelligible even to their immediate carers. A wide public understanding of the problems of living with schizophrenia can therefore make a great difference, helping both sufferers and carers to bear the burden of exhaustion and empathy.

Up to the 1950's, many of those with symptoms of schizophrenia were kept out of sight in grim institutions, some for up to fifty years, only a small proportion of them showing any tendency towards violence or psychosis. The arrival of effective medication meant that most asylums were closed in the 1960's, and by the 1970's, 'care in the community' with tailor-made medication became common, only those deemed to be a threat to themselves and others having their liberty curtailed by being sectioned.

Many problems remain however. Many schizophrenics now wander our streets, their symptoms merely masked, not cured. About a fifth 'make it' and forge some sort of deal between a dislocated self and a difficult society. They must continue to take drugs however, mainly chlorpromazine or Largactil, ten million prescriptions for which have been written since 1953.

Schizophrenia and crime
Medication and therapy allow many schizophrenics to manage their symptoms and lead as normal a life as possible. With the right treatment they are no more likely to commit acts of violence that anyone else, and even in their paranoid state, they are not moral wantons. They know the difference between right and wrong, paying their bills at the checkout and stopping at red lights like the rest of us.

They commit far fewer acts of violence than popular opinion imagines. Only around fifty incidents of aggression against members of the public by mentally ill patients are recorded in the UK each year, a fraction of violent crimes against the person nationally, but when they do happen, they make the news, provoking fear and outrage. 'Normals' are far more likely to be violent than schizophrenics, especially when they tank up with alcohol. Compared to levels of crime in the wider community, schizophrenics are relatively harmless, more likely to self-harm than lash out indiscriminately. Most of their battles are with their own demons, not other people, approximately ten per cent of them going on to take their own lives.

Schizophrenia is at its most dangerous when delusion and impaired impulse control are coupled with lack of empathy. Male schizophrenics are at least three times more likely to murder than female, but only a tenth of total murders are committed by people with some symptoms of schizophrenia, which doesn't say much for the other nine tenths of us who take a life while in our right minds.

Schizophrenia is largely unrecorded in history because most sufferers died ignored or unnoticed, before anyone could diagnose their condition or write their story. The disease's association with crime is probably an echo of the historical reality that most schizophrenics were abandoned to the streets or asylums, where they were more likely to be not the perpetrators of violence, but its victims.

The Mirror of the Mind

Schizophrenia is higher in immigrant communities.

The disease seems to be largely post-industrial, leading us to ask whether it is the curse of feeling anonymous and alienated in large cities, especially for those at the lower end of the social scale, living in 'transit zones' that house the lonely, jobless, and dispossessed. There is definitely a social dimension to diagnosis, with more referrals for psychosis among the poor and homeless than in the middle classes, who tend to be labelled eccentric. There is also some evidence that schizophrenia is higher in immigrant communities, who feel unwelcome in a new country, stranded between cultures and cut off from family ties.

These social factors mean that psychiatrists might struggle to meet the needs of schizophrenics, and cultural differences can lead doctors to misinterpret symptoms. Schizophrenia can be masked or mis-diagnosed in ethnic minorities, who are more likely to have difficulty adjusting to the ways of the dominant culture, or feel alienated by power structures that seem to exclude them.

The causes of schizophrenia lie much deeper however than emotional turmoil during a search for self knowledge. There are distinct physiological and genetic causes, often running in families, found in all cultures. It is not nurture at fault, but nature. Nurture merely exaggerates the symptoms, to which we all unwittingly contribute when we treat schizophrenics as 'other', thereby exaggerating their sense of alienation. Schizophrenia is for instance statistically higher in the children of mixed marriages (nature), but the cause may lie in the fact that these same children might face greater conflict of identity in their peer group (nurture).

Schizophrenia and genius

Schizophrenia is not to be confused with manic depression, which is a mood disorder, the result of cyclical changes in software or brain chemistry leaving the sufferer 'low' for long periods (unipolar) or experiencing occasional bursts of feeling 'high' (bipolar). During depressed times there can be acute despair and sense of helplessness, but in the 'manic' phase there might be euphoria and heightened sensory awareness.

Many artists and scientists are bipolar, enjoying intense bursts of creativity when they are 'up'. Their visions may have a hallucinatory quality, such as a new way of looking at clouds, or understanding the mystery of dark matter. What is

171

also required however is the discipline in the 'down' phase to express these insights in a form we can all understand.

Schizophrenics share some of these symptoms, but there are crucial differences from depression. Schizophrenics generally feel an external force is assuming control over them, whereas in mania and depression, sufferers are more likely to credit themselves for their 'highs', or blame themselves for their 'lows'.

Schizophrenics might experience unusual associations of ideas, but these tend to retain their hallucinatory quality. Creativity and the advancement of thought require a rational mind to fit blurry visions into the sharp edges of reality. It's one thing to see patterns in everything, another to connect these loose associations into finished feats of intellect. There must be an executive capacity to knock ideas into shape.

John Nash
1928-2015
Nash is often upheld as a schizophrenic who was also a genius. The two are not however necessarily linked. Many of his mathematical insights came to him before his illness set in.

The Mirror of the Mind

In acute schizophrenia, this facility is lacking. Few schizophrenics therefore, unable to integrate their neural networks of self, intellect and imagination, have given us great paintings, novels or scientific theories. The brilliant mathematician John Nash, the subject of the 2002 film 'A Beautiful Mind', suffered acute symptoms of schizophrenia, but these were not the secret of his genius. Most of his mathematical insights came to him before his illness set in.

Another mathematical genius from an earlier generation, Srinavasa Ramanujan, had only an elementary mathematical education, but he came up with theorems that stunned his Cambridge professors. He said he had no idea where his inspiration came from. For all he knew, it came directly from the gods.

Does tranquilising schizophrenic patients run the risk of
Extinguishing potentially ground-breaking moments of genius?

Ramanujan was neither schizophrenic nor manic, and took no medication, so his genius is as 'natural' as it gets. Before his illness claimed his sanity, Nash claimed that his theorems came to him by the same pathway as his hallucinatory visions. This raises a difficult the question: does tranquilising schizophrenic patients run the risk of extinguishing potentially ground-breaking moments of genius and reality-changing thoughts?

The important difference between schizophrenia and manic depression is that, though they share some symptoms such as bursts of insight, heightened perception and flamboyant behaviour, depressives, unlike schizophrenics, are always aware of what is happening to them, whatever state they are in, and are seldom psychotic or violent. Unlike schizophrenics, many manic depressives are able to choose their own medication, or decide to take none at all.

Seeing sanely

Let not your heart be troubled

Anxiety – hysteria – Freud and psychoanalysis – Jung and depth psychology – alternative therapies – psychiatry – the Diagnostic and Statistical Manual – R D Laing and anti-psychiatry – modern approaches to mental illness

- Evolution has programmed us to be constantly on the alert, but worry without a specific object can become energy-sapping anxiety.
- Nervousness has nothing to do with our nerves, but everything to do with our emotional settings for fear and uncertainty.
- Hysteria originated as an 'explanation' of woman's fickleness, but it has been exploded as a male fantasy.
- Freud revealed core truths about women's sexuality, but he failed to acknowledge the reality of sexual abuse in their lives.
- His 'talking cure' of psychoanalysis dominated therapy for over a century, but many question its core assumptions about our unconscious demons, and its efficacy as a treatment
- Jung sought a more holistic psychological integration and nurture for his patients, based on a more positive reading of our spiritual journey.
- Together, Freud and Jung drew back the curtain on our hidden mind, and transformed the way we understand mental illness.
- Freud and Jung's disciples split into a bewildering range of rival factions.

The Mirror of the Mind

- Despite operating a more medical model of the mind than psychotherapists, psychiatrists face many complex challenges in 'doctoring' the mind.
- They stand accused of medicalising every psychological blip or oddity, and of over-prescribing mind-altering drugs.
- This approach triggered an 'anti-psychiatry' movement in the 1960's, but by treating mental illness as a social construction, and madness as a journey of liberation, many sufferers were denied the care and medication they needed.
- Psychiatrists now clinically diagnose, tailor their therapy and prescribe psychoactive medication on an individual basis, but there is much about the nature of 'madness' that continues to elude them.
- In addition, despite increasing affluence, levels of depression and unhappiness are on the rise, especially in the young.

Being worried

Fear is an inherited emotional state, in that every animal that has ever lived has had to face a precarious existence. Sexual rivals have to be defeated, food must be found regularly, and predators are always on the prowl. When one is sighted, some animals freeze, while others self-startle, as if they are set on a hair trigger.

Both tactics are useful in thwarting the attentions of a hungry lion, but the response has to be in proportion to the threat. It makes sense to be wary of a shadow in the grass, and assume it might be a lion, even if it means keeping up a high level of vigilance. Herbivores that mistake a lion for a shadow do not live long enough to pass on their genes.

Chronic fear however allows no reset to default. The gazelle does not spend every waking moment in a state of high stress and constant anxiety. As soon as the lion is seen to lose interest, or pass on by, its heart rate drops, and it goes back to peaceful grazing. Fear is a response to a particular threat, which subsides when the danger is over. There's no point staying on high alert, as this is an exhausting waste of energy.

The Mirror of the Mind

We have much more highly evolved brains than a gazelle: we think much more about our predicament, which means that anxiety is potentially chronic. Fear is a reaction to a specific danger, but anxiety is indiscriminate. We can worry about absolutely anything, even worry about having nothing to worry about. At a low level, this isn't problematic, but when worry impacts on our everyday functioning, with no object or end in sight, we can be diagnosed with 'general anxiety disorder'.

Some of us worry about having nothing to worry about.

Our brain and emotional settings are oriented to second-guessing the future. Modern life satisfies most of our material needs, but it has introduced many more, which rolling news keeps in the forefront of our mind. In many ways our sensitivity to threat is higher than for our ancestors on the savannah. The gazelle lives in the present, and quickly resumes grazing when the immediate danger passes, insouciant about the future. We fantasise about a hundred 'what if' scenarios which we can't control, and will almost certainly will never happen.

Fear evolved to help us more forward, which we can't do if it holds us back. Anxiety and stress are like salt: we need them in the right amount, in the right dish, at the right time, about the right problem. There are things we can't change, such as getting ill, growing old, or what happened in the past, so there's not much point worrying about them, other than doing what is necessary to give ourselves the best shot at what is to come. Other things we can change, such as our attitude, self-absorption or possible future, so it's worth giving them a bit of productive worry. In the film 'Bridge of Spies', a Russian spy facing a possible death sentence for treason is asked why he doesn't appear to be worried. 'Will it help?' is his reply.

There's no point fretting over whether we will get cancer, or whether the world will end tomorrow. Other than watching our diet, or recycling our plastic, we have no influence over such matters. Nor can we keep a tight rein on what others say or think about us. Our time is better spent focussing on areas where we can make a difference, such as our desires, opinions and consumer spending.

The Mirror of the Mind

Feel the fear
We have reason to be anxious when one of these is in the vicinity, or on our tail. But there's no point staying on high alert, or letting one stalk our dreams.

We are the worrying species, and our history is full of mass outbreaks of panic, paranoia and hysteria that we are living in the end times, especially at the turn of each century and millennium. It's as if we are always facing the Last Judgment. We maintain large armies and cough up for expensive insurance policies on the basis of threats that *might* come to pass.

Our 'worry level' depends on our personality, emotional thermostat, childhood experiences and coping strategies, so we're not all necessarily chronic worriers. We find our own ways of responding to evolution's daily menu of fight, flee, freeze, feed and fornicate. There is an element of choice involved, not mere reaction to brain chemistry, unconscious urges, Darwinian drives or Pavlovian stimuli.

Worry which prompts us to avert a potential crisis is self-justifying, but not when it chips away at the very mental resources we need to cope, paralysing us into inaction or triggering a panic attack. We come kitted out with powerful emotions, but it is within our gift to manage them. They evolved to be our guardians, but if we're not careful, they can become our jailers.

We are constantly bombarded with signals, far more saying 'this is safe' than 'this is dangerous', but our failsafe position is wariness, especially in unfamiliar surroundings. For our ancestors, a snake bite was something they needed to fear, but the legacy for us is a general aversion to creepy-crawlies, the vast majority of which we need not fear. The best therapy in these situations is to separate the thing we fear from our irrational reaction to it, otherwise what we end up fearing is fear itself.

Needless to say, this is much more easily said than done, but it's worth persisting, because excessive worry and irrational fear compromise our ability to process incoming information calmly, block our access to working memory, and upset our ability to respond rationally. We feel trapped in a brain war, our frontal cortex telling us 'everything is okay', our amygdala screaming 'oh no it isn't'.

We have to accept an element of risk in life, because uncertainty comes with the territory. As the quip goes, the only certainties are death and taxes. If we don't take a chance every now and then, we're locked indoors. If we don't choose, we make ourselves the playthings of fate. Pop psychology urges us to feel the fear and do it anyway. Only then will we find out what we are capable of.

Many myths from across the world taunt us with the idea that there was once a golden age, free of worry, disease, death and sweating the small stuff. Our parents cushion us as long as they can, but life soon confronts us with a more complex reality. By and large, evolution has gifted us the mental resources to cope with our expulsion from Eden, because the cost of failure is so high. Phobias, traumas and compulsions result if we can't find the 'off' switch, or if we are unable to temper the strength of a threat with an analysis of the real danger we are in.

Anxiety leaves us powerless, unable to move forward or back. Ivan Pavlov is famed for showing how to condition a dog to salivate on demand, but less well known are his demonstrations of how far he could push a dog before it became a quivering canine wreck. In what would now be regarded as an unethical experiment, he made one dog so afraid of drowning that the sight of a mere trickle of water into its cage sent it into a paroxysm of fear.

Feeling nervous
Unless we're being chased by a rabid dog, we don't instinctively have a nervous breakdown or go into an emotional tail-spin, but reflect on what our feelings mean in a symbolic life-world. We know our response is not knee-jerk, because we can modulate it, making ourselves happy when we think of a pleasant memory, or sad when we think of a departed loved one.

It pays to stay emotionally chilled, as advised by the world's philosophers, because worrying doesn't change anything. In the Second World War, government posters urged the British public to 'keep calm and carry on'. Worry might prime us for action, but it doesn't win the war. Nor does it make us wealthy or add an inch to our stature. The Bible urges us to be like the lilies of the field, which simply need to bloom, not to fret over their sowing or reaping. To which the worrier replies, yes, until along comes a cow that tramples and eats them.

In the nineteenth century, fear, anxiety and depression were attributed to vague conditions such as neurosis, neurasthenia, hypochondria and hysteria. Today they are more likely to be put down to living in an age of conspicuous consumption: are we suffering from status anxiety?

The dictionary lists fifty synonyms for feeling anxious.

We still talk of feeling nervous, or of our nerves being on edge. These terms have largely been dropped, on the grounds that our nerves are designed to carry electrical messages, not to modulate our moods. They are either on or off, and the neurons or nerve cells in our brain offer no 'picture' of what distorted thinking or distressed feeling looks like. The dictionary defines neurosis as 'morbid psychic activity', which is as vague as it gets.

Thinkers of all hues have attempted to explain worry, anxiety and nervousness as inescapable aspects of the human condition, reflected in the thesaurus's list of fifty synonyms for our edginess. Religious teachers put our fractious state down to our being flawed and alienated creatures. Shakespeare calls us 'poor players strutting and fretting our hour upon the stage'. Psychologists of a certain hue describe us as fundamentally insecure, weakly attached and estranged from ourselves, struggling to separate ourselves from our parents, leaving us feeling helpless in a hostile world.

Evolutionary psychologists attribute our angst to the legacy of living in a 'demon-haunted world', jumping at every thunder crack, lightning strike and rustle in the bushes. We are still hunters at heart, constantly on the alert, even in a quiet urban street, checking out stimuli and pursuing goals. Anxiety is the price we pay for being conscious. The existentialist philosopher Søren Kierkegaard put a slightly different spin on this: anxiety is the price we pay for being free.

The Mirror of the Mind

Acting hysterically

Hysteria, like neurosis, was another vague nineteenth century ailment with little biological foundation. It was attributed exclusively to women, and diagnosed exclusively by male doctors. At the very start of Western medicine, Hippocrates suggested that the female sexual organs cause hysteria, which means 'womb madness', a peculiar instability of a woman's body which compromises her ability to reason.

He might have been familiar with a contemporary play, which told the story of Medea. She was so furious with her husband Jason's adultery that she killed their two children in revenge. Modern feminists might baulk at the manner of her retaliation, but not at her feistiness. It is still the case in the age of the 'Me Too' movement, non-disclosure payouts and powerful men doing what they like, that women are likely to be criticised for complaining about sexual abuse in the first place. Given how they dress and behave, what else do they expect?

Medea's dilemma and solution cannot be compared with the real-life psychosis of a modern mother who feels an urge to murder her child. She is motivated not by hatred or revenge, but is suffering a fit of post-natal depression. She is not hysterical but mentally ill, afflicted by a hormone imbalance. What she needs is a compassionate family, an accurate diagnosis and the right drugs. She is not a lunatic mother, an evil harridan or a vile witch, just a woman who needs help.

Nevertheless, the notion of a woman's physical constitution being fundamentally weak, despite her being able to endure childbirth, lasted for two millennia, and women's sexuality remained a male fiefdom. In Victorian times, some doctors recommended clitoral stimulation as a 'cure' for a woman's listlessness, and a typical male put-down for a woman standing up for herself was that she had 'a touch of the vapours'.

Women have always held an ambivalent place in the male imagination. On one side is the nurturing mother, exemplified in the Virgin Mary, but on the other is Jezebel, the traitorous harlot. The female sexual organ was seen ambivalently as the seat of male pleasure, but also as a pit of slimy secretions. In the manner of the female spider eating the male after sex, men have long been irresistibly drawn to the 'femme fatale', despite their secret fear of being devoured by her.

The Mirror of the Mind

Medea's fury

For centuries, women have been regarded as subordinate, weak and expendable, expected to be chaste but obliged to put up with make adultery. This was not good enough for Medea. 'Dumped' by her husband Jason for another woman, she took revenge by murdering their two children.

1690's New England saw an outburst of hysteria in which women were singled out as the villains of the piece. Although the Puritans had fled the Old World to escape its prejudices, they recreated them in the New World. In their tight community, they became convinced that certain women were 'dancing with the devil'. In the Salem Witch Trials, as many as twenty five 'goodwives' were executed on the say-so of a few screaming teenage girls.

Religious mania was certainly at work, but so were copy-cat fainting fits, fabricated hysteria, and fear among the male accusers that their own adultery would be exposed. Frightened or dead women tell no tales. Much more prosaically, there is a possibility that the whole community was 'high' on a fungus that was attacking the wheat they used to make their bread.

Arthur Miller wrote his 1953 play 'The Crucible' about this, capturing the perfect storm of hysteria, anxiety, paranoia, delusion and conspiracy theory that was sweeping America at the time, on this occasion nothing to do with women at all. Senator Joe McCarthy was convinced that 'Reds under the Bed', or dangerous Communists were infiltrating key institutions, from government to Hollywood. Needless to say, Miller's name was on the blacklist.

The Mirror of the Mind

For centuries women were seen as virginal,
lascivious or hysterical.

As feminists readily point out, until very recently it has been a man's world. A woman was essentially an inferior being or failed man, long seen in the eyes of the law as a 'chattel' or possession of her husband, expected to know her place. In 1837, Mary Heaton was confined to the local madhouse for forty one years for presuming to challenge the authority of the local vicar, who was of course a man.

'Gaslighting' involved undermining a wife's sanity to the point that she could be committed to an asylum. Many ended up like the 'mad' Mrs Rochester in the 1847 novel 'Jane Eyre', or Blanche Dubois at the end of the 1947 play 'A Streetcar Named Desire'. She is broken like a butterfly by men's duplicity, carried off by orderlies in white coats to the local mental institution, where she can spend the rest of her life inventing strange fantasies to make sense of her senseless incarceration.

Many women felt abused, psychologically and sexually, displaying various symptoms of disturbed behaviour as defence mechanisms, but this did not amount to 'moral insanity', as some male accusers insisted. The burden of childbearing, poverty, boredom, loneliness, lack of opportunity and sexual abuse in a loveless marriage drove many women to the edge. In what is known as 'conversion disorder', the symptoms might have manifested as fainting fits, paralysis or constant weeping, making doctors even more puzzled about the underlying physical cause.

'Female hysteria' as a diagnosis is now consigned to the history books, but the problem has not gone away. The sense of abandonment and cry for help manifests in new ways, whether as chronic fatigue syndrome, eating disorders or clinical depression. Many women in rural India find their situation so intolerable that they choose suicide as their only escape.

Freud's legacy
Sigmund Freud's legacy lingers in our modern ideas of healing a disturbed mind, but he was a man of contradictions. He was a medical doctor, committed to finding physical causes for mental illness, but he also came up with such inventive myths of child and adult sexuality that he reads more like a prophet and a novelist

than a scientist. To him we owe the tropes of the Oedipus complex, anal retentiveness, oral dependence, Freudian slips and the guilt left behind by the primal murder.

He was on the side of women, in the sense that he rejected the male confabulation of female hysteria, but he did them a great disservice by not acknowledging the reality of the sexual abuse they have had to endure in all cultures and at all levels of society. He pulled back the curtain on female sexual desire, which up to then had been a mystery to many men, but he cluttered the picture with so many chauvinist speculations about women's sexuality that it took three generations to set them straight.

To his credit, he turned his back on the powerful male doctors of his day who he felt were too ready to hypnotise female subjects in front of a male audience, making a peep show of their hysterical fragility, sexual fantasy and heaving bosoms. He also rejected electro-shock therapy and drug treatment.

Freud did not believe his female patients
when they talked of sexual abuse.

Unfortunately however he did not believe his female patients when they talked of sexual abuse, which we now know is both real and universal. Instead he accused them of 'acting out', or living out the fantasies of their dreams. His most famous patient, Dora, eventually left his care because of this.

If he had been more proactive in exposing sexual abuse, he might have saved generations of children and women from paedophiles and rapists, whose defence was that their victims were 'making it up'. Instead, he propagated a series of myths about little girls that arose from his own imagination, not from any research he carried out. They are castrated boys, suffering from penis envy, and destined to have inferior orgasms to boys. The little boys didn't escape scot free. They are in love with their mothers, hate their fathers as sexual rivals, and suffer from a castration complex.

Our ordinary unhappiness

Childhood sexuality was an important starting point for Freud's 'take' on the human condition, because he believed we need look no further for the causes of

183

our adult neuroses than the cradle. As the poet Philip Larkin put it so memorably, 'They fuck you up, your mum and dad'. We are born too soon, dragged screaming into the world, never quite getting to finish the difficult business of growing up.

One disappointment at a time, we gradually lose our childhood sense of omnipotence, our superego puncturing our oceanic bubble. Unable to wean ourselves off our parents, we grow up with a parent-shaped hole at the centre of our life, finding whatever substitute we can for wetting the bed, sucking our thumb and going to sleep with the light on. This includes belief in God, which Freud also dismissed as a childhood fairytale.

Given the strength of our unruly drives for food, love, power and sex, he concluded that we have to do a deal with life, because we can't get our way with everything. Constant sublimation of our childhood drives leaves us with unresolved 'hang ups'. He extended this argument to society at large: civilisation itself depends on all of us sublimating our urges, otherwise we would not be able to walk down the street without fear of assault.

On a personal level, to protect our ego, and as a defence mechanism, our wilder passions have to be buried deep in our unconscious. There they lie hidden from conscious awareness, but they are capable of popping up any time, especially in our dreams, sometimes awkwardly gate-crashing our waking life, leaving us feeling confused, guilty and frustrated, without knowing why. This means that the self we present to the world is never what it appears on the surface, but a front for a soul at war with its instincts. It is an artefact of constant repression, merely 'good enough' to get by without embarrassing ourselves in public.

We are angst-ridden, parent-hating spoilt brats.

Freud believed that we are sick animals, stranded between a craving for love and a death wish. There is no cure for this disease, only the adoption of certain ways of coping. The job of the therapist is to enable us to 'convert neurotic misery into ordinary unhappiness'. He particularly admired artists for their ability to exorcise their demons and externalise their neuroses. That devout painting of the Madonna is really a yearning to be mothered, loved and sexually understood.

Most reject Freud's portrayal of us as angst-ridden parent-hating spoilt brats pining for a lost paradise. We are in a position to do so however only because he gave us the insight and courage to 'come out'. It was he who dragged sex into the open, especially child sexuality, and the sexual fantasies of adulthood. He confronted us with the painful truth that our past never loses its hold over us. He alerted us to the potency of our dreams, and the savagery that lurks just beneath our civilised exterior, no matter how highly we regard ourselves.

It's good to talk

Freud is best known for pioneering his 'talking cure' of psychoanalysis, which involves far more than relieving tension by having a heart to heart with a friend. He did not present it as a total cure, but as the best stop-gap measure until science can identify the neural causes of mental illness, or come up with safe psychoactive drugs.

As an archaeologist of the mind, he was convinced that, to function well as an adult, we need to get right back to the source of our neurosis, which is our fundamental sense of guilt that we drag around with us like original sin. If not, pressure builds inside us, and we explode, because we can't live in a state of perpetual denial. We have to 'let it all hang out' every now and then.

This means putting our thoughts and feelings into words, which is therapeutic in itself, because it enables us to become narrators of our own story. Talking by itself is aimless however unless it is carefully directed. Sometimes words simply get in the way. First we start rambling, then we get lost in half-remembered loops of self-pity. It's good to get something 'off our chest', but just as often it is better to let sleeping dogs lie. Some of our 'forgotten' thoughts might be locked out of sight for a good reason.

The flip side of too many words is not having enough, or any at all, because our feelings are wordless. If our memories are preverbal, laid down in childhood before we can string many words together, we change their nature when we start recasting them as word-perfect images. This is a great problem for therapists who explore 'recovered memories' in trauma victims, or sufferers from childhood abuse. How do we know that the memories are not backward-projections of present distress?

Freud developed the talking cure on the back of two traditions. Firstly, as a Jew, he heard the cry of Job from the Old Testament: why do we suffer? He felt that psychoanalysis could offer some consolation, as 'chicken soup for the soul'.

The Mirror of the Mind

But he did not judge his patients, promise them forgiveness, give them easy answers, or present the couch as a substitute altar. His optimism was tempered by pessimism, and even stronger determinism: we are capable of a degree of change and control, but we have to accept the human condition as given.

Secondly, he belonged to the Enlightenment tradition of belief in reason, trusting the power of the word to tame the raw energy of emotion: it's good to talk. He asked his patient to lie on a couch, facing away from him with no eye contact or touching. This was to avoid the danger of transference, a difficult situation in which the subject starts to fall in love with the therapist. The therapist's role is to listen, encouraging a free association of ideas, but offering nothing personal back.

We cannot see ourselves for what we are.

He believed the 'conscious' work of talking was necessary to bring up ideas buried in the unconscious, there but not yet spoken. His job was to spot patterns, speaking only to probe more deeply. This sounds a straightforward process, but it requires skill, commitment, honesty and insight on both sides of the couch. The dialogic nature of the encounter is important, because it doesn't work if we try to self-analyse. We cannot see ourselves for what we are.

Criticisms of psychoanalysis

Psychoanalysis has faced many criticisms in its one hundred year history, dismissed as 'psychobabble' by sceptics. As a lengthy process, it is an extravagance that only the wealthy can afford. Its personal nature means that it is not open to objective scientific analysis, leaving it neither verifiable nor falsifiable.

Its critics find themselves in an irrational loop that they can't escape from. Their antagonism to psychoanalysis proves they are in denial about some aspect of their psyche, in need of the very thing they are attacking, which is a session on the couch with a trained therapist.

As proof of the giddy nature of its subject, psychoanalysis has split into dozens of rival factions that cannot agree on what aspect of our nature or part of our anatomy is to blame for our malaise. For Freud it was the genitals, for Jung our

The Mirror of the Mind

alienation from the dreamtime, for Adler our inferiority complex, for Erikson our need to establish basic trust, for Reich our inability to orgasm freely, for Klein our detachment from the breast, for Fromm our reluctance to let go of our fear.

Even more bewildering is the proliferation of 'alternative' therapies: Rolfing, astral planning, colonic irrigation, primal screaming, rebirthing the psyche, crystal healing, wilderness experience, orgone therapy, encountering our inner child, neurolinguistic programming, Reiki, bioenergetics, taichi, mindfulness, the Hoffman process, yoga, object relations theory, transactional analysis and gestalt therapy, to name but a few.

If we don't fancy any of these, we can settle for our grandmother's remedies, which come free of charge: helping other people, sustaining our relationships, enjoying our job, eating well, going for a jog, pursuing a passion, or simply dancing in the sunrise.

When we're at a low ebb, most of us will try anything.

Follow-up research suggests that, where any therapy works, it is because the patient believes in it, and trusts the practitioner. When we're at a low ebb, most of us will try anything. Psychoanalysis is not particularly at fault here. It works well in combination with other therapies, and some therapists swear by it, even with psychotic patients for whom no other treatment has worked.

The therapist Melanie Klein regarded paranoid schizophrenia not as a disease but as a paranoid-schizoid psychological disturbance, the mind split between the good and the bad breast. The bad breast symbolises all those times that our mother withheld the breast, making us feel unloved. Unless we work these feelings through, we end up loading all of our frustrations and fears onto a hate object inside ourselves. Severe cases tormented by voices in their head need more than words and the good breast however. They need medication too.

Some point out that the success rate of the talking cure is no better than regularly taking the dog for a walk. Many return to it, as if on a repeat loop, and some relapse or deteriorate during treatment. Others simply get better anyway, because the mind is a self-regulating and self-healing mechanism with its own rhythms and cycles.

187

The Mirror of the Mind

Melanie Klein
1882-1960
Were we breast or bottle fed? On demand or four-hourly? Did we get enough of it? Are we the product of the good breast or the bad breast? Does any of this matter?

Finally, the talking cure is inevitably solipsistic, all about *me*, my authentic self, and who I can blame for my shortcomings. If we're not careful, therapy encourages victim culture and learned helplessness, and since we're the ones paying the bill, our therapist is tempted to reflect back to us what we want to hear, not what we need to be told.

Jung and the Shadow

Carl Jung was initially a disciple of Freud, but he found his mentor's take on the human condition too gloomy, and his proposed remedy too introspective. Where Freud saw anxiety as the default, he believed in a spirit of hope. Where Freud was quasi-scientific, he was mystico-religious. Where Freud seemed fixated on the legacy of early sexual experience and later fragmentation, he was more concerned with psychic integration in the second half of life. He not only wanted to show how each of us is charged with finding a true path, but also how to find it.

The Mirror of the Mind

When the gods die, they return as diseases.

This does not mean that he had a tin ear for the darker voices in our nature. The son of a Swiss pastor, and the survivor of a nervous breakdown, he worried about the psychic consequences of the loss of religious belief, remarking prophetically that, when the gods die, they return as diseases. He needed only to look at the politics of neighbouring Germany to see the fulfilment of this prophecy. He also talked about the Shadow, the nearest he got to Freud's idea of a murky unconscious that stalks our dreams.

Unlike Freud, Jung did not read us as sex-obsessed infants, but proposed that our psyche has more power to heal us than to weigh us down. Our mind contains a treasure trove of ancient wisdom in the form of symbols and myths, which can nurture us on our spiritual quest. Freud read into the story of Oedipus an ancestral obsession with incestuous feelings for our parents, but Jung focussed on the second half of the myth, in which Oedipus achieves a kind of self-knowledge. This is painfully won, but it is redemption of a sort.

He agreed with Freud in the power of the unconscious, but he added 'collective' to it, hinting at a 'Great Memory' of inherited wisdom in the hinterland of our mind, answering a deep longing in all of us. These healing and revitalising stories are passed on through the folktales, myths, rituals and dreams, recurring in all cultures as naturally as language or family life.

He called these 'epics of individuation', in which heroes go out on arduous journeys to find themselves, achieve wholeness and reconcile opposites of fear and hope, betrayal and trust, abandonment and belonging. 'I am just an old African these days who finds God in his dreams', he remarked.

He disagreed with Freud that our dreams are libidinous, dark and chaotic, locking us in a fearful past. He saw them more creatively, as integrating symbols that arise naturally in our imaginations, pointing us to a positive future. Each night in our dreams we re-enact the history of the race, showing us truths that lie deeper than those given in our experience. He saw the progress of our species and each individual as a spiritual journey from the African savannah to modern civilisation. Instead of Freud's forced childhood compromise between desire and denial, he looked to the hard-won wisdom of our later years,

The Mirror of the Mind

Finding our solitary way

Jung believed that the psyche has a healing potential to help us achieve self-acceptance without feeling alienated from our 'other side'. Our task in life is individuation or self-making, a kind of striving for psychic unity, but we're not on our own. We get help from an on-board guru who initiates us on our journey into a symbolic life-world.

This is replete with symbols and myths which are encoded in our culture, told to us as nursery rhymes and fairy tales, preparing us for the challenges ahead. Where Freud saw 'Little Red Riding Hood' as a parable of the threat posed to young girls by male sexual predation symbolised in the wolf, Jung celebrated the girl's resourcefulness in rescuing her grandmother.

> **Red Riding Hood**
> We all know the story, which is told in many cultures. Today it's treated as a harmless fairy tale, but it contains strong adult themes. Freud highlighted the powerful threat of the predatory male wolf to a young girl's sexual innocence, symbolised in her red cloak, while Jung talked up her resourcefulness in defeating the wolf and saving her grandmother from its jaws.

Jung would have read much into Shakespeare's play 'The Tempest'. Prospero is the Wise Old Man or magus looking to right past wrongs, Miranda is the female Anima who will give birth to a better future, Ferdinand is the male Animus looking to build a new kingdom, and Caliban is the Shadow, threatening to undermine the whole project.

190

The Mirror of the Mind

Seen this way, stories, dreams and myths are not irrational messages from a dark past, but intuitive glimpses into a light-filled future, rewarding careful study and interpretation. For these reasons Jung was particularly interested in the mandala, a circular eastern symbolic visual representation of the stages we must negotiate in our passage through life.

There are shadows imprinted across the human psyche.

Jung's take on anxiety was that, just as all small birds panic at the silhouette of a soaring predator, so there are shadows imprinted across the human psyche, which we must turn from objects of fear into nurturing sources of psychic energy. Such a notion is anathema to a brain scientist or geneticist, for whom there is no evidence of neural DNA that can carry the archaic folk wisdom of the race from one generation to another.

But there is the reality of cultural transmission, an idea which receives support from anthropology and the arts. Claude Levi-Strauss identified kinship systems and myth-making as the unwritten grammars of all societies. These are ways of organising our unconscious, as if an atavistic distinction between clean and unclean is written into our neural software. Jung was eighty when the spiral helix of DNA was unravelled, too late for him to think in terms of psychic genes, but we do seem to possess some common cultural symbols that frame a cosmic narrative, operating as story-making algorithms.

If we look at the plots of our soap operas, we realise that Freud is right: they are obsessed with trust, betrayal, sexual infidelity and revenge. If we look at our myths, we realise that Jung is right too: they feature the testing of the hero, the overcoming of obstacles, the completion of the task, the destruction of evil, the triumphant homecoming.

Our cinematic epics feature common heroes defeating uncommon enemies such as Saruman, Voldemort, Darth Vader, the Magisterium and the Evil Empire. Timeless conflicts between good and evil, male and female, light and dark, oblivion and survival, are captured in countless sagas about wizards, dragons, time-travellers, special operatives and inter-galactic star-sailors. Like Adam and Eve expelled from Eden, we have to find our solitary way. Like David defeating Goliath, we have to overcome our Shadow. But unlike David, we are not alone.

191

The Mirror of the Mind

Ministering to the mind

If our doctor finds our body difficult to heal, our psychiatrist (if we ever need one) finds healing the mind doubly so. Minds and their owners are unpredictable subjects, not law-obeying massy objects. We can see a broken arm, but we can't see a shattered mind. 'Canst thou not minister to a mind diseased' asks Shakespeare, or 'raze out the written troubles of the brain'? Our answers to these agonised questions have barely advanced in four hundred years.

Perhaps the last general physician to see his patients as psychic wholes was Sir Thomas Browne in the seventeenth century, author of 'Religio Medici'. Medicine at that time was close to religion, and healing was as much spiritual as corporeal, traditionally left to God.

Doctors today have to make a secular diagnosis, combining the art of mending the mind with the science of curing the body through a long tradition of healing dating back to Hippocrates in Ancient Greece. He was among the first to treat illness as physical malady, not as possession by evil spirits.

Physical ailments, once objectively diagnosed, are treatable, but subjectively experienced mental illness is much harder to pin down. Our doctor has to decide whether to treat us conventionally by prescribing psychiatric drugs (brain as part of mal-functioning body-machine), or leap the gap into alternative treatments such as therapy and counselling (mind as hurt self and emotions).

Societies differ over the extent to which we must be our own physicians in these matters. Life is full of challenging transitions that we must self-manage: adolescence, first love, pregnancy, divorce, illness and bereavement, to name a few. News bulletins are replete with enemies we can neither see nor fight: cyber-hacking, environmental Armageddon, immigration, pandemics, corporate takeovers and collapses, post-truth politics, weapons of mass destruction. As material wealth has risen, so have expectations, and yet happiness levels have stagnated. We have become the 'worried well', obsessed with our fitness trackers, sleep profiles and body-mass indices.

Governments are caught between discouraging 'learned helplessness', and leaving the vulnerable to the mercy of their circumstances. Matters are complicated by those in society who, through no fault of their own, enjoy less opportunity, are exposed to tougher challenges, or feel higher levels of alienation.

The Mirror of the Mind

There are incontrovertible links between poverty, homelessness, joblessness, social inequality, levels of mental illness and number of psychiatric referrals.

It has become a badge of honour for public figures to be open about their problems with depression.

Another issue is the extent to which it helps to acknowledge and talk about the problem. Old soldiers are notoriously silent about their combat traumas. On the other hand, millions are helped by public discussion of the importance of mental health, and how to receive help rather than suffer in silence. It has now become a badge of honour for public figures to be open about their problems with depression.

Psychological ups and downs are only to be expected in our tempestuous journey through the life, which makes soul-doctoring a theoretical minefield. Psychiatrists look for chemical imbalances in the brain, psychoanalysts try to free us from the burden of the past, psychotherapists look to release us into a self-nurturing future, and neuroscientists hunt for structural defects and functional failures in the brain.

It doesn't help that there is little agreement what exactly mental illness is, or whether it exists at all. If the diagnoses fall short, essential treatment is denied to those who need it. If they over-reach, every glitch in our life becomes medicalised. On one side are 'rugged individualists' who insist that what we really need is to be left to 'toughen up' and solve our own problems. On the other are tender-hearts who can't bear to see anyone reduced to sleeping on a park bench.

It's not uncommon to hear that a quarter of all western children and teenagers suffer some kind of 'mental health problem', but the fluidity of the criteria means it could just as easily be a tenth or a half. Self-harming in the young seems to be on the increase, and the annual health bill in the adult population for psychosomatic illness, self-diagnosed or otherwise, runs into untold millions.

It's impossible to say whether these psychological storms are normal rites of passage, or harder to weather than a generation ago. Opinions differ on whether life is more stressed, we are less resilient, or we have poorer coping strategies. It's too glib to say that we are all constantly on the edge of an episode of mental illness. Some mental disturbances are very real, extending far beyond our personal duel with reality.

Soul-doctoring

Psychiatry has taken a long time to earn its credentials, taking over a century to find its identity. Is it a proper science, a branch of the humanities, a lackey of the pharmaceutical industry, or an instrument of social engineering? If the therapist over-focuses on the mind, the diagnosis is brainless, in the sense of ignoring the physiological cause. If only the brain is prioritised, the treatment could be mindless, in the sense of ignoring the predicament of the sufferer.

No wonder psychiatry has been the butt of many jokes, such as 'If you're thinking of visiting a shrink, you need to get your head examined'. Psychiatrists have been accused of charlatanry, and encouraging a culture of learned helplessness. Their critics include Friedrich Nietzsche, who insisted that we are on our own, and just need to get tough. Victor Frankl, an Auschwitz survivor, believed that the answer to our self-absorption is to find a meaning beyond ourselves. Jean Paul Sartre urged us to be authentic, or true to ourselves, less concerned about what others think of us.

Psychiatrists are not unaware of these sentiments. Most believe that the best therapy is transpersonal, because it comes from life's core truths: our relationships with important others hold the key, it is better to give than to receive, and we need to find ways to contribute towards a more just society.

We're not given a workshop manual at birth, so we have to become our own mechanic and life-coach, expert at identifying what helps us to move forward strongly, and knowing how to jettison the baggage that is holding us back. It is not our demons we need to master, but our resistance to taking responsibility for our lives.

It might not be a shrink we need, but a sage. Our existential angst might be generated more by wayward thoughts than by unruly feelings. We need not just emotional affirmation, but also a more hard-boiled way of thinking. Instead of hankering after meaning, wanting to feel more authentic and craving to be noticed, we need to start asking totally different questions about ourselves, and looking elsewhere for answers.

The Mirror of the Mind

This tension is reflected in shifts in psychiatric clientele, which therapists note has changed since Freud's day. As a sign of the times, repressed and neurotic individuals have been replaced by those battling issues of self control and impulsivity, manifesting as addiction to gambling, sex, violence or drugs.

Psychiatry has 'arrived' as a profession because it has smartened up its act. Its practitioners must complete a medical course before they choose to specialise in 'soul-doctoring'. It takes a particular mindset and character to follow the path because, unlike surgeons who can operate and then walk away, psychiatrists might find themselves going on difficult journeys with clients (as they prefer to call their patients), lasting months or years.

They might be called upon to act by turns as life-coaches, sleuths, counsellors, gurus and confessors as more and more of us turn to them in a post-religious age to help rebuild our life, search for something missing, or find forgiveness for the vague sin of failure. The one thing they cannot offer however is absolution. They have to be ready for the possibility that, after hours of therapy, a client may simply walk out of the office, the burden of anxiety heavier than ever.

Soul-sleuthing
Sherlock Holmes used deduction to solve his cases. When you've eliminated the impossible, and all that. But problems of the heart and mind are of a different order altogether, existential, not amenable to logic.

They have to be good detectives, but they are not lawyers or logicians. Instead they need empathy to help them understand and share their clients' existential burdens. They cannot treat clients as friends, or harder still, treat friends as potential clients. They must be able to detach themselves after a day of intense concentration on other people's suffering, and yet, because their clients choose

The Mirror of the Mind

them as much as they choose their clients, they must also be capable of building a relationship of trust and caring. Finally, policing the borderlines of sanity is a heavy responsibility. There are potentially lethal consequences if a psychotic patient is prematurely declared as 'cured', and then released into the community.

Diagnostic Statistical Manual

The nexus between bodily disease and mental instability has been known since the nineteenth century, syphilis and pellagra showing how they can disturb a patient's sanity. A tumour on the brain can induce murderous behaviour if it is not treated. It took a long time however to shake off the notion that mental illness was a punishment for bad genes, weak character or social deviance. Are left-handedness, homosexuality, criminality and madness divine punishments, possession by demons, learned behaviours, treatable maladies or natural conditions?

Some answers are found in the Diagnostic and Statistical Manual (DSM for short), the bible of the psychiatric profession, updated five times since its first publication in 1952. Reading it, we can get lost in the maze of symptoms of around a hundred and fifty mental disorders, organised into seven major categories covering childhood, personality, mood, adjustment, delusional and sexual disorders, to name but a few. No causes or cures are itemised, because most of the mental states described have no physical or neural signatures. Substance abuse leaves a clear paper trail, but personality disorders baffle even the most careful sleuth.

Naming something is not to comprehend it.

It is an odd thought that, before 1960, no-one suffered from autism, dyslexia, bulimia and bipolar. These terms did not exist, so there was no mental space to entertain them. However recent or approximate, these labels are at least an advance on vague out-dated medical diagnoses of fluxions, rheums, distempers, apoplexies and agues, but naming something is not to comprehend it. 'Road rage disorder' is no defence for dangerous driving, nor are 'sick building syndrome' and 'allergy to the twentieth century' excuses for not turning up to work. How does it help to diagnose a teenager with anger management issues as having

196

'oppositional deficit disorder', or a shy one as showing symptoms of 'social anxiety disorder'?

The DSM's critics doubt that the mind can be cut so neatly at the joints. What are the borderlines between syndromes, disorders, traumas, disturbances, deficits, phobias, conditions, psychoses, difficulties, problems and organic malfunctions? Where into these designations do we fit bad sleepers, gambling addicts, bed-wetters, anorexics, compulsive shoppers, the chronically fatigued, and refuseniks of any kind?

In the early days of medicine some diseases were described as 'iatrogenic', or cooked up by doctors to bolster their status. We didn't feel ill *until* we went to the doctor. We have seen how hysteria was invented as a male conspiracy against women. The DSM has targeted non-conformist men too, listing homosexuality as a 'mental disorder' until its removal in 1975.

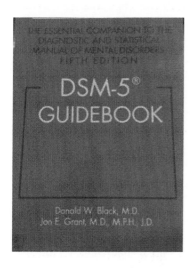

DSM 5 2013
Listing hundreds of mental disorders, the Diagnostic and Statistical Manual is the bible of the American Psychiatric Association. But who decides what is in and what is out? Some say that there will never be a sixth edition.

DSM 5, the latest edition published in 2013, is much improved on earlier versions, giving psychiatrists around the world common criteria to work from. It is still accused of over-medicalising behaviour, creating a host of false positives, inventing new ways of being unhappy, arriving at truth by agreement rather objective science, and placing the needs of insurance and pharmaceutical companies before the patient, but modern psychiatrists are very aware of these shortcomings.

Most use a judicious mix of approved medical diagnosis, appropriate psychotherapy and carefully chosen drugs to treat their clients as individuals with unique histories. They understand that mental illness is no respecter of class, gender or religion, and that each treatment must focus attention on the life of the sufferer.

Anti-psychiatry

The pharmaceutical revolution of the 1950's transformed treatment for millions and forced psychiatrists back to their medical roots, but it also exposed them to accusations of being manipulators of the mind, curtailers of freedom, conspirators against the sane, and generators of huge profits for investors in pharmaceuticals.

Doctors who devote themselves to curing heart disease, cancer or Alzheimer's receive no complaints about their methodology, because they are using medical science to target specific ailments of the body. Psychiatrists face the much harder challenge of defining what we consider to be mentally normal behaviour. Except in extreme cases, this is almost impossible, because we all know one or two 'odd' people who, despite our disapproval, seem quite happy and able to make a success of their lives.

By the 1960's and 70's, a rebranding of psychiatry became essential. It had fallen into disrepute, unsure of its status, role and remit, accused of equating 'mentally normal' with 'socially acceptable'. In 1960's Soviet Russia, 'sluggish' schizophrenia became a convenient label to imprison activists whose only 'illness' was to disagree with communist dogma. Andrei Shnezhnevsky was responsible for committing thousands of so-called misfits and deviants to long spells in re-education and rehabilitation camps, where they could be cured of their 'delusion'.

In the United States, a few therapists assumed a god-like control over their clients, triggering protracted legal cases for malpractice or abuse of clients. John Rosen's radical cures courted controversy for decades, and he was finally struck off the medical register in 1998.

In 1973, David Rosenhan sent shock waves through the psychiatric profession when he sent 'normal' volunteers incognito to self-present to mental hospitals, where they complained of hearing voices in their head. A worryingly large number were assessed as 'abnormal', and invited to stay. Fortunately, despite being asked to take anti-psychotic drugs, the stooges self-discharged before they were reduced to institutionalised zombies.

This theme had already been explored in Ken Kesey's 1962 novel 'One Flew Over The Cuckoo's Nest', about a secure unit in which patients were tranquilised, or had their cortices zapped, whether they needed it or not. The message was clear: psychiatry is a form of control. The only sane people are those identified as deviant, because only they see through the conspiracy against them.

If involuntary electroshock treatment sounds bad, lobotomy was far worse. In 1949 Egas Moniz was awarded the Nobel Prize for pioneering this practice, though he never performed it himself. In its crudest form it entailed the wiggling of an ice pick behind the eye. The intention was to remove 'offending' brain cells in psychotic patients, but it also caused massive collateral damage and personality change. In hindsight, the only defence of this barbaric neuro-assault is that no other cures were available at the time, and no therapeutic drugs had been found.

Our mental breakdowns are normal features of life's journey,
which psychiatrists should leave well alone.

In 1961, Thomas Szasz pushed the anti-psychiatry movement to the fore with his charge against the psychiatric profession of promulgating a 'myth of mental illness'. He suggested that most of us solve our 'problems of living' from our own resources. Our mental breakdowns are normal features of life's journey, which psychiatrists should leave well alone.

He saw 'mental illness' as a way of stigmatising those who do not conform to some imagined norm. The dispossessed already start from a position of disadvantage, without scapegoating them or compounding their woes. This notion received support in 1975 from the philosopher Michel Foucault, who regarded psychiatry as part of the apparatus of state control over citizens. Mental illness is invented by 'normals' to give them power over 'abnormals', by incarceration if necessary.

If levels of mental illness are high, suggested Szasz, it may be the fault of society, not the citizen. It would be better to remove the causes of mass unhappiness, such as grasping capitalism, surveillance cameras, inequality and

The Mirror of the Mind

lack of opportunity. It wouldn't take much to transform the mental woes of millions. It's better and cheaper to change the political system with some enlightened social policies than to manipulate everyone's consciousness with stupefying drugs or mind-numbing entertainments.

R D Laing

The psychiatrist R D Laing is best known for his alternative views on the treatment of schizophrenia, which he saw as an existential problem, not a medical one. It marked the struggle of a 'divided self' to find meaning while also having to conform to a dehumanised world. Given time, understanding and space, the illness can lead to redemption and insight, not disintegration and madness. Schizophrenics are not psychotic basket-cases, but potential geniuses, innovators and revolutionaries, seeing visions beyond the rest of us.

He saw the schizophrenic patient not as a diseased mind, but as a pilgrim seeking a self-cure on life's journey, like a hero completing a quest. From Eastern religions he took the idea that mental illness might be the mark of spiritual transition, not madness. Alternative states of mind might be creative trials of sanity, breakthroughs to exciting new worlds, and necessary ordeals that need to be endured before emerging stronger on the other side.

R D Laing
Laing (1927-1989) became a guru of the anti-psychiatry movement, arguing that mental illness was often the result of social alienation or exclusion. Unfortunately this approach did not help those who needed medication, not theorising, to relieve their suffering.

The Mirror of the Mind

Adolescence in particular is a testing time of upheaval, especially if it also involves an attempted breakout from a dysfunctional family. It is a rite of passage in search of an answer, requiring not drugs or institutionalisation, but mentoring and support, even if this results in patients rolling in their own excrement in lengthy therapy sessions.

He saw his own profession of psychiatry as white-coated agents of repression, part of the 'system' designed to sedate and control, never mining down to deeper causes, or understanding the psychic transformation of the sufferer. Shortly after Laing, two French writers, Deleuze and Guattari, lauded schizophrenia as an emblem of a society that was experiencing fragmentation, celebrating multiplicity and seeking difference. Madness is self-liberation from an oppressive system.

Laing described insanity as 'a perfectly radical
response to an insane world'.

An anti-psychiatric stance causes as much harm as good however, denying expert clinical help to those who need it. Insisting that mental illness is a social construction, and promoting psychosis as a vehicle for personal growth, political reform and social change, imposes a heavy toll on those suffering acute mental distress, in real pain, and in need of medication.

Unfazed by these criticisms, Laing described insanity as 'a perfectly radical response to an insane world'. Perhaps those we label 'perverts' are the ones who think what we think but dare not admit to. Perhaps the residents of the asylum are misunderstood eccentrics, their perceived paranoia a perfectly legitimate survival strategy in the face of adversity.

The ones we label mad are the true 'normals', the only ones who are truly sane, reacting normally to life's abnormal afflictions. They see the rest of us for the insane bunch that we are, because we believe that normal life is all there is, and not to be challenged.

Paranoid schizophrenia is however more than a 'social illness' or trendy bid for freedom: it is a clinical condition with a real signature in the brain, requiring antipsychotic medicines and cognitive therapy. Laing found himself having to revise his views on schizophrenia as a journey of self-discovery and psychic transformation when his own son developed symptoms of the disease.

201

That way madness lies

Madness – sanity – genius – eccentricity – lovesickness – normality – deviance – madness in culture – madness in history – bedlam – asylums – care in the community - optogenetics

- 'Madness' is too vague a term for psychiatrists, and lawyers prefer insanity.
- Shakespeare introduces us to various degrees of madness, but his characters never completely lose their reason.
- Rather than thinking in terms of going mad, there is more to be gained from contemplating how we become sane.
- The motions of the mind cannot be predicted as accurately as the orbits of the planets.
- We rely on geniuses and iconoclasts to see things we can't, so long as they are able to explain their vision to us.
- 'Normal' is a slippery term, usually used to exclude those who don't think like us.
- We tend to tolerate eccentrics, so long as they keep their peculiarities to themselves.
- We all need to let our hair down every now and then.
- Throughout history, different cultures have licensed madness in particular ways, usually with a view to keeping it under control.
- The nineteenth century was a time of asylums, eugenics, and harsh treatment for the cognitively divergent.
- Modern pharmaceuticals allow many mental patients to live in the community, but a large number fall below the safety net, and are abandoned.

Hairs in the palm of the hand

'Madness' is not a term that yields easily to definition. It derives from *mutare*, meaning change, which is something our mind does all the time, not least in our

The Mirror of the Mind

dreams. One day we might wake up like Gregor, in Franz Kafka's story 'Metamorphosis', transmuted by the alchemy of imagination into a giant beetle.

Plato attributed madness to an excess of emotion, and two millennia later we still give 'anger management' lessons to teenagers who struggle with 'schooling' their passions. Aristotle opted for a deficit of reason as the cause: a disordered mind is caused by ignorance, or illogical compulsion.

Both thinkers treat us as rational maximisers who know deep down what is best for us. Modern utility theorists also presume that we act in our own best interests, but this view is of no use when our inner world collapses, our thought and feeling are in conflict, and we lose touch with other minds.

Other schools of philosophy don't do much better. The empiricist says that the only true madness is to claim that we know things that we know we don't. The rationalist believes we are mad not to be able to make sense of what we do know. The existentialist is not impressed by either of these positions: life is intrinsically absurd, its only meaning being what we give it by our choices and actions.

Nor is 'madness' a useful term for psychiatrists. They prefer 'psychosis', which they regard as a clinical condition traceable to chemical causes in the brain. Lawyers opt for 'insanity': were we in our right mind at the time of our lapse from grace?

Except in the case of degenerative brain disease, it's rare to 'lose our mind' completely. There is a joke that if the second sign of madness is hairs in the palm of the hand, the first sign is looking for them. But to 'get' this joke, we need all of our brain cells working.

The mind is supported by the brain, which can't afford to go mad or have a breakdown. No matter how 'mad' we appear on the surface, the core brain functions that keep our body alive must perform to the last. When we starve ourselves, our body conserves the energy of the brain at the cost of all other organs.

Essential cognitive functions can however be blitzed by fever-induced delirium, or in Van Gogh's case, possibly by late-stage syphilis, a sexual disease which can attack core brain areas. He veered between bouts of sublime creativity and self-mutilation, attempting to cut off his ear a year before his suspected suicide at the age of thirty. Whether we classify him as sick, normal, insane or a

The Mirror of the Mind

frustrated genius, the paintings he left are among the most sought-after in the art world, and we are mad not to want to share his vision.

Starry Night
Painted by Van Gogh in 1889 while he was staying in an asylum, 'Starry Night' leaves us aghast at the beauty of his vision, but clueless about his state of mind when he painted it.

Even psychopaths and serial killers are
capable of talking sense.

The faculty of speech, the emblem of logic and sanity, stays with us to the end. If our speech is garbled, it is more likely that our feelings are strained, not our ability to think straight. Sometimes we get so angry that we stumble over our words. Unless our speech areas are damaged, even in our madness we talk coherently, which is a sign of order and sanity, though we may make little sense. Even psychopaths and serial killers are capable of talking sense, thinking straight and sending emails. They can be frighteningly rational. What they lack is emotional warmth to humanise their icy logic.

What fools these mortals be
Shakespeare's tragic heroes are not psychopathic, because they remain at all times aware of their folly or cruelty, which is beyond the awareness of a psychopath. They do however hover on the brink of madness, in the form of losing control of their destiny. Lady Macbeth is traumatised by the sight of blood, and stricken by

The Mirror of the Mind

guilt. She starts to sleepwalk, blurting out secrets of the murder she knows that she should not have abetted.

King Lear's tragedy is that he is forced to witness his own descent into mania, largely brought about by his own foolishness. 'O let me not be mad', he pleads. But his 'madness' is not a random affliction: he is an old king at the end of his powers, showing tell-tale signs of dementia, making strategic errors and leaving a political vacuum behind him. He has been subjected to great emotional stress by those nearest and dearest to him, compounded by his own poor judgment.

Madness comes slowly to Lear, but for other Shakespearean characters, it can be sudden and violent. They become 'mad with love', are blinded by jealousy, gripped by a passion, overtaken by a compulsion or consumed by vanity. After their emotion subsides, reason and order are restored, but it is too late for the protagonists to make amends. That is their tragedy. They have either killed the ones they love, brought about their own death, or both.

Shakespeare prefers to 'show' us our own natures rather than 'tell' us how to behave, but the lesson is clear: however good or right they feel at the time, we pay heavily for our moments of madness, loss of composure and abdication of control. The only characters who talk any sense in his tragedies are those who are dutiful, are licensed to play the fool, or assume the mask of the lunatic, behind which they can peer out to see clearly the antics of others.

Shakespeare also warns us of the dangers of simplifying the causes of madness. Polonius was convinced that he knew the cause of Hamlet's strange behaviour: he was besotted with his daughter Ophelia. The true cause lay much deeper, and in the end Ophelia found herself a victim of the Prince's 'antic disposition', not the solution to it.

*We are still as confused as Polonius in finding
any method in madness.*

Today, with all our sophisticated knowledge and procedures, we are still as confused as Polonius in finding any method in madness: it remains a muddle of causes, symptoms, diagnoses, treatments and classifications. We have no tests or cures for it. We can't agree whether it is a genetic bad prize in the lottery of life, a self-afflicted learned condition, the mark of the beast, or all three. We're not sure

205

whether to turn for treatment to the priest, the doctor, the therapist, the neuroscientist or the politician.

We do better to bask in the sunshine of Shakespeare's comedies as a counterbalance to the darkness of his tragedies. Here too we see characters temporarily losing their minds, but the comic universe is more forgiving. Suffering and silliness can end in redemption and a new beginning, not retribution and death. For this to happen, we must see ourselves for the fools that we mortals are, and accept others for the flawed beings that they are. That is not just the human condition, it is the condition of being human.

The mask of sanity

Given that our brain chemistry is so easily disturbed by the slightest whim, it is a miracle that we can lay any claim to knowing our own minds in any meaningful sense. In the cradle, madness is our default, and we have to learn little by little to be sane, in the sense of conforming to what the world expects of us. Even then, only part of us is sane, usually in brief internals between periods of madness. We can't be sane all the time, or we would go crazy.

Instead, we put on the mask of sanity, allowing us to put on a show, which fools most of the people most of the time. Just as it is very difficult to prove insanity in a court of law, so we cannot prove we are sane outside the courtroom. We just rely on our senses and the corroboration of other minds to stay as close to reality as our sanity allows.

Lovesickness is a celebrated rite of passage on life's journey, but 'going crazy' for each other is also a temporary insanity, or out-of-control passion. Society allows this suspension of reason, as it does not last long, and is easily cured by marriage, which quickly readmits reality to the relationship. As 'acute attachment disorder' however, sexual passion can lead to stalking behaviour, misogynistic abuse, coercive control, all-consuming jealousy and even murder, stealing our reason and blinding us to reality, as the story of Othello shows. An infatuation that is delusory, does not subside and becomes threatening is classed as a psychosis.

As well as the passions, the intellect can undergo difficulty with reality-testing, brought on by dullness of thought. We might find ourselves looking for a lost coin at night under a street lamp, where the light is good, even though we know we dropped it in the dark several yards away. Albert Einstein's definition of

The Mirror of the Mind

madness was to do the same thing over and over while expecting a different result, without having the wit to change tack. Scientists have been known to spend years searching in the wrong place for a 'killer proof' of their theory.

Men do not stick to fixed orbits, as planets do.

Isaac Newton was under no delusion of the fickleness of the human mind, remarking 'I can calculate the movement of the stars, but not the madness of men'. Men do not stick to fixed orbits, as planets do. He should know as, although he wrote one of the founding texts of modern physics, he also lost money in a stock market stampede, and wrote thousands of words on theology.

Science and technology as advanced by Newton have transformed the material condition of our lives, but our mental health has not kept pace. We now have the capacity to alter our genome, upload our brain, colonise space and live forever. The theoretical physicist Freeman Dyson worried whether we can play God and still stay sane, because despite our fiendish cleverness, we have not evolved the moral wisdom to wield such power wisely. Any civilisation that stockpiles enough nuclear weapons to obliterate itself several times over, while ignoring the destruction of the planet's biosphere, must question its sanity.

Rasputin
1869-1916
Would you take advice from this man? He was a self-proclaimed visionary and healer who won the confidence of Czar Nicholas II and his wife. All modern leaders have their 'mad monks' who whisper darkly in their ear.

The Mirror of the Mind

Such madness might be a pathological design fault: to feel secure in our bed at night, we have to point weapons of mass destruction at strangers, *just in case* there is a threat. We can behave irrationally while still claiming to be sane. No wonder the acronym for 'mutually assured destruction' is MAD. Kings, tsars and autocrats have long consulted madmen and clairvoyants for guidance, Rasputin being the most famous. Even democratically elected leaders cling to the oracular whisperings of their advisers, and hold prayer meetings in secret.

To define true madness

Charles Mackay's book 'Extraordinary Popular Delusions and the Madness of Crowds', written in 1841, is still a depressingly relevant inventory of what drives people to abandon their reason when blood rushes to the collective head, especially when power, passion and identity are thrown into the mix, as in nationalist and populist electioneering.

Mackay makes the point that the great advances in human thought come not from group-think, but from the voice of the lone child who dares to say that the emperor is not wearing any clothes. If we don't think for ourselves, we become like ants following their own pheromones, wheeling themselves to death in ever-tighter circles.

Evolutionary psychologists believe that aberrations of thinking may once have been useful mutations: the unstable and eccentric mind is more likely to innovate or push the edges of survival. Permanently compliant people tend not to be iconoclasts or world-changers, but those who think outside the box are more likely to find a new reality. Think how impoverished our history would be without the strange visions seen by Moses, Buddha, Plato, Jesus, Joan of Arc, Newton and Einstein.

It's almost as if a breakthrough in thinking demands a breakdown
in the normal relations of mind and body.

Many of our greatest works of art were created in what to most of us would feel like a manic state, which is not the same as having freak brain pathology. The genius of these visionaries was not just to drift into another reality, but to return and tell us what they saw in a language we can understand. Most of us are not so

208

The Mirror of the Mind

gifted. We allow others to take risks in our stead, seldom chancing the journey ourselves.

Those who have stood out in our history have been characterised by a kind of divine madness, controlled folly and non-conformity to fate. Many had unusual childhoods, problems of socialising and strange adult habits, but these 'abnormalities' were balanced by extraordinary abilities to abstract new realities from experience. It's almost as if a breakthrough in thinking demands a breakdown in the normal relations of mind and body.

This is far from saying that all geniuses are mad, or have lost their reason: on the contrary, they seem to have far more reason than the rest of us can handle. That said, Newton had two nervous breakdowns, though they might have been totally unrelated to his mathematical genius.

What characterises genius, both scientific and artistic, is not a breakdown of mind, but fitting things together differently, not a fragmentation of personality, but extending the boundaries of body and mind, not an estrangement from reality, but integrating eternity and matter in a new way.

Artists often find themselves paying a higher price for this privilege than scientists. Mark Rothko's 'black square' paintings capture the void of existence, the unknowability of experience and the emptiness of self. He was found dead in his apartment in 1970 having over-dosed on anti-depressants, though he had been ill for some time. By comparison, few scientists lose their minds or commit suicide over a mathematical formula.

We can lose our minds physically as well as psychologically. Alzheimer's is a degenerative disease of the brain where friends and relatives watch the person they know and love slip away, leaving behind the shell of the body and a naked brain stem, though this might be preferable to a physically wasting disease which imprisons a conscious mind.

We can lose our minds artificially and temporarily through mind-altering experiences: lovers rely on roses and chocolates to stimulate natural hormones, while others rely on recreational drugs for 'out of mind' experiences. Those who fast or ingest sacred herbs often claim 'out of body' illumination, though they struggle to tell the rest of us what they saw after they have 'come down'.

The Mirror of the Mind

Establishing what is normal

At the fairground one of the most popular attractions is the hall of mirrors. Instead of reflecting the image we expect, the curved looking-glasses give us gross caricatures of ourselves, with elongated legs, crushed heads and distorted torsos. Such incongruity makes us laugh, but it also makes us question how we arrive at an image of ourselves that we might regard as 'normal'.

'Mental illness' doesn't show up on a brain scan or in an autopsy, but it exerts great power as a meme, determining what we consider to be 'normal' behaviour. The problem with establishing a norm is that it automatically marginalises those who are not like the rest of us. How do we set the norms of normality? Little about human beings is statistically average, and most of us talk to ourselves, hear voices or harbour dark secrets of one sort or another.

Our mental state is always on the move, reflecting our complex relationship with other minds. It matters whether we live alone, have money troubles, are meaningfully employed, in a settled relationship, worried about money, in trouble with the law, socially excluded, devoted to a project greater than ourselves, or convinced that others are against us. Given these variables, we might agree with the philosopher David Hume that 'abnormal' madness ought to be the rule, not the exception.

It is dangerous to judge our sanity in relation to
what the majority think and do.

The danger is that 'normal' soon ceases to be a statistic. It quickly becomes a term of moral approval, constantly redefined in line with medical findings and political priorities in each generation. It is dangerous however to judge our sanity in relation to what the majority think and do, or base it on what was thought yesterday, because the minority are just as likely to be right, or at least as rational.

History is littered with those we have rejected as 'abnormal': malcontents, dwarves, refugees, heretics, lunatics, imbeciles, malingerers, immigrants, the vanquished, the disabled, the feeble minded, the degenerate, the mentally retarded, troublemakers, the educationally subnormal, the differently gendered and the differently coloured. Deep in our ancestral past lurks an ancient instinct to expel deviants who threaten to pollute the group mind or subvert the social order.

The Mirror of the Mind

Ironically it is our laughter that betrays our intolerance, not our sneering. We tend to laugh at those we feel are on the outside, and by our laughter we assure ourselves that we belong on the inside. Those who don't laugh at our jokes prove their alien status, making it easy to attack them from within the safety of the crowd.

Drapetomania
Slavery thrived for so long because plantation owners were convinced that it was a rational and morally justified practice. Any slave who tried to escape was by definition mentally ill, suffering from drapetomania.

In the Middle Ages, such clannishness was driven by religious superstition. As many as two hundred thousand witches were drowned, hanged or burned for trafficking with the forces of darkness. By the nineteenth century, a more 'rational' explanation was needed to justify the bigotry of the moral majority against those who marched to a different drummer, and this came in the catch-all reject-box of 'mental illness'. Runaway slaves were deemed to be afflicted with a morbid desire to abscond, dubbed drapetomania. Which slave in his or her right mind would want to run away from their rightful master or mistress?

Such thinking reached its nadir in the twentieth century. Between twenty and thirty million Russians were 'purged' in Stalin's re-education programmes for those whose thinking was not deemed to be ideologically pure. Not to be left out, the American government introduced extraordinary rendition, water-boarding and deradicalisation programmes for its enemies in its 'war on terror'. Each society perfects its own ways of shoring up its prevailing ideology, protecting its perceived norms, and demonising its enemies.

Accepting difference
We have on the whole been more welcoming to eccentrics, whose 'off-centre' antics we find amusing. We don't mind the shuffling bag lady, the wacky artist or

211

The Mirror of the Mind

the flamboyant dresser, because they have chosen their madness freely, rather than having it forced upon them. We allow them to hold bizarre views about the world, so long as they keep them to themselves, and their deviance stays within bounds.

We don't feel threatened by them. We might even learn a thing or two from their alternative perspective, or just smile at their iconoclasm. The sage Diogenes both entertained and disturbed the citizens of ancient Athens by carrying a lantern through the streets in broad daylight, claiming he was looking for an honest man.

We need our licensed insanities, tomfoolery,
madcap comedies, raves and carnivals.

Perhaps we are all slightly unhinged, living on the edge of reason. We need our licensed insanities, tomfoolery, madcap comedies, raves and carnivals, when we can let our hair down and turn the world upside down, if only for a brief while. The priest can be made to ride on a donkey, and the serf can be allowed to dine at the lord's table. We can 'go mad' and splash out on that sports car we've always wanted to be seen driving. It's a mad world, my masters, and we all sail aboard a ship of fools.

We can take a lesson from Don Quixote, the 'hero' of an early seventeenth century novel by Miguel de Cervantes. He believes he is a knight-errant performing chivalrous deeds, but he is merely mounted on a donkey, tilting at windmills. His friends, in their wisdom, leave him to his search for sanity in an insane world. He may be deluded, but he is not unhappy, and he harms no-one.

This is not the case with ideologues, radicals, fundamentalists and terrorists, who are prepared to deny others freedom of thought, even to kill and maim, in order to impose their utopian or paradisal vision. At heart they are insecure loners, but they borrow their courage, zeal and passion from emotional rallies, tight-knit cells or isolating cults, where they suffer anxiety by contagion: when one faints, all faint.

The only escape is to break free, exposing ourselves to the oxygen of difference. As the hysteria passes, 'normal' service is resumed, proving that fanaticism is a passing social fad, not a malfunction of the brain. It is more akin to brainwashing than insanity, a temporary aberration of the mind which does not absolve the 'believer' from inflicting suffering on others in the name of a private cause, no matter how great.

Madness in culture

Madness is defined by the culture we are born into. In some places, insects and dog meat are regarded as delicacies on the menu, in others eating such things is anathema, a disgusting abdication of reason. In some communities it's polite to smile in public, in others it's a sign of madness to smile with nothing obvious to smile about. In some cultures it is 'normal' for men to run amok occasionally (a Malay term to describe a wild rampage) until their rage has passed, in others any display of rage is seen as a breach of the social fabric.

Public approval or disapproval of our antics depends on our social status. When working class youngsters go 'mad' on a drunken spree, they are called uncouth yobs, but when their privately-educated peers at university 'let their hair down', they are just having high-spirited larks. In some societies, public drunkenness is seen as normal conduct, while in others it is regarded as a loss of self-control that brings shame on the family.

Madness has historically been a matter of letting in spirits or casting out demons. Our ancestors used to visit special dark chambers where they were drugged by a shaman, allowing them to be 'enthused' by the deity, and to enjoy the 'ecstasy' of standing outside their normal experience. They might become 'seers', the geniuses of their day, who saw what others could not see.

'Those whom the gods would destroy, they first make mad'.

If the visitations turned out to be malignant, the local shaman could exorcise the demons. Jesus once drove evil spirits out of a demoniac into a herd of swine, which then stampeded over a cliff edge, which seems a bit harsh on the pigs. The 'madman' was possibly an epileptic, which means being seized by a spirit, leading some to regard the condition as the 'sacred disease', indicating possession by a god.

We are still superstitious about such things: we put our hands over our mouths when we yawn to prevent spirits entering us, and we bless each other when we sneeze or expel a demon. In traditional societies, madness is seen as a punishment for breaking taboo, operating as a form of social control: we must stay within the time-honoured traditions of the tribe, for fear of the consequences. Those who lay claim to a special revelation outside permitted tribal lore face a stern challenge: 'Those whom the gods would destroy, they first make mad'.

Dionysus
Known to the Romans as Bacchus, Dionysus is the god of wine and revelry. Every so often we need to let our hair down. The assumption however is that this marks only a temporary departure from sanity, reality and responsibility.

In Ancient Greece, Dionysian revels permitted temporary release from the tyranny of normality, during which frenzied dancing took place. Many Greek cults used dance to enter a trance or state of delirium, and the Romans linked the tarantella to the psychotropic bite of the tarantula spider. St Vitus' Dance, an involuntary shaking of the limbs, was originally seen as a manifestation of evil spirits, but we now know it is caused by a bacterial infection of the brain. Religious devotees such as the Whirling Dervishes still dance themselves into a mystical stupor or spiritual frenzy, emulated by enthusiasts at modern rock concerts. Enthusiasm originally meant to be filled with the spirit of a god.

The Mirror of the Mind

Hermits traditionally shut themselves away in a cave or the desert, awaiting their passage through the dark night of the soul, without which there can be no revelation of the divine light. Intent on leaving the world and the body behind, they fasted to starve their brain into receptivity, and avoided all human contact, which serves only as a distraction from what is essentially a spiritual quest.

In the Middle Ages, Christian worshippers saw their hopes and dreams writ large in Sunday sermons, stained glass windows, holy rites and religious festivals. Prayer and faith were the best protections against madness, and the only medicine to ward off low spirits and distracting thoughts. The greatest sin was doubt, the most feared symptom was loss of hope, and the worst punishment was to be excommunicated, or exiled from the communion of believers. Sack cloth and ashes, though humiliating, were the only cure that permitted the sinner to be readmitted to the fold.

By the seventeenth century, there developed an unspoken link between genius, insanity and divine possession, as the gateway to art and progress: 'Great wits are sure to madness near allied', wrote the poet John Dryden. As traditional religion declined, inspiration became a private neurosis or emotional crisis, which no amount of reason could assuage.

Romantic poets deliberately courted madness in order to commune with their muse. Some took narcotics to exalt their sensibility and fire their genius in a twilight zone of the imagination. Their spirit lives on in rock stars, eccentrics and radicals, whom we idolise or ostracise depending on how much we like what they do.

Madness in history

No period in history has been without its share of madness, its label being used as a term of abuse or containment, seldom sympathy or understanding. Cures have been elusive if not non-existent, quack doctors employing a number of cures to trick the gullible. Attitudes towards it have been even more mercurial. Lunatics were dismissed as moon-gazers whose stars are temporarily out of joint, while lepers were driven out of the village, beyond the pale.

Attitudes to madness began to change in the eighteenth century. For centuries, monastic guilds and almshouses had sheltered society's unfortunates, but purpose-built asylums gradually became sinks for rejects and retards, which meant those

215

who did not fit in, could not look after themselves, or had offended public morals in any way, including young girls bearing illegitimate babies.

Newtonian physics had shown that the universe is governed by physical laws. By similar reasoning, the mind was deemed to be a machine working on rational principles which, if broken, could be fixed, no matter how brutal the repair job. Bethlem, from which we get the word bedlam, was a notorious London madhouse, closed in 1770, though some Victorian asylums remain in use.

Bethlem's inmates were routinely chained to the wall, dumped in cold baths, or given bleeding and vomiting purges. It became a pastime for the rich on Sunday afternoons to gawp from a viewing gallery at those whom society had discarded, but was doing its charitable best to 'cure'.

This brutality was challenged in 1792 when the French physician Philippe Pinel struck the chains from some of the residents of his local asylum, noting that they became immediately calmer, some even staging a recovery. They were not animals insensitive to cold, pain, nakedness, restraint and punishment, but human souls who needed care and understanding. Some may have been guilty of no more than homelessness, or falling on hard times. If they weren't insane when they were admitted, they certainly were on their release, if that ever came.

Unfortunately Pinel's humane attitude did not prevail through the nineteenth century. Increasing numbers were being driven by industrialisation from the countryside into fetid urban slums, where they not only fed the rapacious factory system, but also swelled the asylum populations. Doctors persisted in seeing mental illness as feebleness of the will, fevered emotion or moral insanity.

Eugenic ideas were explored on both sides of the Atlantic.

Darwinian thinking complicated matters further. 'Social' Darwinism (not a view to which Darwin himself subscribed) was used to promote the principle of the survival of the fittest. Society will always have its dropouts, dregs, parasites, vermin and throwbacks, and these need to be weeded out, or at least prevented from breeding out of control. If madness is passed on through degenerate genes, this is justification for sterilisation of imbeciles, morons and idiots, of whom there are always too many, threatening to dilute genetic strength and purity. Eugenic ideas were explored on both sides of the Atlantic, reaching their nadir in Nazi

216

The Mirror of the Mind

Germany, where a quarter of a million mental patients were gassed in the name of racial hygiene.

In the true Hippocratic tradition of doing the patient no harm, the medical profession had meanwhile been making steady progress in understanding the aetiology of mental illness and madness. There had to be physical causes. The extraordinary brain injury of Phineas Gage in 1848 left surgeons in no doubt about the impact of cortical damage on cognitive function and mental health. In anticipation of the explosion of pharmaceutical cures in the 1950's, there was a growing belief that neuroses and psychoses could be reduced to fundamental principles of brain chemistry.

The hunt for genetic biomarkers goes on, but it has not proved easy to pin any specific psychiatric disorder to a specific gene. A complex combination of genes is at work, waiting to be triggered by something in our experience or environment. Mental illness shows high heritability in families, perhaps but not necessarily traceable to excess or deficiency of key hormones at the foetal stage.

Care in the community

We are all occasional and harmless visitors to 'cloud cuckoo land', but if we become too embarrassing, we can be hidden within the family, sent to the workhouse or locked in an asylum. If we are to be made a public example, we can be strapped in the ducking stool, put in the stocks or flogged in the market place. We might simply be left to wander the streets, where keeping an eye on us can take up to a third of police time.

In the developing world, there is often no word for
mental illness, depression, despair or suicide.

Madness elicits various responses because it is always relative, determined by local expectation, political priority and ethnic identity, not measured by any absolute standard. In predominantly white communities, black males find themselves six times more likely to be referred to a psychiatric unit. By contrast, in the developing world, there is often no word for mental illness, depression, despair or suicide. When someone is ill, the whole family becomes a medical and therapeutic support unit.

217

The Mirror of the Mind

In traditional societies, families look after their old and vulnerable, but in post-industrial society, the family is atomised, no longer the principal protector of the needy or those going through difficult times, so it looks to the state for support. In return, the state decides what kind of care is affordable, and how much 'care in the community' should happen, which can mean reducing the provision of 'beds', and putting people out on the streets to save public funds.

The Workhouse
Nobody wanted to be sent to the Victorian workhouse, as happened to Oliver Twist. For many however, mentally ill or not, that's where they ended up.

For those with no family support network to fall back on, and in times of austerity, the psychologically vulnerable become even more at risk. They are least able to fight their own corner, and because they are disenfranchised, they tend not to vote, so there is no-one to represent them. This is not a new phenomenon: withdrawal of parish poor relief since mediaeval times foreshadowed modern attacks on 'benefit culture'.

It suits cash-strapped government to dismiss mental illness as a social construction or moral lapse, but as we all live for longer, with a wider range of mental health issues, we will increasingly have to take collective responsibility for the needs and suffering of those who deserve compassion, care and medication. Solutions to mental health problems are shared societal challenges, not off-loadable onto single parents, the low-paid, politicians or society at large. Psychopathy, which we consider in our final chapter, poses a particular problem for public safety, and requires a specific whole-society response.

The distorted mind: Psychopathy

- A psychosis is a disorder of thought and emotion in which we lose contact with external reality.
- Obsessive compulsive disorder is not a psychosis, but a personality disorder with organic causes.
- Psychoanalysis is not effective in treating compulsions and phobias, which respond much better to cognitive behaviour therapy and drugs.
- In rare cases, delicate neurosurgery can help, but there are risks.
- Multiple personality disorder shows some psychotic symptoms, such as hallucinations, but it also acts as a psychological defence against stress and abuse.
- Psychopathy is a neuropsychiatric disorder distinguished by low or zero awareness of other people's feelings.
- In extreme cases, hurting others is not seen as wrong, and may even be enjoyed.
- Not all psychopaths are violent, though the ones that are tend to end up in prison or psychiatric hospitals.
- Many jobs in society require low levels of empathy in order to be decisive and get the job done, but not all efficient bosses and punctilious traffic wardens are psychopaths.
- Viking berserkers showed that, as well as pumping themselves up with battle frenzy, they could also calm down afterwards.
- We are primed by evolution with emotional blocks not to kill in another human being in cold blood or face to face.

- Serial killers do not show such compunction. Their repeat killing is a rare form of psychopathy, but when it happens, it hits the headlines.
- Psychopaths are clever enough to hide their feelings and manipulate others, but they tend to get caught, because they don't care enough about their own futures.
- Psychopaths don't know they are psychopathic. If we think we are psychopathic, we are not psychopathic.
- If psychopathy seems to be more common these days, it may be because more of us are 'bowling alone', leaving us feeling excluded and isolated.
- Anders Breivik was judged to be in his right mind when he shot dead seventy seven young people on the island of Utøya in 2015.
- Psychopathy, serial killing and mass murder are wrong because they are evolutionary dead ends. A society of psychopaths would quickly remove everyone in it from the gene pool, including themselves.
- Psychopaths, extremists, terrorists and fanatics give off early warning signs, which it is the duty of all of us to spot and report.
- Soldiers are trained to kill, but they are not natural born killers.
- The last thing to give a psychopath is a gun, or a job that makes it easy to prey on others undetected.

The Mirror of the Mind

You have been feeling listless lately, struggling to get out of bed, less attentive to your personal appearance and hygiene. You feel strangely different, irritable and anxious, but you can't put your finger on how or why. Some days your thoughts seem to be racing, others you have difficulty concentrating, as if you're weirdly elated one moment and inexplicably struck down the next. You can't build up enthusiasm for anything, feeling emotionally flat most of the time. You keep forgetting things, sleeping less well and not enjoying your food. You're spending much more time alone. You're not getting on so well with the people in your life, or even seeing them as people any more. You put up a front in their presence, pretending to be normal, but not really caring one way or the other. In fact, you're starting to suspect them of plotting against you, and you're imagining doing nasty things to them to put a stop to their scheming. Nothing seems to make sense any more. Occasionally things get so bad that you think of ending it all.

This is what it is like to be in the early stages of a psychosis.

A curse that lasts a lifetime

A psychosis is a severe mental disorder in which thought and emotion are so impaired that we lose contact with external reality. Many forms of madness are brief phases when our sanity goes on a short holiday, but psychoses have deeper organic causes, and usually last a lifetime. After onset, diagnosis and treatment, there can be a period of recovery, but rates of relapse and recurrence are high.

We all have moments of road, trolley and
parking rage, but we soon recover.

Some psychiatrists believe there is a sliding scale of psychoticism: we all have moments of road, trolley and parking rage, but we soon recover. If our outbursts become frequent, and we can no longer control our temper tantrums, we are on the cusp of a psychosis, in this case intermittent explosive disorder. Post-natal psychosis, where a mother wants to harm her baby, can be treated with medication, but many psychopathologies, too numerous to mention, are permanent features which may be treated, but never cured.

We can bring a psychosis on ourselves, perhaps putting on an 'antic disposition' to deceive others, as Hamlet does. During the Second World War, some prisoners of war feigned madness as a way of being repatriated on medical grounds. This was a dangerous ploy however: in a phenomenon known as the Ganser syndrome, some of them actually went mad, and never regained sanity.

Many psychoses are rare, caused by malfunctions in the brain, not by traumatic life events. Psychiatrists debate long and hard about the boundaries between psychoses, anxiety disorders and personality disorders.

Obsessive compulsive disorder (OCD) is classified as a personality disorder that locks about one per cent of the population in cycles of distressing controlling thoughts, causing futile repetition of an action. It is a debilitating curse, involving far more than an irresistible urge to be tidy. It feels like a bully inside the head, setting the mind at loggerheads with its own brain.

It has been linked to a desire to minimise risk, which is a natural thing to want to do. Normally, after we have checked that the door is locked before we go out, a loop in our brain is completed, and synaptic gates are closed. Our house is safe from burglars. But what if we fall victim to misplaced heightened conscientiousness? Are we *sure* we locked the door?

So we go back to check. Unless our brain 'turns the page', this fretting could go on all day. Our door-locking actions become ritualised with none of the usual closures and satisfactions. The compulsion becomes self-defeating. We want our house to be secure, but then the fear returns, over and over in a tormented stream.

The only way to deal with this nagging anxiety is to check the lock again, by which time the repeated act has become addictive, and we have lost the cognitive flexibility to extinguish the urge. Instead of free will, we have free won't, or an inability not to act, and when we do act, it is pointless. We are condemned like Sysiphus eternally to push the boulder up the mountain, and eternally to slip within inches of the summit. We slide all the way back down to the bottom, at which point our labour has to start all over again.

The Mirror of the Mind

If we fixate on an object, it can become a fetish: we can't sleep, make love or go on a journey without our amulet or talisman. If we fixate on an action, it can become a ritual: we can't relax until we have scrubbed the step three times. If we fixate on a person, it can become a menace: we turn into a sex stalker. If we fixate on a habit, it becomes drudgery, like Queen Victoria wearing black for forty years after the death of Albert, never varying her wardrobe.

Lucky charms
We all have our black cats, white rabbits, voodoo fetishes and sacred mascots. They protect us and help us control the future. If we're not careful however, our behaviour can become similarly ritualised and superstitious.

From the brain's perspective, it is all a matter of attention: our arousal-exciters that normally fade after our initial interest has been captured fail to do so, and our inhibitors that move us on to the next thing don't kick in. This also happens when we are stressed: we lose some control over our synaptic on/off switches, and that is when we are most likely to hallucinate, seeing and hearing things long after the original stimulus has vanished.

Compulsions and phobias
A similar principle applies with phobias: automatic reflexes are activated before the conscious brain is able to assess the risk or prevent the behaviour, paralysing the body with fear, convincing us that something harmless is going to cause us great harm. We might develop an irrational fear of scissors or the number thirteen,

The Mirror of the Mind

perhaps because of some now-forgotten experience that scarred our memory. It is the memory of an object or event that we are in thrall to, not the thing itself.

We can be taught to stand back from our behaviour.

In compulsions and phobias, the brain appears to be locked. The good news is that the brain is plastic, and can be remoulded with careful cognitive behaviour therapy (CBT): the mind has the power to rewrite part of its brain. We can unlock the neural padlocks. This sounds difficult, but we can be taught to stand back from our behaviour, to see it as a mis-wiring of our brain, probably genetic in origin, something that can be fixed. Compulsions and phobias are not psychoses, moral failings or character defects, because we can be made aware that it is not our mind at fault, but a malfunction of our brain.

Compulsion works on the principle that the more we get, the more we want, which makes our condition worse. But we can train ourselves to avoid the triggers, choose alternatives, learn distraction techniques, even to live with the things we hate. Through techniques of relabelling, refocussing and revaluing, we can use our mind to reconfigure our brain. We can reason with ourselves that, once we've checked that the door is locked, and seen it to be so, we can recalculate the risk of burglary, and unlock the fear that is shutting us in.

Some compulsions are distinctly organic in origin. Involuntary tics of various kinds affect around one per cent of the population, most of them harmless. They are not psychotic in nature, or signs of mental illness, but neuro-mechanical malfunctions which, in the case of Tourette's syndrome, can cause distress and suffering for those affected, and for those they live with. Involuntary outbursts of bad language or offensive behaviour occur when inhibitory mechanisms fail to kick in. This was enough in previous times to get us strapped in a straitjacket, but nowadays a scan can identify not just the specific neural circuit causing our problem, but also the specific neurons.

Ordinarily we learn to control our swearing, muttering expletives under our breath if we have to, but only if we have control over the hair-trigger settings of the urge to let rip. Psychoanalysis is not appropriate in these cases, but drugs can manage the condition, especially clomipramine, and cognitive therapy can help to call non-affected parts of the brain to the rescue.

The Mirror of the Mind

When this fails, delicate neurosurgery might be able to free the neural logjam, much more subtle than the crude lobotomy of two or three generations ago. In a process called optogenetics, delicate probes can be targeted deep into the brain, using light to activate or deactivate neurons, sometimes just a single one. Needless to say, such treatments are highly risky, and have to be precise to avoid collateral damage. They are not always effective, but they offer a lifeline for those whose lives are miserable to the point of suicide without effective relief.

Multiple personality disorder

A psychosis we have become familiar with in recent years is multiple personality disorder (MPD), also known as dissociative identity disorder. Some psychiatrists say that, while sufferers manifest psychotic features such as hallucinating, the disorder is not a full psychosis. Others insist that the illness is a psychological defence against abuse, real or imagined, with no organic markers. Nothing shows up on a brain scan.

How can one mind house more than one person?

It is problematic when a condition such as MPD suddenly achieves greater prominence. What factors are causing personality disorders to become more frequent and complex? Are they cultural fads, reflecting the neuroses of the time, or have they always been there, but not noticed, at least not in this form? We know the fences that edge our delicate sense of self can occasionally tumble, and that our usually clear associations between perception, memory and thought can become muddled. But how can one mind house more than one person?

For us to function socially, we need an autobiographical self to provide unity, continuity and consistency. But we are also capable of dissociating one part of our self from another. Spies are skilled at leading double lives, as are bigamists and confidence tricksters. At Auschwitz, camp guards insouciantly went about their business herding Jews into gas ovens during the day, then went home to the domestic charms of their family at night. We seem to possess an unnerving ability to dissociate different aspects of our personality, as if one part of our mind is hiding its secrets from another.

225

The Mirror of the Mind

Less harmfully, our imagination allows us to wear several identities simultaneously. 'I am multitudes', wrote the poet Walt Whitman, and our arts offer our singular 'I' many creative ways to be a multiple 'we'. We put on a number of faces in a typical day, or through our life course, as partner, colleague, parent, student or consumer, and we like to dress up occasionally. 'All the world's a stage', as Shakespeare said, but this poetic licence works only if we have a core self to come home to.

Actors offer us a range of alter egos, Alec Guinness playing nine different roles in the film 'Kind Hearts and Coronets'. Voluntary 'pretend' play is very different however from the unwilled compulsion of MPD, in which masks are worn not for fun, but to hide or escape from abuse and unhappiness.

Taking flight

Fugue is a state of being in flight from a perceived threat. Some people temporarily lose their memory and go missing, taking on a new identity, much to the distress of their loved ones. This can be caused by a neurological blip, or a subconscious decision to flee the burden of the present. In one instance, as a way of living with her daily trauma of physical and sexual abuse at home, a young girl created a fantasy that she was a secret agent protecting vital information, and her parents were Russian spies trying to steal it from her.

Some MPD sufferers lay claim to as many
as twenty different personalities.

There seemed to be a flurry of MPD in the late twentieth century, confirming its copycat nature, with some sufferers claiming as many as twenty different personalities. The origins of the disorder lie in the late nineteenth century. It has long been known that parents can be physically and emotionally cruel to their children, but gradually the Victorians grudgingly recognised domestic sexual abuse as a social reality too.

Since then, in what appears to be a re-calibration of the nineteenth century diagnosis of female hysteria, MPD has been seen as an attempt, mainly by young female sufferers, to create one or more alter-egos or personalities to dissipate the

226

The Mirror of the Mind

anger and shame of childhood abuse. This gives the everyday adult ego a chance to function normally and live with itself, hiding away the hurt. Rape victims also might resort to cultivating an alter ego as a scapegoat to bear their pain.

These so-called 'conversion disorders' do not mean that there are several persons inhabiting one body. It is more like several sets of memories or cognitive fictions, each taking over temporarily, a bit like a cast of actors being called on stage at will. As far as the brain is concerned, there is only one organism to control, but psychologically there are several 'fronts', as explored in the film 'The Three Faces of Eve'.

Jekyll and Hyde
In line with Robert Louis Stevenson's 1886 story, we might sometimes feel as if our 'evil' side has taken over. But not even in our dreams do we roam the streets at night wantonly killing people. Or do we?

It remains a mystery how one mind can contain different 'selves' that have no access to each other's memories. The first case of MPD was reported in 1885, a year before R L Stevenson's fiction about the split personality of the good Dr Jekyll and the evil Mr Hyde. It is not a defence when we get in trouble with the law however to say 'my evil side did it'. There is only one of us standing in the dock, not separate selves that can be put on trial individually.

When given the choice, few of us want to 'wipe' any of our memories, or any part of our personality, because in so doing we change who we are. Many MPD sufferers are aware of their condition, which means they are not psychotic. When asked if they want treatment to erase their troublesome alter egos, especially the bad ones, they say no, because they know that removal of a part will compromise the identity of the whole.

Psychopathy

A psychosis we fear the most, because it stalks our dreams and news channels, is psychopathy. It means 'disease of the mind', but it is a very specific neuropsychiatric disorder, marked by lack of empathy, impulsivity and antisocial deviance, by no means always accompanied by violent or criminal behaviour.

By no means are all criminals psychopaths, because they are able to control their impulses, some choosing to 'go straight' on release, but as many as a fifth of the prison population show some symptoms of psychopathy. They are overwhelmingly male, not necessarily given to aggression, and possibly suffering from a related psychiatric condition.

Not all criminals are psychopaths, and
not all psychopaths are criminals.

This raises the question of what prisons are for. Apart from serving as a place of punishment, if they are largely to protect the public from those with disordered feelings or defective reason, they are no more humane and no less cruel than the lunatic asylums of old, punishing people for drawing a short straw in the genetic lottery. Prisoners with psychopathic symptoms are fifteen times more likely to reoffend on release, testimony to the fact that the links between crime, poverty, social exclusion and psychiatric illness are very strong.

Having a low empathy-count is no more an offence than wearing our heart on our sleeve. Autistic individuals may not be able to feel empathy, but they are by no means psychopathic. Schizophrenics are not necessarily psychotic, and even less likely to be psychopathic, while few psychotics or psychopaths are schizophrenic.

We are surrounded by people in everyday life who hide their feelings well, keep them buttoned down, or have none to speak of. We may well be one of them. We tend to call such people sociopaths, not psychopaths. On certain reckonings, many chief executives, entrepreneurs, politicians, police, military personnel and emergency workers fall into this category.

The Mirror of the Mind

Society needs its share of people with 'low affect', or tight control over their feelings. If our job requires us to make tough decisions, tell people they are no longer needed, shut down parts of the business that are no longer profitable, operate weapon systems capable of exterminating thousands, work in a bomb disposal squad, stand on duty in front of a baying crowd without taking sides, or face a daily diet of human pain and suffering, it doesn't pay to be over-sensitive. Ruthlessness, single-mindedness and detachment serve us much better.

If we are lucky enough to live in a democracy, we might be thankful that we are not ruled by a bullying autocrat who thinks nothing of eliminating opponents. Even in democracies however, we end up voting for leaders who blatantly claw their way to power by any means, prepared to make exaggerated claims and ride roughshod over other people's feelings. In these cases, it's not just empathy they lack, but shame. The more power they accrue, the more they are cushioned from the kind of shunning that our ancestors used against those who rose above their station, or treated others badly.

It is a bald reality that, in the bear-pit of modern politics, bloody-mindedness pays, and too much conscience gets in the way, or causes dithering. It is usually said that power corrupts, but more importantly, it closes the mind to ordinary people's feelings. Then again, wilting violets do not get noticed, do not realise their ambitions, and do not feature in our history books. We vote for these people *because* they persuade us that they are prepared to knock heads together.

Sociopaths in positions of power outnumber those in the general population by a factor of about six, and we rely on them to do our dirty work for us, because we know we could never do the job ourselves. We grant prison guards, hired henchmen or secret service torturers enhanced powers of control, but they still have to stay within the bounds of 'reasonable force' in pursuing their job. By standing at the top of the chain of command, they are given licence to be nasty on our behalf. They just happen to be working *for* the law, not against it.

Going berserk

Northern Europeans possess a stiff upper lip, keeping their emotions under control, while Southern Europeans wear their hearts on their sleeves. This gross generalisation is disproved by the Viking warriors of the so-called Dark Ages. They were famous for going berserk, an Old Norse word meaning 'wearing a bear

229

shirt'. What made them frightening was their ability to 'psyche' themselves up into a frenzy during a battle, so that they felt no pain. Crucially however they were also capable of 'psyching' themselves down afterwards, returning to being husbands and fathers, so that their default setting was *not* to kill.

Aggression and how it is expressed is culturally moulded.

Blood-curdling Vikings were the forebears of modern Scandinavian peaceniks and lovers of liberal democracy, where violent psychopaths are exposed as dangerous outliers. Aggression and how it is expressed is therefore culturally moulded, not an ineradicable curse or flaw in human nature. To that extent, it is a tap that can be turned on or off, not 'in the blood' in any sense. The cultural context is crucial. In a warrior society, fearless killers are lionised, and in Nazi Germany, an opportunistic psychopathic minority was promoted to high office, with tragic consequences for those who did not fit the Aryan profile of racial purity.

Viking berserkers
Famous for winding themselves up into a battle frenzy, Viking warriors were also able to wind themselves down. They formed the first parliament in 930, and their descendants are peace-loving democrats.

The Mirror of the Mind

The psychopaths that make the headlines are the serial killers, mass murderers and torturers who haunt every culture. Merely to mention their names is to give them the kind of notoriety they crave, but do not deserve. Are they born, or made? The organic causes of their psychopathy are unknown, because the neurology is complex. They may have a lower resting heart rate than usual, helping to deaden their feelings. Their amygdala, the seat of their fear network, may be smaller than usual, though in wild animals it is usually larger. Their hippocampus may be structurally abnormal, compromising their memory and social functioning.

The 1960 Alfred Hitchcock film 'Psycho', notorious for its shower murder scene, toyed with the subterranean Freudian causes of the psychopathy of motel owner Norman Bates: a tortured childhood, perverted sexuality, and a fixation on his mother's corpse in the attic.

This is a fiction in a double sense. Norman Bates never existed, and millions successfully overcome early abuse, emotional trauma and rank injustice without growing up to be dropouts, freaks or killers. That said, the psychologist John Bowlby identified 'separation anxiety' in children who were denied consistent mothering for more than six months in their first five years. Many of them experienced difficulties forming secure attachments to people in later life.

Inside the mind of a killer

Hours of watching television crime series make us aware that the law distinguishes between spur of the moment murders, and those planned in advance. It's one thing to kill in a moment of passion, another to be cold-blooded about it. Most of us can't do that, because evolution has primed us with a host of emotional blocks against it.

To steel herself emotionally to participate in the murder of King Duncan, Lady Macbeth has to obliterate her natural feelings, or what she calls 'compunctious visitings of nature'. At one point, she says she would be prepared to dash out her baby's brain if it meant getting what she wanted, which is to wear a queen's crown.

But she is wrong: she is not as tough as she thinks, and it's not that easy to turn herself into a callous killing machine. Although she doesn't commit the murder herself, she is plagued afterwards by nightmares which steal her sanity. She ends up sleepwalking, blurting out her guilt, and taking her own life to end her misery. Psychopaths, say psychologists, don't have this problem, because they are not like the rest of us. Lacking right-brained feelings, they feel no remorse, so killing people feels no different from shelling nuts.

Humans have always had a ghoulish fascination with cruelty, or our capacity to do terrible things to each other. The Roman emperor Caligula was notorious for his barbarous acts, and Shakespeare's play 'King Lear' features unspeakable acts of cruelty performed on stage. In modern times, the Theatre of the Absurd and the Theatre of Cruelty have explored our inhumanity towards each other, and the internet is awash with 'dark matter', despite attempts to censor it.

The callous cruelty, distorted behaviour and perverted sexuality of 'morally insane' serial killers continue to shock modern sensibilities, nearly always men, but occasionally women. Love, violence, death and control become gruesomely intertwined, as corpses are violated, installed in the living room for company, sunk into lakes, cut up and stored in bin liners, buried under the floorboards or eaten as a delicacy.

Serial killers account for only one per cent of all murders.

Fortunately, serial killers are rare evolutionary freaks, accounting for only one per cent of all murders. They share our logic, and even know the wrongness of their actions, but they lack key emotional brain circuitry: they just don't care about the suffering they inflict. They are unable to block the incitements to anti-social behaviour that the rest of us confine to our dreams and computer games, so in that sense they never reach emotional maturity. They tend to come from psychopathic backgrounds, and because of their high-risk lifestyle, they usually die young, unless they are caught first, in which case they die in jail.

Some serial killers use their murdering spree to satisfy a psychological need, which raises the question of whether they are mad (they can't help it) or bad (yes they can). The problem for the rest of society is that, if they are criminally insane, no deterrent will stop them, and if they are mentally ill, no therapy will cure them.

Too clever by half

Psychopaths are undoubtedly clever: they need to be to plan their killing. But as Aristotle said, cleverness is dangerous unless it is also accompanied by virtue. It's not reason that makes us big-hearted, but common humanity. 'The madman has lost everything except his reason', remarked G K Chesterton. An overdose of reason constitutes its own kind of madness, making us too reasonable by half, deaf to our feelings.

If the elimination of undesirables is our goal, we can defend atrocities such as pogroms, ethnic cleansing and extermination camps as rational and coherent strategies. The Holocaust was promoted as the 'final solution' to the 'Jewish problem'. Doing things with bureaucratic efficiency comes at a heavy price however: people are no longer seen as valued ends, but expendable means.

Psychopaths are smart enough to know how to mask their lack of feeling by simulating empathy, enabling them to manipulate their victims and get away with their crimes. Such is the stuff of horror movies and nightmares: the unassuming guy next door, the attentive nurse in the maternity ward, the friendly classroom teacher and that charismatic television entertainer turn out to be serial child molesters, sex offenders or killers with several corpses in the basement.

Britain's most prolific serial killer, Harold Shipman, was able to murder around two hundred and fifty people only because of his position as a family doctor, the epitome of responsibility. He could kill so many because his patients were generally elderly, dependent on his help, totally trusting, and had no reason to doubt his care for them. What is most remarkable about his case is not the tally of his victims, but that it took so long for him to be exposed and stopped.

If you think you're psychopathic, you're not psychopathic.

Shipman kept below the radar, but many psychopathic killers, keen to prove their cleverness, play a cat and mouse game with the police, until they eventually get caught. Cleverness is no substitute for conscience, which takes a longer view. Locked in the present, their recall of the past is poor, and they have no life plan for the future. They are not held in check by guilt, and don't feel enough fear of being found out. They are clever enough to manipulate other people's feelings, but they come unstuck because they treat themselves as unfeelingly as they do others. If they are ever released into the community after serving their time, their re-offending rates are three times higher than other prisoners.

The Mirror of the Mind

Psychopathy involving violence against others is so extreme and totalising that, if you think you're psychopathic, you're not psychopathic. Psychopaths don't know they are psychopathic, because they can't realise that they lack what they cannot feel, which is empathy. If they are aware in any sense of their psychosis, they either don't care, or they live in a state of denial.

Bowling alone

What appals us most about psychopaths is their ability to kill in cold blood, devoid of pity and love, breaking the primal social contract of sympathy and relationship. Not only do they see no wrong in killing, they also get a thrill from it. They are deaf to the whispering of the Golden Rule: we owe each other kindness, not wanton harm. They are social isolates, frozen in their hearts, unable to enter the minds of their victims, therefore impervious to their suffering. They tend to live on their own, and if they laugh at all, they laugh alone, usually at people, never with them.

We need the constant confirmation of friends,
and the correction of critics.

Sociologists describe a modern social phenomenon called 'bowling alone', where fewer people join clubs or engage in the community. This might have created a growing army of male lone wolves, 'incels' or involuntary celibates, cut off from the tenderising company of family, friends and women. To stay in touch with reality, they need the constant confirmation of their mates, and the correction of critics.

Instead, they feel shunned by their peers and community. Exile is a political punishment, a physical banishment from the country of our roots, but ostracism is worse, a moral isolation and rejection by those closest to us, even if the withdrawal is self-imposed.

The Mirror of the Mind

Bowling alone
Ten pin bowling is a sociable sport, conducted in teams, or played against a rival. We bowl not just to win, but to engage in gossip and banter, keeping ourselves in touch with community goals and values. It is a worrying sign if all the lanes in the alley, including our own, are booked by lone bowlers.

Many are lost in a 'shoot-em-up' cyber-world, nursing real or imagined grievances against society. In a culture where guns are easily available, this is a recipe for tragedy. Investigation into the backgrounds of high school 'shooters' in the USA reveals that they nearly always feel motivated by revenge, alienated from the mainstream, rejected by peers and marked down by teachers. Their killing spree is a desperate attempt to force people finally to acknowledge them.

Anders Breivik

Merely to mention Anders Breivik's name is an offence to the memory of the seventy seven young people he murdered in a shooting spree with automatic weapons on the island of Utøya off the coast of Norway in 2012. Fame and notoriety were precisely what he craved.

His agenda was clear enough, because he posted it online before his attack. He subscribed to a twisted populist/nationalist ideology that opposed the perceived 'Islamisation' of his country, caused by a 'flood' of immigrants who were stealing local jobs, scrounging benefits and diluting white cultural identity. He fell for far-right propaganda about Muslims intending to take over public institutions, impose Sharia law and sexually prey on white girls.

His mass shooting was clearly premeditated, because he planted bombs in two buildings in Oslo before he set off to the political rally of left wing activists committed to a liberal agenda of open borders and globalisation, whom he despised as his enemies. The explosions in the city were designed to divert police attention, so that his attack on his real target, the young people on the island, could be more deadly.

Psychopathic or not, Breivik was a sane killer.

The crucial question at his subsequent trial was whether he was in his right mind at the time of the massacre. The jury decided that, because he had planned his attack meticulously, and claimed to be pursuing 'rational' political motives, he was in full possession of his cognitive faculties, and therefore knew what he was doing: psychopathic or not, he was a sane killer.

Psychiatrists were divided over his mental state, and Norwegian public opinion was split over whether he should be placed in a prison or a mental institution. The public were generally pleased that Breivik was declared sane, because it meant that he could be held fully to account for his crimes. He is not a heroic political radical, or latter-day Crusader prepared to martyr himself for the Christian cause. He is a vicious, violent killer who committed mass murder for personal reasons.

The peaceful nation of Norway had to become quickly aware of a violent new reality in their midst, the threat of ideological extremism. If they were to avoid such an atrocity ever happening again, they needed to understand what motivated Breivik. They needed to redraw their political landscape to include those who felt angry, alienated and abandoned.

Breivik was delighted to be declared sane, as it meant the state had no right to pump him full of mind-altering or sedative drugs. They did however have the right to deny him his freedom, and what he craved most of all: access to the media, so that he could continue to spread his pernicious views.

What is so chilling about Breivik is that any human being, sane or insane, rational or disturbed, right or wrong, moral or mad, can be capable of pulling the trigger on seventy seven young people as a means to a political end, without compassion and with such precision. It offends and frightens us that we all possess a mind that can contemplate the stars one moment, and execute in cold blood the next. The challenge in such cases of appalling madness in the midst of so much sanity is to identify which part of the brain or personality has gone so terribly wrong, and why.

236

The Mirror of the Mind

As 'normals', we like to distance ourselves from psychopaths like Breivik: he is not like the rest of us. We cannot conceive of a mind like Breivik's, persuaded that any political cause can be worth a single life, let alone seventy seven. But the warning signs were there. Breivik's father left him as a child, and he grew up to be a very angry young man. He was a loner, spending many hours at computer games.

He had certain legitimate political views, such as an objection to the feminisation of society, but these were compromised by several dangerous delusions which classified him as mentally deranged and in need of psychiatric help. He had a distorted view of what it meant to be a real man, and he imagined that he was the leader of a secret order of knights. It's one thing to fantasise about being the saviour of the world, another to believe that one actually *is* the saving hero, especially if 'saving' amounts to murdering so many innocent and unarmed people.

A society of one
Breivik's mistake was to believe that he was the only sane person on earth, or that other people's sanity was a function of his reality. He was neither liberal nor democratic: he lived in a society of one, and he would have killed until he was the last man standing if it meant getting his way.

Solipsism is always doomed to failure.

He liked to propagate his views online, but words depend for their meaning on mutual exchange, not private obsession. Solipsism is always doomed to failure, as any nursing mother knows. Love is based on reciprocity and renewal, but it also thrives on risk and opposition. The one true madness is to believe that everyone else thinks like us, or should be forced to do so. Our physical and moral evolution depends on voluntary difference, not enforced conformity.

Pumping bullets into warm young bodies with their whole life in front of them breaks every bond and value that we hold dear. We know that psychopathy is a moral breach because we cannot generalise it: if we did, we would all be dead in a week. A society where everyone was a callous easily-bored risk-taking thrill-

The Mirror of the Mind

seeking macho extrovert would quickly remove itself from the evolutionary gene pool, because it could never nurture its young.

What might Breivik's passion and intelligence have achieved if he had dedicated them to saving lives, not destroying them, or if he had seen his young compatriots as kindred spirits, not enemies of his fantasy state? It wasn't particularly his politics at fault, but the lengths he was prepared to go to get his way. There is no arguing with someone who is prepared to kill until he is the last man standing.

He showed no sign of remorse at his trial, only a complacent smirk. The only consolation that the rest of us can draw from Breivik's heinous crime is not a quickened desire for justice and revenge, but a renewed commitment to a morally intelligible world in which human beings of all persuasions may flourish. Breivik confirms the direction we choose *not* to take.

Nelson Mandela
1918-2013
Mandela performed terrorist acts as a young man, for which he served twenty seven years in prison. During that time, he turned from violence to peacemaking. On his release, he went on to lead South Africa away from retribution and reprisal towards truth and reconciliation.

And yet understand his madness we must, because Breivik is one of us, and his descent into depravity might help us to keep other young minds safe. Sick or healthy, his brain was not an isolated agent, but a mind with a childhood, brought up in an agreed set of values in a free society.

The Mirror of the Mind

So what went wrong? A huge contributing factor was his social life, or lack of it. He lived in a society of one, and had barely any friends. This is important, because they might have tempered his extremist views or warned the police if they felt he posed a danger to the public.

This is a lesson for how we can defend ourselves against political terrorists and religious fundamentalists. Can we spot their anger and madness in advance, or rehabilitate them before they murder and maim in the name of their beliefs?

The difficulty is that we cannot second-guess the futures created by their ideological zeal. Today's freedom fighter prepared to kill for the cause might be tomorrow's revered politician, as happened with David Ben Gurion of Israel and Nelson Mandela of South Africa. On the other hand, if Josef Stalin and Adolf Hitler had been assassinated early in their dictatorships (there were attempts to do so), millions of lives would have been saved.

Early warning signs

Modern terrorists and jihadists are able to instil so much fear because they can abuse the freedom and trust of the society that nurtures them. Apart from having access to deadlier weapons, they work in tight-knit cells, reinforcing each other's bigotry and isolation by denying themselves the oxygen of difference. This does not make them clinically insane, but it does flood their mind with dangerous dogma to the exclusion of all other perspectives or interests. Whatever their ideology, they remain fully responsible for the suffering they are prepared to inflict on others in pursuit of their private paradise. Their deviance from the norm is not a tolerable aberration but a deadly delusion.

We cannot be arrested for crimes we have not yet committed, but we may give off ominous signs that we are willing to cause serious harm to others in pursuit of our convictions. Detecting the signs of psychiatric disturbance or ideological fanaticism early is crucial, difficult though it is, with the concomitant risk of prejudging people's mental state or danger to the public. After Anders Lubitz had flown a German passenger plane into the Alps in 2015, killing all one hundred and fifty people on board, it was revealed that he had known psychiatric problems. He had hidden them from his employers, and his doctors had failed to report them.

Post-crash, some feared that all mentally ill people would be tarred with the same brush, as potential mass-murderers who are out to deceive us. But there is no obvious path from mental illness to crime or mass murder. It is easy to scapegoat the mentally ill as killers, scroungers and malcontents, but the facts tell a different story: they are far more likely to be self-destructive than to take others down with them.

There is no obvious path from mental illness
to crime or mass murder.

Most of them are not suicidal, aggressive or intent on murdering others. On the contrary, they hurt badly and feel powerless, beyond love and help, often homeless and jobless, far more likely to suffer in silence and be the victim of crime than the perpetrator of it.

If there are lessons to be learned from the tragedies of Breivik and Lubitz, one is the need to detect warning signs which can start in early childhood. 'Avoidant' children whose emotional development lags behind, for whatever reasons, can be identified through their unwillingness to engage in simple social activities, such as tapping a ball backwards and forwards with a partner. In these cases, albeit belatedly, reciprocity can be learned, and dormant mirror neurons fired into action. By the teenage years, the vigilance of parents, friends, doctors, teachers and social workers, acting like priests in the confessional who see into the heart, can help to spot when someone poses a wider threat to the community.

Trained to kill

Military personnel face a difficult psychological challenge. During combat they are trained to kill on command, but while on peacekeeping duties, they are expected to win over hearts and minds by smiling and playing with local children. Soldiers are not natural born killers, or able to kill without compunction. We pay them to do our killing for us, but they are no more likely to be psychopaths than nurses or teachers.

Research after World War Two showed that many soldiers deliberately fired to miss their human targets during combat, so appalled were they by the prospect of living with the blood of another on their hands. They could not live a lie, or reconcile the morally conflicting ideas of achieving liberty for some at the expense of taking the lives of others.

The zoologist Konrad Lorenz worried that modern technological warfare makes us more deadly killers, less likely to hold back, because we cannot see the face of our enemy. Those who control drones to destroy camps and villages remotely are playing a kind of enhanced video game. At least the Viking berserkers could see the faces of their victims.

Recruitment officers for the armed forces want youngsters tough enough to kill on command, but soft enough to fit seamlessly back into society when their tour of duty is over. Many struggle to perform this emotional volte-face, and suffer severe depression as a result. Governments spend millions training fighter pilots, but barely anything on rehabilitating troops returning from combat. To ensure the money is well spent, pilots are subjected to intense psychological profiling to ensure that, once they get the enemy in their sights, even if it is potentially a civilian target, they don't bottle out.

The worst thing to hand to someone with psychopathic tendencies,
military or civilian, is an automatic weapon.

Occasionally we hear of military personnel stepping over the mark in the line of duty, unlawfully killing non-combatants. Some are prosecuted for abusing the power vested in them, tried to the same standards as civilians regardless of the circumstances. The rest of us, cocooned from the dangers of minefields, snipers and IED's, struggle to comprehend the stresses of being miles from home, losing comrades, and living in the macho culture of the platoon.

For these reasons, and many besides, recruiting officers work hard to identify and exclude young soldiers with psychopathic tendencies at the training stage. The worst thing to hand to someone with psychopathic tendencies, military or civilian, is an automatic weapon, and a violent psychopath in a uniform is a grave liability to any code of honour.

On the other hand, psychopathy flourishes where it is culturally sanctioned, enabling it to seep like a cancer into ordinary minds. Historians have long noted that the gods a society chooses to idolise are generally projections of the aspirations of their human creators, in which case it helps if justice and kindness are selected as desirable values. But what if a society chooses a 'psychopathic god', as the poet W H Auden believed was the case in Nazi Germany?

Heinrich Himmler, one of the leading architects of the Holocaust, praised his SS troops as 'decent fellows' for persisting with the unpleasant task of rounding up Jews. After the defeat of the Nazis, what struck prosecutors in the Nuremberg war trials was not the obvious beastliness of the masterminds of the Holocaust. It was their 'banality', or ordinariness. It's as if they simply weren't thinking about what they were doing, just doing their job and going along with the popular mood. They were not obviously mad, because their minds were in full working order. But nor were they obviously bad, because they loved their families and admired the music of Bach.

Nuremberg War Trials
Just a bunch of older men sitting in a court room in 1945. But they had masterminded the deaths of six million Jews. Were they mad, bad, or just sad?

And yet they had gassed Jews, children included, while Bach played in the background. This was not madness. It was evil because, however banal, it was a knowing choice to hurt, maim and commit atrocities. This was why the international court found them guilty and passed the death sentence. The challenge was to keep them alive before they committed suicide, so that justice could be seen to be done.

The Mirror of the Mind

The lesson seems to be clear: there is no 'real' or 'essential' human nature, only choices made by particular societies, and the individuals within them. Human beings are capable of great kindness or terrible cruelty, depending on what is culturally sanctioned. Psychopathy is part of the human condition, waiting like a virus for the right social conditions to flourish.

If war has a lesson to teach, it is surely this: nations lying cheek by jowl, disputing their borders, parading their identity, promoting their superiority and sequestered in their hate behind a blustering leader, are far more likely to inflict terrible suffering on each other than those who talk to each other, trade goods and exchange tourists.

Reflections

At the end of our long gaze into the 'false mirror' of the mind, we might feel a little less confident about our 'normal' take on reality. We begin to realise that Bacon's warning about our mind distorting and discolouring what it sees applies not only to autistic people, schizophrenics and psychotics. It applies to all of us.

Bacon's main concern was to give us a sharper view of the material world, without which science cannot flourish. But as we have seen, science is only one lens through which we view reality. We have many other ways of seeing and believing, and these too need to be polished and clarified.

We also need to realise that being 'realistic' about anything is not straightforward, as realism rather confusingly has two opposed meanings, depending on who is using it. To a materialist exploring the natural world, the real is what our senses feed to our brain. To an idealist, the real is the show we put on in the theatre of our mind. No wonder we are so divided between pessimism and optimism, determinism and free will, caution and gay abandon.

If we want to be more empathic and less isolated, more rational and less deluded, more connected and less paranoid, it pays to illuminate all of our ways of being and knowing. If Bacon is right, that we are creatures who mingle our mind with the nature of things, we need to study not just the mind that peers into the mirror, but also what lies behind the glass.

Bibliography

As the field covered by 'The Mirror of the Mind' is so vast, I have divided the bibliography into topic areas, and included only those texts that have contributed in some way to the writing of this book.

Anxiety and its antidotes
Aurelius, Marcus – *Meditations* 170CE The classic Stoic text on how to school our emotions, or 'keep calm and carry on'.
Dalai Lama – *The Art of Happiness* 1998 A Buddhist perspective on how anxiety can be quelled by systematic training of the mind.
Dunant, Sarah – *The Age of Anxiety* 1996 Ten prominent thinkers reflect on why worrying seems to be on the increase.
Frazzetto, Giovanni – *How We Feel 2014* An exploration of how we can manage our feelings to help us to cope with anxiety.
Fromm, Erich – *The Sane Society* 1955 A critique of 'me first' capitalism as a principal source of our psychological malaise.
Haidt, Jonathan – *The Righteous Mind* 2013 Why we are so divided on politics and religion.
Holloway, Richard – *A Little History of Religion* 2016 Religion's strengths and weaknesses in allaying our concerns, laid bare by a sceptical cleric.
Kolk, Bessel van der – *The Body Keeps the Score* 2015 The effects of stress and trauma on the mind/brain.
Le Doux, Joseph – *Anxious* 2015 A neuroscientist explores the biochemistry of fear and anxiety.
Linden, David – *The Accidental Mind* 2008 Why we shouldn't fret too much over love, memory, dreams and God, because they are 'accidents' of evolution.
Rycroft, Charles – *Anxiety and Neurosis* 1968 How anxiety can prepare us for action or weigh us down.

The Mirror of the Mind

Shermer, Michael – *The Believing Brain* 2011   Whether we worry or not, our brain is a belief engine that puts assumptions before explanations.

Wax, Ruby – *Sane New World* 2013 How the incessant chattering of our mind can be the source of our anxiety and stress.

Autism and theory of mind

Astington, Janet W – *The Child's Discovery of the Mind* 1993 How young children discover theory of mind, and start to put it to use.

Bakewell, Sarah – *At the Existentialist Cafe* 2016   How phenomenologists and existentialists have explored theory of mind.

Baron-Cohen, Simon – *Mindblindness* 1971   The links between autism and theory of mind.

Baron-Cohen, Simon – *The Pattern Seekers* 2020 How the genes for human inventiveness and aspects of autistic thinking might overlap.

Barrett, Lisa F – *How Emotions are Made* 2017 The brain's role in constructing our perceptions and feelings.

Berne, Eric – *Games People Play* 1964   How our social interactions are different types of mind game that we play to get our way, get even or get on.

Bogdashina, Olga – *Theory of Mind* 2005 Perspectives on aspects of autism and Asperger's.

Byrne, R and Whiten, A – *Machiavellian Intelligence* 1988   The book that introduced the idea that social manoeuvring, not tool making, drove human intelligence.

Frith, Uta – *Autism* 2008 What we know about the condition, and what we have yet to find out.

Godrey-Smith, Peter - *Other Minds* 2016 An insight into the development of consciousness and 'other-mindedness' in animals, especially cephalopods.

Grandin, Temple – *Thinking in Pictures* 1995 Growing up and working with autism.

Humphrey, Nicholas – *The Inner Eye* 1986 The close links between our primate ancestry, theory of mind and the evolution of consciousness.

Machiavelli, Niccolo – *The Prince* 1532 The classic text on how to second-guess the intentions of political opponents, and how to out-manoeuvre them.

The Mirror of the Mind

Silberman, Steve – *Neurotribes* 2015   A study of autism and plea for neurodiversity.

Tammet, Daniel – *Embracing the Blue Sky* 2007   Life from the perspective of someone with autistic savant syndrome.

Madness, sanity and psychosis

Bentall, Richard – *Madness Explained* 2003   A study of schizophrenia and psychosis.

Cleckley, Hervey M – *The Mask of Sanity* 1941 Interviews by a psychiatrist with institutionalised patients diagnosed with psychopathic personality disorder.

Foucault, Michel – *Madness and Civilisation* 1961   Argues that society, medicine and law use madness as a form of control.

Hart, Bernard – *The psychology of Insanity* 1916 An early and prescient attempt to get to grips with a puzzling and complex phenomenon.

Hobson, J Allan – *Dreaming as Delirium* 1999   A sleep researcher and psychiatrist compares the brain states of nightmares and psychosis.

Leader, Darian – *What is Madness?* 2011 What separates the sane from the mad, and how do we know?

Persaud, Raj – *Staying Sane* 1997 How to maintain a healthy attitude in the face of unrelenting pressure.

Phillips, Adam – *Going Sane* 2005 What does it mean to claim to be sane?

Porter, Roy – *Madness* 2002 A brief medical, social and cultural history.

Scull, Andrew – *Madness* 2011 Why madness haunts, disturbs and frightens us.

Yellowlees, Henry – *To Define True Madness* 1953 England's chief medical officer at the time gives his assessment of what we understand by madness.

Psychiatry

Albert, Gail – *The Other Side of the Couch* 1995 A sympathetic series of interviews with experienced psychiatrists, highlighting the challenges they face.

American Psychiatric Association – *The Diagnostic and Statistical Manual* 2013 The fifth edition lists over one hundred and fifty mental disorders.

Bentall, Richard – *Doctoring the Mind* 2009 A sceptical view of medicalising mental illness without also treating the person.

The Mirror of the Mind

Burns, Tom – *Our Necessary Shadow* 2013 Why we cannot live without psychiatry.

Clare, Anthony – *In the Psychiatrist's Chair* 1993 Radio interviews in which well-known figures open up about themselves

Lieberman, Jeffrey – *Shrinks* 2015 How psychiatry has gradually taken on the lessons of neuroscience.

Hacking, Ian – *Rewriting the Soul* 1998 A study of multiple personality disorder, and its relation to recovered memories.

Leff, Julian – *The Unbalanced Mind* 2001 How advances in biotechnology may be able to uncover the causes of mental disturbances.

Luria, Alexander – *The Man with a Shattered World* 1994 A case study of a man with a serious brain wound.

Ropper, Allan – *Reaching down the Rabbit Hole* 2014 A neurologist describes some of the extraordinary psychoses of his patients.

Szasz, Thomas – *The Myth of Mental Illness* 1960 A challenge to psychiatry as a form of power and control over the patient.

Psychoanalysis, therapy and healing

Baggini, J and Macaro, A – *The Shrink and the Sage* 2012 A philosopher and therapist pool ideas on how to face life's challenges.

Berne, Eric – *A Layman's Guide to Psychiatry and Psychoanalysis* 1975 Does what it says on the tin.

Burns, Tom, and Burns-Lundgren, Eva – *Psychotherapy* 2015 Covers the range of therapies on offer, their history and effectiveness.

Easthope, Anthony – *The Unconscious* 1999 An exploration of the concept that is fundamental to an understanding of psychoanalysis.

Freud, Sigmund – *The Psychopathology of Everyday Life* 1901 The grand master of the unconscious lays bare the slips and blips that reveal what is really going on in our mind.

Jeffers, Susan – *Feel the Fear and Do It Anyway* 1987 The bestselling self-help book that encourages positive and assertive thinking.

Jung, Carl – *Modern Man in Search of a Soul* 1933 The guru of depth psychology offers a diagnosis and a cure for our modern neuroses.

The Mirror of the Mind

Kovel, Joel – *A Complete Guide to Therapy* 1976 A clear summary of different approaches, from psychoanalysis to behaviour modification.

Masson, Jeffrey – *Against Therapy* 1988 A critique of psychotherapy and its effectiveness.

Moyers, Bill – *Healing and the Mind* 1993 The book that accompanies the television series about how we can self-heal by bringing body and mind closer together.

Orbach, Susie – *In Therapy* 2016 Why we might choose to see a therapist, and what happens when we do.

Perls, Fritz – *Gestalt Therapy* 1951 Introducing the therapy that encourages a more hands-on approach to managing our mental health.

Rieff, Philip – *The Triumph of the Therapeutic* 1966 An exploration of how psychoanalysis became a substitute for religious faith after Freud.

Schwartz, J and Begley, S – *The Mind and the Brain* 2002 The importance of neuroplasticity in therapy.

Sigman, Mariano – *The Secret Life of the Mind* 2015 A neuroscientist considers why we worry, what we dream about, and how we make our decisions.

Symington, Neville – *The Analytic Experience* 1986 An exploration of the relationship between the analyst and patient in clinical practice.

Van der Post, Laurens – *Jung and the Story of Our Time* 1975 Reflections and insights from a long friendship between Jung and the author.

Wilber, Ken – *Integral Psychology* 1994 A rare attempt to pull all aspects of our consciousness and well-being together in one theory.

Yalom, Irvin D – *Becoming myself* 2017 An experienced psychotherapist casts a shewd eye over his own development as a therapist.

Psychopathy and violence

Arendt, Hannah – *Eichmann in Jerusalem* 1963 Having escaped Nazism, the author reports on the 'banality of evil' she saw in the prosecution of Nazi war criminals.

Banks, Iain – *The Wasp Factory* 1984 A grim fictional foray into the mind of an isolated psychopathic teenager.

The Mirror of the Mind

Baron-Cohen, Simon – *Zero Degrees of Empathy* 2011 Why it's not moral evil that makes us 'bad', but biological lack of empathy.

Bavidge, Michael - *Mad or Bad?* 1989 How do we decide culpability in the mind of a serial killer?

Bregman, Rutger – *Humankind* 2020 A challenge to the assumption that we are violent by nature, debunking many myths along the way.

Dostoyevsky, Fyodor – *Crime and Punishment* 1866 The classic Russian novel about murder and guilty conscience: there's no getting off scot free.

Easton Ellis, Bret – *American Psycho* 1991 A chilling novel which takes us into the mind of a successful Wall Street banker who gets his kicks from serial killing.

Golding, William – *The Lord of the Flies* 1954 A fiction about a bunch of marooned English choirboys lapsing into cruelty and violence.

Lorenz, Konrad – *On Aggression* 1963 A zoologist gives his views on the dangers of aggression in an age or automated warfare.

Montagu, Ashley – *The Nature of Human Aggression* 1976 Argues that human aggression is not innate, but influenced by sociocultural factors.

Raine, Adrian – *The Anatomy of Violence* 2013 Crime has biological roots, which explains why kids from good neighbourhoods can grow up to be killers.

Ronson, Jon – *The Psychopath Test* 2012 'A journey through the madness industry', exploring the boundaries between sanity and insanity.

Storr, Anthony – *Aggression* 1968 Captures the fascination with our violent nature that prevailed at the time, but overtaken by subsequent research.

Wrangham, Richard – *The Goodness Paradox* 2019 A primatologist considers why, although our species values goodness, there is also evil and violence in the world.

Reality

Andersen, Truett – *Reality isn't What it Used to Be* 1990 How new technologies are challenging and changing our perception of reality.

Baggott, Jim – *A Beginner's Guide to Reality* 2015 As it asks on the book's cover, how do we know this book is real?

The Mirror of the Mind

Berger, P and Luckman, T – *The Social Construction of Reality* 1966 How we make our 'human' realities through language and culture.

Blackmore, Susan – *The Meme Machine* 1999 How the passing on of memes or 'sticky ideas' shapes our understanding of reality.

Bostrom, Nick – *Superintelligence* 2014 How and why there may be realities beyond those we can see.

Cary, Joyce – *Art and Reality* 1958 A novelist's account of how artists of all kinds create their version of truth and reality.

Cohen, Jack and Stewart, Ian – *Figments of Reality* 1997 A biologist and mathematician unveil the realities our mind has evolved to see.

Deutsch, David – *The Fabric of Reality* 1996 A physicist opens our eyes to layers of reality beyond our senses.

Hoffman, Donald D – *The Case Against Reality* 2019 How our brain evolved to give us a 'good enough' picture of reality, but not necessarily an accurate one.

Kastrup, Bernardo – *The Idea of the World* 2019 A challenging but stimulating argument that reality is mental, not reducible to physical data.

Lewens, Tim – *The |Meaning of Science* 2015 How scientists establish the 'scientifically real'.

Penrose, Roger – *The Road to Reality* 2004 An eminent mathematician takes us on a tour of the realities of the physical universe.

Ricard, Matthieu – *The Quantum and the Lotus* 2000 A molecular biologist turned Tibetan monk takes us on a mind-expanding tour of reality.

Rovelli, Carlo – *Reality is not What it Seems* 2014 A quantum physicist describes the vast universe waiting to be discovered.

Sacks, Jonathan – *The Great Partnership* 2011 A powerful analysis of how religion and science give us not opposing but complementary views of reality.

Sutherland, Graham – *Irrationality* 1992 Shows how social and emotional factors get in the way of a rational understanding of reality.

Tomlin, Sarah – *What would Freud Do?* 2017 How different psychologists and psychotherapists have approached the mind's construction of reality.

Westerhoff, Jan – *Reality* 2011 A short introduction to different aspects of reality.

Whorf, Benjamin Lee – *Language, Thought and Reality* 1956 A linguist explains the role of language in shaping our perception of reality.

The Mirror of the Mind

Winnicott, Donald – *Play and Reality* 1971 A study of the value of play in helping children draw the boundaries of reality.

Woolley, Benjamin – *Virtual Worlds* 1992 Investigating the hype and reality of hyper-reality.

Schizophrenia and hearing voices

Blackman, Lisa – *Hearing Voices* 2001 How hearing voices is not necessarily a sign of mental illness.

Fernyhough, Charles – *The Voices Within* 2015 A different perspective on the voices in our head.

Frith, Chris – *Schizophrenia* 2003 A short introduction to symptoms, causes and treatments.

Horrobin, David – *The Madness of Adam and Eve* 2001 How schizophrenia was present in Eden, and has cast its long shadow over human history.

Jaynes, Julian – *The Origin of Consciousness* 1976 A bold theory that we became fully conscious only when the busy voices in our right brain invaded the quieter processing of the left.

Laing, Ronald D – *The Divided Self* 1960 Case studies of schizophrenia, attempting to see psychosis as part of a personal journey.

Nettle, Daniel – *Strong Imagination* 2001 The relationship of schizophrenia to madness and creativity.

Pullman, Philip – *Daemon Voices* 2017 The acclaimed novelist describes how writers imagine, hear and interpret voices.

Snyder, Kurt – *Me, Myself and Them* 2007 A young person's account of living with schizophrenia.

Index

The Mirror of the Mind

The Mirror of the Mind

Printed in Great Britain
by Amazon

54519877R00147